DEPORTATION AND EXILE

Also by Keith Sword

THE FORMATION OF THE POLISH COMMUNITY IN
GREAT BRITAIN, 1939–50 (*with N. Davies and J. Ciechanowski*)

* THE SOVIET TAKEOVER OF THE POLISH
EASTERN PROVINCES, 1939–41 (*editor*)

THE TIMES GUIDE TO EASTERN EUROPE (*editor*)

* *From the same publishers*

Deportation and Exile

Poles in the Soviet Union, 1939–48

Keith Sword

Lecturer in the Social Science Department
School of Slavonic and East European Studies
University of London

in association with
SCHOOL OF SLAVONIC AND
EAST EUROPEAN STUDIES
UNIVERSITY OF LONDON

Published in Great Britain by
MACMILLAN PRESS LTD
Houndmills, Basingstoke, Hampshire RG21 6XS
and London
Companies and representatives
throughout the world

First edition 1994
Reprinted (with alterations) 1996

This book is published in the *Studies in Russia
and East Europe* series

A catalogue record for this book is available
from the British Library.

ISBN 0–333–59376–6 hardcover
ISBN 0–333–66860–X paperback

First published in the United States of America 1994 by
ST. MARTIN'S PRESS, INC.,
Scholarly and Reference Division,
175 Fifth Avenue,
New York, N.Y. 10010

ISBN 0–312–12397–3

Library of Congress Cataloging-in-Publication Data
Sword, Keith.
Deportation and exile / Poles in the Soviet Union, 1939–48
/ Keith Sword.
p.   cm.
Includes bibliographical references and index.
1. World War, 1939–45—Deportations from Poland.   2. World War,
1939–45—Concentration camps—Soviet Union.   3. Poles—Soviet
Union—History—20th century.   4. World War, 1939–45—Forced
repatriation.   5. Poland—Relations—Soviet Union.   6. Soviet Union–
–Relations—Poland.   I. Title.
D810.D5S88   1994
940.53'15039185047—dc20   94–31934
                                                                                                    CIP

Printed and bound in Great Britain by
Antony Rowe Ltd, Chippenham, Wiltshire

Contents

List of Maps

Preface

This book is the result of work carried out under the aegis of the Polish Migration Project at the School of Slavonic and East European Studies, University of London. An earlier fruit of the Project's work was a general study of the circumstances under which Poles travelled to Great Britain following the outbreak of war in 1939, and the means by which a large number were resettled in this country in the late 1940s.[1] In its original conception the present volume was to provide a complementary study. It was to focus on one of the routes – perhaps the most significant in terms of numbers and impact – by which Poles travelled to Britain during the 1940s: forced deportation from homes in eastern Poland to the Soviet Union and, thereafter, a trek which led via Persia, the Middle East, Italy and, for some, East Africa.

The original plan for this volume changed due to a number of factors. The first arose from the question of where and when to end it. Initially the evacuations of General Anders' troops to Iran in 1942 had seemed a logical point to draw the line. For many of the émigrés, whose memoirs I had read, their experiences in the Soviet Union cease at this point. However, I later reflected increasingly on those who had been left behind, following Anders' departure. If Polish Government estimates of the period are to be believed, then less than 10 per cent of the Poles deported from Eastern Poland by the Soviet authorities in the period 1939–41 made their exit from Soviet territory in 1942. Even if some 20 per cent had fallen victim to starvation and related diseases and were no longer alive in 1942, there would still have been several hundred thousand Polish deportees remaining.

These reflections concentrated my attention on the gulf in historical writing which developed in the postwar period. The field became divided between the 'émigré' and the 'homeland' (communist) histories of Poles in the Soviet Union during the 1940s. The émigré accounts tended to dwell on the years 1939–43, dealing with the Soviet occupation of Eastern Poland, the Katyn massacre, the mass deportations from Polish territories and the fate of the deportees. This chapter of events closed either with the evacuations of 1942 or, at a formal diplomatic level, with the break in Polish–Soviet relations in April 1943. The 'communist' studies concentrated on the period 1943–47. They glossed over many of the earlier events (without ignoring them

completely) and concentrated on what they regard as the more positive aspects of Polish–Soviet relations – that is, between the Soviet
Government and Polish communists – after the 1943 break in diplomatic relations.

The period as a whole takes in the formation of two Polish armies on
Soviet soil and the mounting of two welfare initiatives for the needy,
uprooted, civilian Poles. However, in its historical writing, each political camp has concentrated on one aspect of the period and tended to
play down the role of the other. My decision was therefore to attempt
to bridge this gulf and include chapters on the role of the Polish communists in the USSR, including the repatriation process by which hundreds of thousands of Poles moved west in the period 1944–48.

The second factor was the decision to include material on the thousands of Polish underground activists and civilian personnel deported
by the Soviet security forces in 1944–45. Their story has, until recently, been less well-known outside Poland and, even today, relatively little is available on this episode which is not written in Polish.
The reasons for this are perhaps obvious; by contrast with the 1940
deportees, large numbers of whom made their way out of the USSR
in 1942 and were subsequently able to write about their experiences
for a wider audience, the voices of the 1944–45 deportees were sti-
fled. There was no general amnesty for them, no independent Polish
Government in Warsaw with the power to intervene on their behalf.
Those who were released from Soviet labour camps, and allowed to
return to their homeland, were still almost as effectively gagged in
communist Poland as they would have been had they remained on
Soviet territory.

As I read and researched, I became increasingly aware of the degree of continuity between exile policies as they evolved under successive Tsarist regimes and those of the Stalinist period. This became
evident from the repetitive nature of the 'Siberian Odyssey' experience that Poles underwent during the war years. Although the
deportations of the Stalinist years surpassed in size (numbers taken)
and in its horrors previous forced exile movements, Poles of previous generations had undergone similar experiences of involuntary
uprooting. Norman Davies has drawn attention to this pattern of
movement in his general history of Poland:

> Each generation of Poles that was dumped in the tundra or the steppe
> in 1832, 1864, 1906, 1940 or 1945 has talked of encountering Poles
> of an earlier generation who had shared the same fate.[2]

This is something that almost every Pole knows, of course, since it is not only a part of the nation's history, but also part of the history of most Polish families.

By way of example, Jan Plater-Gajewski, spokesman for the Polish community in Kazakhstan, explained during 1988, in an interview with a Warsaw journalist, how four generations of his family had been exiled by the Russian, and later Soviet, authorities:

> Family fortunes were linked to the Polish Risings and the democratic movements. My great-grandfather was exiled to Siberia as a result of the 1831 Rising; great-grandmother went with him and my grandfather was born in Siberia. He (grandfather) returned several years later to the family estate in Lithuania and became involved with the 1863 Rising, as a result of which he was exiled to the Yakutsk *gubernia* and from Vilnius, travelled there on foot and in irons. He later returned to Poland – not to Lithuania, but to Podolia, to the estates of my grandmother. Finally my father was sent to Siberia for his participation in the democratic movement and collaboration in forming a Polish underground press at the turn of the century. He was sent to Sołowka, from where he escaped and crossed the Russian border into Austro-Hungary.

Plater-Gajewski himself was born in the Austro-Hungarian Empire and returned to Poland only in 1924. From there he in turn was deported by the Soviet authorities in 1939–40. Taken over the four generations of the family, the total period each spent in Siberia was: great-grandfather, seven years; grandfather, 11 years; father, five years; himself (J.P-G), 17 years.[3]

An interest in this cyclical 'pattern' of exile, this rhythm of movement to the east, prompted me to write an introductory chapter on historical background. I thought it important that the reader should understand something – however superficial it was to be in the space available – of the traditions of the Tsarist exile system in which the Stalinist deportation of whole classes and nationalities had its roots – traditions from which past generations of Poles had suffered over centuries.

Inevitably, perhaps, by extending the scope of the study in this way, I accumulated too much material and was in the end forced to jettison both this and other material. Consequently, I have limited the attention devoted to the 'main waves' of 1939–41 deportees. For example, I have left out a separate chapter on the exile experiences of the 1940 deportees (in labour camps, 'special settlements' and state

or collective farms). There is also relatively little space allocated here
to the Katyn massacre – largely because I felt that an already considerable literature is available and much of it is in English. I had
thought at one time to have separate chapters on the formation of the
two armies – Anders's and Berling's – but in both cases this material
has now been subsumed into other chapters.

The book which has resulted concentrates on the movement of
populations – involuntary, state-inspired uprooting; refugee flight from
armed conflict; migration to join armed forces (and to leave captivity);
large-scale exodus across state borders; state-organised repatriation.
This is shown against a background of political decision-making –
both decisions which led to those migrations and those which attempted
to alleviate the consequences.

The drafting and redrafting of this book has in a sense been overtaken by events; the emergence of Poland from communist rule in
1989, and the disintegration of the Soviet Union in the course of the
following three years. A number of consequences have flowed from
these events. First, the artificial division between émigré and homeland historiography has disappeared. There has been in Poland a bur-
geoning interest in researching and writing about the 'eastern experiences'
of Poles from the 1940s onwards. This comes from a younger gen-
eration of historians who, in general, were educated in ignorance of
this chapter in their nation's history, or learned about it by word of
mouth. By contrast with Poles' experiences at the hands of the Germans during the 1940s, many areas of Polish–Soviet relations had been
a taboo subject. A considerable volume of such literature was published in exile, but this has only recently become generally available
to a readership in Poland.[4] There has also been an unexpected freedom for some scholars to consult Soviet archival materials which were
previously kept well-hidden from public view. Several documents have
appeared from the archives of the Soviet security forces – some through
official channels, others via private channels.[5]

The task of gathering historical material is all the more urgent in
that the surviving witnesses to these episodes in Polish history are
now elderly. Attempts have been made to establish contact with the
survivors and to elicit written memoirs – partly through the help of
competitions in Polish periodicals. One of the major initiatives in this
respect is the creation of the 'Archiwum Wschodnie' (Eastern Archive),
which was set up in 1987 to coordinate the collection and catalogu-
ing of such materials and has since received the support of a group of
eminent university historians.[6]

The renewed interest in the fate of ethnic Poles in the east is of more than purely historic interest, though. Their welfare, and that of their descendants, has become a much-discussed issue in Poland. Press articles have appeared about the situation of Poles in several of the former Soviet republics, most frequently in the neighbouring republics of Lithuania, Belarus and Ukraine. Academics are increasingly undertaking sociological studies. Most frequently, these focus on attempts to retain Polish language and culture against the assimilatory pressures from the central or republican authorities. Several initiatives have been set in motion to help the Polish minority – by sending literature and teachers, inviting children to Poland on holiday camps, inviting adults (especially teachers) on courses, university exchanges, and so on. But, in addition, there are pressures for many of these Poles in the former Soviet republics to be allowed to return to Poland.

The prospect of further repatriation on a mass scale is one that has been exercising the Polish Government. Although public opinion is generally sympathetic to the repatriation of such people, since 1990 there have been worries at official level about an uncontrolled stampede which might accompany political or economic collapse in the east. While these fears have not fully receded, the improving economic situation in Poland itself following the transition from communism has allowed consideration of a graduated repatriation plan. If such a plan is put into motion, it seems likely that, barring emergency situations, such as a civil war or ethnic conflict, those who live in the most remote parts of the former Soviet empire will have precedence. A recent issue of the English-language newspaper *Warsaw Voice* suggests that such movement may begin as early as 1994, if the Polish Foreign Ministry can prepare legal and organisational rules for the operation in time.[7]

The name 'Belarus' is used here in referring to the modern republic which emerged following the break-up of the USSR. Throughout the remainder of this book, however, the form 'Byelorussia' is used in historical references, e.g. 'Byelorussian SSR', 'Western Byelorussia'.

Preface to the 1996 Reprint

This reprint is substantially unchanged from the hardback edition published in 1994, except for a number of minor corrections. It has not been revised or rewritten. Indeed, given that the period which elapsed between the appearance of the first edition and the writing of this new Preface is so short (eight months), no reviews have yet appeared of the book. I have been unable therefore to benefit from the suggestions of reviewers.

In my original Preface I drew attention to the work being done by Polish scholars on the subject of Poles in the USSR. Disappointingly, relatively little has appeared in print. Most related scholarly work that has come to my attention has been on the Soviet occupation of Eastern Poland, between 1939 and 1941. An exception is the recent book by Albin Glowacki, *Ocalić i repatriować. Opieka nad ludnością polską w głębi terytorium ZSSR.* (Łódź, 1994).

Soviet archival material on the subject has continued to appear. The Warsaw journal *KARTA* carried an article in its No. 12 (1994) issue by Russian historian Aleksander Guryanov. Guryanov located NKVD archival records of the rail transports which set off from Polish territory between February and June 1940. The tables he has reproduced in his article contain dates of transports, their starting points and destinations, number of deportees in each, and even the commander of the NVKD contingent accompanying the train. On the basis of these records, the author estimated that the total number of people deported in these operations from eastern Poland was some 320,000 – far less than the figures advanced by emigré sources. (See pages 25–7 of this volume.) Doubtless the veracity of Guryanov's materials will be challenged in due course.

There is a further item which may be of interest to readers. This is the 1994 reissue of a book that has become a classic study of wartime Polish experiences in the Gulag – *Sprawiedliwość Sowiecka* (Soviet Justice). In the bibliography to this volume it is listed under the pen-names originally used by the authors – S. Mora and P. Zwierniak. The use of *noms de plume* by emigré authors was customary during the communist period if they wished to protect relatives in Poland from possible reprisals, or wished themselves to visit Poland without trouble. The reissued paperback version has been published in Warsaw under the authors' true names – Kazimierz Zamorski and Stanisław Starzewski.

Acknowledgements

Too many people have helped me in the course of working on this book for me to thank all of them individually, but I would like to express my particular gratitude to Andrzej Suchcitz, keeper of records at the Sikorski Institute in London, Dr Zdzisław Jagodzinski and his staff at the Polish Library in Hammersmith, the staff of the Public Record Office in Kew and to the library staff at the School of Slavonic and East European Studies who have at all times fielded my requests for materials with courtesy and good humour.

I am grateful to the Controller of Crown Copyright for permission to quote from official documents in the Public Record Office.

Many thanks also to Ed Oliver of Queen Mary College for drawing the maps.

Finally, a debt of gratitude is owed to the Leverhulme Foundation and to the M. B. Grabowski Fund, without whose financial support this study would not have been possible.

List of Abbreviations

AK	(Pol) Armia Krajowa (Home Army – Polish underground movement owing allegiance to the Polish Government in London)
AL	(Pol) Armia Ludowa (People's Army – communist underground movement)
GULag	(Rus) Glavnoye Upravlenye Ispravitelno-Trudovikh Lagerei (division of the NKVD responsible for labour camps)
ITL	(Rus) Isprivitelno-Trudovikh Lagierei (Soviet corrective labour camp)
KOP	(Pol) Korpus Ochrony Pogranicza (Frontier Defence Corps)
KPP	(Pol) Komunistyczna Partia Polska (Polish Communist Party – prewar)
KRN	(Pol) Krajowa Rada Narodowa (Homeland National Council)
MO	(Pol) Milicja Obywatelska (Citizens' Militia)
NKVD	(Rus) Narodnyi Komisariat Vnutrennikh Dyel (People's Commissariat for Internal Affairs)
NSZ	(Pol) Narodowe Siły Zbrojne (National Armed Forces – right-wing formation)
OSO/OSSO	(Rus) Osoboye Soveschanie (Special Tribunal – for sentencing more serious offenders against the Soviet penal code)
PKWN	(Pol) Polski Komitet Wolności Narodowej (Polish Committee of National Liberation)
PSK	(Pol) Pomocnicza Służba Kobiet (Women's Voluntary Service)
PUR	(Pol) Polski Urząd Repatriacyjny (Polish Repatriation Office)
TRJN	(Pol) Tymczasowy Rząd Jedności Narodowej (Interim Government of National Unity)
UB	(Pol) Urząd Bezpieczeństwa Publicznego (Security Office)
UNRRA	United Nations Relief and Rehabilitation Administration
WW	(Pol) Wojsko Wewnętrzne (Interior Force)
WOS	(Pol) Wydział Opieki Społecznej (Social Welfare Division – of the ZPP)
ZPP	(Pol) Związek Patriotów Polskich (Union of Polish Patriots – in the USSR)

1 The Mass Movement of Poles to the USSR, 1939–41

CATEGORIES OF THOSE DISPLACED

When the Soviet Union occupied the eastern half of the Polish Republic in September 1939 it took over an area containing some 13 million people.[1] Following the Red Army's campaign, and the final establishment of the Nazi–Soviet demarcation line at the end of September, the Soviet authorities set about formally annexing the conquered territories and establishing their own administration. The elections organised during October 1939 followed by the decision by the two National Assemblies (of the Western Ukraine and Western Byelorussia) to ask the Supreme Soviet that the regions be incorporated into the respective Soviet republics are generally recognised to have been a sham – an attempt to persuade world opinion that the democratic will of the local inhabitants had been sought.[2] It could not have been otherwise, of course. Stalin could not afford to trust the democratic process. He would hardly have sent the Red Army into eastern Poland, merely to have seen it withdrawn on the basis of a vote by the local population. The fact is that the fate of the region had been decided in advance. This much is clear in pronouncements made by Soviet dignitaries – and is clear from the terms of the Nazi–Soviet agreements of August–September 1939.[3] Stalin had rejected the idea of a rump Polish state well before the 'elections' were carried out. Moreover, the warning issued by the two allies in Moscow against Polish resistance to the new order not only precluded any 'democratic' resolution of the situation, it foreshadowed the harshness of what was to come.

It is significant that, following the agreement of the Supreme Soviet on 1 and 2 November 1939 to accede to the National Assemblies' requests and incorporate the occupied Polish territories into the USSR (Ukrainian SSR and Byelorussian SSR), Soviet law was applied to the region and to its inhabitants. All those 'former' Polish citizens who were in the territory formally annexed by the Soviets on 1 November (Western Byelorussia) and 2 November (Western Ukraine) were

1

thenceforth regarded as having acquired Soviet citizenship. This much was made clear in a decree issued by the Presidium of the Supreme Soviet of 29 November 1939.

The imposition of Soviet rule triggered involuntary population movement on a large scale. Apart from the large number of people seeking to escape from the Soviet–controlled area, there was internal upheaval and displacement. Widespread expulsions from houses and apartments took place in order to create living space for the thousands of incoming Soviet officials and their families.[4] The involuntary uprooting was brought about by the notorious paragraph 11 frequently inserted into the identity documents issued by the Soviet authorities. This forbade the bearer from residing within 100 km of major cities or the state border.[5] Sudden enforced homelessness resulted in tragic circumstances for large sections of the population and the internal migration of many thousands – to relatives, to friends, to the countryside.

Most residents of eastern Poland had little experience of travel. Many rarely ventured beyond the confines of their village or parish. The kind of uprooting and displacement they faced therefore was an experience fraught with anxiety. But the mass transportation of Poles to the Soviet interior was of a different order than the ejection of people from apartments, houses and towns. The Soviet authorities removed in one fell swoop and in a surgical fashion whole classes of Polish citizens. Moreover, the movement was organised, controlled and directed. The victims of this action were not simply left to the whims of fate but were despatched in batches to the vast and empty spaces of the Soviet interior. Those displaced can be divided into several categories, each of which demands some comment.

Prisoners-of-War

In chronological order the first victims of the Soviets were the prisoners-of-war captured by the Red Army during or after the military campaign of September 1939. On the first anniversary of the campaign, the Red Army newspaper *Krasnaya Zviezda* (Red Star) claimed that 181 223 Polish POWs (other ranks) had been taken. In addition to this number 12 generals, 55 colonels, 72 lieutenants and 9227 officers of lower rank had also been seized. Altogether, therefore, 190 589.[6] However, in the more immediate aftermath of the Red Army's campaign, in October 1939, the Soviet Foreign Minister, Viacheslav Molotov, announced to the Supreme Soviet that 230 000 Polish soldiers had been captured.[7]

It is unlikely that this figure would have included the numbers of

Poles (particularly officers, but also those who had offered resistance to the Soviet troops and inflicted casualties) who were summarily executed by Red Army personnel.[8] Molotov's figure would certainly not have included the Polish troops who crossed the north-eastern border to seek sanctuary in Lithuania or Latvia. Although a trickle of these men made their way out of their internment camps and escaped to Britain via Sweden, the majority (some 12 000) fell into Soviet hands only when Stalin moved against the Baltic States in the summer of 1940.[9]

There were in addition many soldiers, especially officers, who went to ground following the Polish collapse. The majority either joined the underground resistance movement or attempted to make their way across the Hungarian and Romanian frontiers to join General Sikorski in France. The Soviets continued to search for such people, and many were subsequently apprehended, especially in the Lwów area where the Polish underground (ZWZ) had been penetrated by the Soviet security forces at an early stage. Others were caught attempting to cross the border, perhaps to join families in the German zone, or else to make their way to join the Polish forces forming under General Sikorski in France. The NKVD was not always aware of the true identity of Poles it captured.[10]

Of those tens of thousands of Polish troops who did fall into Soviet hands, not all were detained. Certain categories were released and allowed to go home, including those younger soldiers of lower rank who were not regarded by their Soviet captors as politically dangerous.[11] It is difficult to find a pattern, however. Some soldiers of non-Polish origin (Byelorussian, Ukrainian), and some Poles who had originated from the central and western districts of Poland, were released quickly. Others were taken to holding camps within the Soviet Union before returning to the west. Recently-released Soviet (NKVD) documents indicate that 42 400 prisoners were 'released from camps and directed to the western provinces of the Ukrainian SSR and the Byelorussian SSR' before the end of 1939.[12]

According to the NKVD report of the transfer, 'all the people received (i.e. by the Germans) were released to return to their homes'.[13] This, however, does not seem to have been the case, since other accounts indicate that Polish prisoners were simply transferred from Soviet POW camps to German POW camps. One group of prisoners, numbering seven thousand, were taken by their Soviet captors under murderous conditions to the Talica camp near Gorky. Several hundred are reported to have died on their march through the forests to the camp.

At the end of October 1939 the prisoners were informed that those whose homes lay to the west of the River Bug were to declare themselves, since they were to be sent home in keeping with the terms of the German–Soviet Pact. Three thousand put their names forward and, in early November were transported west, to be handed over to the Germans at Brześć. On 14 November the group reached Stalag IVB near Dresden.[14]

It must be said that the Soviet definition of 'prisoner-of-war' seems to have been considerably more elastic than that used elsewhere. For example, the fifteen thousand prisoners who were interned in the ill-famed camps at Kozielsk, Starobielsk and Ostashkov included not only regular and reserve officers from the three armed services but officials, landowners, priests, policemen, prison warders, military colonists, military policemen, members of KOP (the frontier defence corps), and border guards. Most of these latter categories were grouped together in the Ostashkov camp.

Most of these POW officers met their deaths at the hands of the NKVD during April 1940. As history has recorded, the victims' fate only became known when a mass grave was found by the Germans near Smolensk in the early spring of 1943. The grave in the Katyn forest contained the bodies of some 4000 Poles from the Kozielsk camp. The Katyn affair has received a great deal of attention from historians – and justifiably so.[15] To Polish minds it became, in the postwar period, a *cause célèbre*, a symbol of the many barbarities committed against the Polish people by an eastern neighbour which posed – after 1941 – as an ally and 'liberator'. Only in the twilight of the Soviet Union's existence as a political entity did the authorities in Moscow admit responsibility for the massacre, and make it possible for the two other mass graves in which Polish victims were laid to rest to be located.[16]

Only a few hundred of the prisoners (some 450) who were interned in these three camps survived, having been selected from each of the camps by the NKVD. Following the segregation, they were eventually placed in a camp at Griazoviets. These were people who were regarded by the Soviet security forces as being more pliant than their colleagues – perhaps more susceptible to indoctrination techniques – as being useful to the Soviets, or quite simply less hostile and dangerous than their peers.

Of those prisoners who escaped a violent end at the hands of the NKVD, one group should be mentioned. This was a group of officers, led by Lt-Colonel Zygmunt Berling, who were evidently regarded by the NKVD as being more pliable, more amenable to the Soviets' designs, and therefore of possible use in the future. The group, which did not number more than twenty, was housed for a time in a villa at

Małachówka outside Moscow. The residence became known popularly as the 'villa szczęścia' (the villa of delight) owing to the relative luxury of the conditions the detainees enjoyed. Although members of the 'Małachówka group' were released in 1941 to join the Polish formations being formed by General Anders, Berling later commanded the 'Kościuszko Division' formed in 1943 under the aegis of the Union of Polish Patriots.[17]

Most of the remaining prisoners were interned in POW camps in the Ukraine, both on former Polish territory, and to the east of the prewar Polish–Soviet frontier – the 'Riga Line'. Almost 100 camps are known to have existed in the western Ukraine although, strangely, no evidence has emerged of any similar holding camps further north – on Byelorussian territory.[18] Some prisoners were employed on construction projects – bridges, roads, airfields – and other activities which demanded hard manual labour (tree-felling, quarrying). With the German attack on Russia in the summer of 1941 they were hurriedly evacuated to the east – in some cases under brutal conditions.

A further group, their number not firmly established, were moved deeper into the Soviet Ukraine and put to work in industries and mining in the Donbas region. In May 1940, however, they were moved north, to the Komi Republic, where they were employed in clearing the taiga and building a railway line. The journey, part of which was undertaken by boat or barge, lasted two weeks. Conditions were harsh and the prisoners were treated cruelly by their guards. One group of 1200 prisoners, which set out from the 'Donbas' industrial region and arrived at 'lagpunkt 24' on the Uchta River, was reduced to 740 by the time it reached its destination.[19]

Those arrested by the NKVD

Within a few weeks of the handover of power from the Red Army, the NKVD had established control over all areas of life in the conquered territories. There were no villages or settlements – not to mention the larger urban communities – in which they did not have either their own officials or trusted nominees. They were represented in all the main offices and bureaus, as well as in strategically important activities such as rail transport and border control. Consequently, it did not take long for the tempo of arrests, which had been sporadic during the early days of the occupation, to increase. In the second half of October 1939 these took on the character of mass round-ups.

The arrested included army officers who had made their way home after evading capture by the Soviet forces during the September campaign, landowners, businessmen (employers), policemen, members of the judiciary and court officials, and local government officials. 'Military settlers' (*osadnicy wojskowi*), those rewarded for their service in the 1920 war against the Bolsheviks by the gift of a parcel of land, or those decorated for former service to the Polish state were obvious targets.[20] Those serving in the many underground resistance movements – in Ukrainian or Jewish resistance groups too – indeed anyone fighting to resist Soviet rule, were regarded as particularly dangerous. Those crossing the borders illegally – in whatever direction – were regarded as spies and were immediately incarcerated. In the case of others, membership of prewar Polish organisations (Teachers' Union, Riflemen's Union, Scouts) was sufficient evidence that the individual had supported the Polish State and was by inference hostile to Soviet power.

Also taken into custody were individuals prominent in social and political life. These included trade unionists and members of political movements and organisations as diverse as the Polish Socialist Party, the right-wing National Democratic Party, the Jewish Socialist 'Bund' and the Zionist movement. On 9 November 1939 Mr Jan Stańczyk, Minister of Labour and Social Welfare in the newly-formed Polish Government in Paris, visited the headquarters of the Trades Union Congress in London. He pointed out that many Polish and Jewish socialists were being arrested by the Soviets for refusing to sign a declaration of loyalty to the Stalinist Constitution, and presented a list of names of those known to have been arrested. They included Henryk Ehrlich – barrister and member of the Jewish 'Bund', arrested at the railway station in Brześć; Wiktor Alter – executive member of the 'Bund', arrested in Kowel; Hersh Himmelfarb – tailor, leader of the Clothing Workers Trade Union; Shoul Goldman – a Bundist member of Białystok City Council; and Anna Rosenthal – a member of Vilnius City Council. Rosenthal was over 60 years old and had been a revolutionary during the days of Tsarist rule. Indeed, she had been sentenced to death by a Tsarist court, although the sentence was later commuted to hard labour. Non-Jewish socialists arrested included Stanisław Grylowski and Mieczysław Mastek – respectively General Secretary and President of the Railwaymen's Union, and Kazimierz Czapiński – a member of the executive of the Polish Socialist party and on the editorial staff of the party's newspaper *Robotnik*.[21]

The speed with which so many key figures in public life and the administration were arrested shows that the groundwork had been laid well before.[22] Moreover the arrest of such prominent figures suggests that the Soviets wished to remove people of influence before the 'plebiscite' of 22 October. Certainly, the removal almost at a stroke of the political, trade union and military elite – the natural leadership element – made it difficult for the subjugated population to mobilise for resistance. Within a matter of weeks the existing prisons were full to overflowing and other premises had to be adapted as detention centres – public buildings such as churches and schools, and even factories. The arrest of one person or group inevitably led to the arrest of others – family members, friends, or work colleagues of the detainee. Names could be elicited in the course of interrogation, but the NKVD used other methods, in order to extend their control and counter organised resistance. One was to recruit caretakers, who reported on all visitors to flats in their block and on the movements of residents.[23] Another method was to take over the house or apartment of a suspect. The residents were placed under house-arrest for a period of 48 hours, while the NKVD waited for further unsuspecting prey to approach.[24]

Apart from the growing 'network' of arrests, though, people were detained purely randomly – as the result of a document search on the street, in a café or restaurant, in a group or alone. Particular attention seems to have been paid to those travelling; perhaps they were engaged in resistance activity? or were fugitives? or involved in smuggling? or speculation? And so railway stations and railway waiting rooms were often the scene of round-ups and document checks. Denunciations also led to arrests and the NKVD offices attracted a growing army of informers who, as often as not, had personal scores to settle or else were attempting to ingratiate themselves with the authorities.

The population rapidly learned about the tricks used by the NKVD. A favourite device was to suddenly detain two people conversing in a public place, and interrogate them separately, asking them in particular what they had been talking about immediately prior to their arrest. If the two depositions did not agree, the suspicion was that they were concealing something and further questioning was the most likely outcome.[25] Counter-measures were developed by quick-thinking Poles. The obvious step (especially when people wanted to talk freely and frankly about political matters or other 'taboo' subjects) was to establish immediately upon meeting what innocent subject they were to declare as the main topic of conversation in the event of sudden arrest.

Where the occupation authorities had already pinpointed a potential candidate for arrest, trickery was often employed to encourage the prey to deliver himself to his interrogators – or, at least, to isolate him from family and friends. Filip Krzyżanowski, a 50-year-old school-head from Pińsk, was requested to travel to the nearby town of Łuniniec supposedly to attend a meeting. Arriving at the railway station, he was arrested at the ticket office.[26] Similarly, Jan Cholewo, an employee of the Polish state railways in Vilnius, was summoned to the railway station supposedly to explain some technical matter concerning the building of a new railway station. He too 'disappeared', his family left without any indication of where or why.[27]

Menachem Begin, later to become the prime minister of Israel, was the subject of a similar attempt at deception. Before the war, Begin had been a follower of Zionist campaigner W. Zabotynsky, and organiser of the Betar youth movement. This was enough to bring him to the notice of the Soviet security services. In the summer of 1940 he received an invitation from the Vilnius municipal authorities to discuss his 'application'. Since he had lodged no application he was immediately on his guard.[28]

Arrests occurred the length and breadth of the occupied territory. Arrests even took place among those soldiers who had been interned as prisoners of war – or among those who were deported with their families during 1940. Most of those arrested were sentenced under Article 58 of the Soviet Penal Code (or its equivalent in the Ukrainian or Byelorussian penal codes). Article 58 had 14 'paragraphs' or subsections, the most significant of which in relation to the Polish detainees were:

2 – high treason, waging an armed struggle against the Soviet Union (sentence: death by shooting)
6 – spying
10 – diversion and propaganda directed against the USSR
13 – historical counter-revolution
14 – sabotage

Paragraph 13 was most frequently employed against those who had fought against communism during the civil war period or else had fought in the Polish Army against the Bolsheviks during the 1919–20 war. Here, as elsewhere, Soviet 'justice' could work retrospectively, i.e. it could cover 'crimes' committed before the Red Army had gained control of the region. Moreover, since Soviet philosophy regarded the Polish 'Sanacja' regime of the prewar years as 'fascist' and corrupt – as counter to the interests of the working class – service or loyalty to this regime was by definition criminal.[29]

Sentences varied, but most received from five to eight years in a correctional labour camp. Exceptionally some received less (three years), or more (10 years). Death sentences were passed and carried out, although some condemned prisoners had the fortune to see their sentences commuted.[30] Those who faced higher sentences (10 years or more) were normally entitled to some form of court process in which they faced their NKVD accusers. Otherwise the sentence would be passed in their absence and frequently read out to them in a prison corridor. Special tribunals or 'troikas' known by the acronym OSO (or OSSO) and consisting of Soviet judges and NKVD officers considered such cases and passed sentence.[31] In many cases, prisoners did not learn of their final sentence until they were in the camps. Beata Obertyńska had her sentence of five years' corrective labour revealed to her in Vorkuta in late 1941, *after* she had heard about the Polish–Soviet Pact and the 'amnesty' for Polish prisoners.[32]

The process of investigation was often lengthy and exhaustive. It involved repeated interrogations – usually carried out at night – in which violence, threats and blackmail were not uncommonly used. Prisoners were often held for months and moved through a variety of prisons – on former Polish territory and within the Soviet Union – before embarking on a lengthy journey to labour camps in the notorious 'archipelago' of the NKVD's Gulag administration. Significantly, although sentences passed upon the arrested also presaged the subsequent deportation of their immediate family, some of those arrested in late 1939 were still imprisoned on Polish territory a year later – after their relatives had been transported to the east. Henryk Poszwiński, the mayor of Zdzięcioł, a small town near Nowogródek, was arrested in September 1939. However, he was not finally consigned to the Gulag camps (Kotlas) until a year later – after he had been repeatedly interrogated by the NKVD.[33] In the meantime hundreds of thousands of people had been rounded up and deported for 'administrative exile' without recourse to a hearing of any kind. It is one of the peculiar contradictions of the Soviet justice system that such painstaking efforts were taken to establish 'guilt' in certain individual cases, while at other times innocent people were despatched to their fate only because they had the misfortune to belong to certain preordained social categories.

Many thousands of Polish citizens were still being held in jails in Lwów, Tarnopol, Stryj and other towns of eastern Poland when the Wehrmacht launched its attack against Soviet Russia in June 1941. Large numbers of the prisoners were shot in their cells, while others were evacuated and forced on long route marches to the east, harried by their NKVD guards and periodically strafed by German aircraft.[34]

Those conscripted into the Red Army

Between 7 December 1939 and 8 January 1940, the registration took
place in the Soviet-occupied territories of all males born between 1890
and 1921. Placed alongside notices of the registration were paragraphs
from the Soviet Constitution, warning that the most severe punishment
would be passed against anyone failing to comply with the requirements of military service. It was not difficult to infer from this rather
unsubtle notification, that the registration being carried out by the authorities was preparatory to the call-up of able-bodied men (aged 18–49) to
the Red Army. On posters appearing at this time were propaganda
slogans such as: 'Service in the Army is an honour.'[35]

Reports reaching the west from Polish underground sources indicated that Soviet propagandists, while giving notice of the recruitment
to the Red Army, promised that Polish units would be formed, that
these would be under Polish command and even subject to Polish Army
regulations. The units would be used, listeners were led to believe,
only in the event of hostilities with the Germans.[36] Although the reports may have been accurate – and it is known that Polish communists were planning to create such a force – there were officially no
such units formed until after the German attack on Russia in 1941,
when they were formed on Soviet soil by the Polish Government.

This registration was completed in March 1940. In September of the
same year three age cohorts – those young men born in 1917, 1918
and 1919 – were called up for the Red Army. Courses were organised
for the recruits which, in some instances, took place before their formal registration (i.e. during July and August 1940). Lecture topics included the Red Army – history and organisation – and civic duty;
sanitation and health; and the Russian language. In Lwów, where courses
took place during 12–31 August, the end of the course was marked by
military-style exercises involving some 3000 people.[37] In December,
three further cohorts, 1920, 1921 and 1922, were also called up. Medical
commissions passed virtually all registered males as fit for frontline
service, releasing only those upon whom their parents depended for
maintenance.[38] Also caught up in the conscription were young men of
Jewish, Ukrainian or Byelorussian ethnic background – including refugees
from central and western Poland. The Polish Government in London
later estimated that the Soviets forced into Red Army service some
200 000 people.[39]

The call-up was accompanied by attempts to intimidate the population. It was made known that refusal to make oneself available for

military service was a capital offence, and the family of the individual concerned would have land and property confiscated before being transported to Siberia. Recruitment took on the character of a mass uprooting, a weeding-out of the young male population of the occupied territories. It was a very clever and a very effective step in neutralising the most likely source of continued resistance to Soviet rule.[40] Polish reports also state that in some cases the work of the recruitment commissions was carried out by NKVD squads, without any help from medical specialists (i.e. there were no accompanying doctors). Even the ages of those being 'press-ganged' in this way were not thoroughly checked, and several cases were recorded of older men, of up to 38–40 years old, being taken. These 'round-ups' to the Red Army took on a mass character as the Red Army retreated before the German advance in the summer of 1941.[41]

The recruits were directed either to the Work Battalions (*strojbataliony*) or to Red Army combat units, in which case they could be drafted to the front. The majority were taken in battalions 250–400-strong – though some numbered as high as 2000 – into the interior of the USSR, beyond the Urals. There they were employed on heavy physical work: building, laying railway tracks, loading ships, factory labour (building of cars, trucks, aircraft), etc. They worked for long hours – 12-hour shifts being common – in a harsh regime which was usually accompanied by some form of political education (*politnauka*). Their living conditions were poor. Often they were living under canvas, in less than adequate hygiene with only subsistence rations.[42] Because of the inadequate selection methods, many youngsters physically unsuited to such work were taken.

Volunteers

The category of 'volunteer' embraces various kinds of motivation for movement to the USSR proper, although in numerical terms it is not large. In the first place it includes those pro-communist or pro-Soviet elements who either migrated to Soviet territory as collaborators during the period of Soviet rule in Western Ukraine and Western Byelorussia, or else fled to the Soviet hinterland in an attempt to evade the advancing German armies in 1941.[43] At the other extreme were those who felt disposed to move to work in the east because they felt under threat and were fearful that the NKVD were closing on them. What better way of evading the clutches of the security forces than taking an assumed name and volunteering for work in the Soviet economy?

But the largest group were those, including both manual workers and professionals, such as doctors, who volunteered for work within the USSR for non-ideological reasons – simply in order to survive. The term 'volunteer' needs some elaboration. Incentives and inducements were offered to recruits which were extremely difficult to turn down – especially to those thousands of refugees from the western regions of Poland. Not only did they have no means of support, but they were required to register for work by the Soviet administration. Since the majority of refugees were Jews, they were eager to put as much distance between themselves and Hitler's armies as possible. A propaganda campaign was waged in the press, including the Yiddish paper, *Der Bialystoker Shtern*. There is even a case on record, from the town of Sokal, which had a large Jewish refugee population, of a Jewish propagandist addressing a synagogue congregation on the Sabbath, calling the refugees to register for work.[44]

The 'volunteers' were sent to a variety of destinations throughout the Soviet Union – from the Crimea with its mild Black Sea climate, to the harsher environment of the northern Urals and Siberia. They were sent to kolkhozes and industrial plants, to mines and forests, to large industrial centres and also to small, isolated villages and settlements. The working conditions they encountered varied immensely. The largest contingent – including thousands of refugees – was sent to the Donbas coalmining region in south-eastern Ukraine. Nevertheless, the conditions the recruits found in the Soviet Union were in general so abysmal that large numbers attempted to return to their former homes on Polish territory – despite the notorious severity of Soviet labour discipline and the penalties they risked by leaving their place of work. A very small group – probably only a few score people – found welcome to Soviet territory as entertainers. The fate of these people in the USSR was far removed from that of most Poles during this period. In some cases they performed for the Soviet élite and were feted and pampered for their services.[45]

Establishing the number of volunteers who moved into the Soviet Union 'proper' (i.e. east of the prewar Polish–Soviet frontier) is problematical. One Polish historian has suggested an overall figure of 30 000.[46] The Polish-language Soviet press in Lwów reported that 15 000 volunteers had left Western Ukraine alone for the Donbas by 21 December 1939, and that new transports were leaving each week – but the report may have been more for propaganda purposes than for information.[47]

THE MASS DEPORTATIONS: ADMINISTRATION AND RATIONALE

By far the largest category of Polish citizens to transfer to Soviet territory were the hundreds of thousands moved *en masse* during 1940 and 1941. The decision to embark on a forcible uprooting and resettlement of the Polish population was taken at an early stage by the Soviet authorities. Released Soviet archival documents indicate that orders from the Soviet Interior Ministry (and signed by Beria) for the deportation of 'osadniks'[48] from Western Ukraine and Western Byelorussia, and their employment in 'special settlements' were approved on 29 December 1939, a mere six weeks before the first major operation was unleashed.[49] However, these documents cover the administration of the journeys and employment of the deportation groups. They say nothing about the criteria for selecting the victims or drawing up lists. So it is likely that such lists – containing tens of thousands of names – were already in existence at this point.

The criteria for selection – for identifying victims for the NKVD's attentions – are contained in documents which reached the west after the war. They comprise instructions drawn up and issued by Guzevicius, Commissar of the newly-sovietised Baltic state, Lithuania, in November 1940. Instruction document no.0054 set out for the communist powers at local level the criteria to be adopted in drawing up lists for transportation from the Baltic States.[50] These were to be people considered to be anti-Soviet and socially undesirable – because of their affiliation to, or membership of, certain organisations; because of whom they had talked to, where they had been, who they were; because of their 'objective characteristics'.[51] It is reasonable to assume that similar documents were issued prior to the deportations which occurred in the occupied Polish territories during this earlier period. In the Polish case, however, included in the category of 'socially undesirable' or 'anti-Soviet' were: university professors, teachers, engineers, the whole of the forestry service, wealthier peasants and smallholders, and certain categories of worker. Families of military personnel outside Poland (e.g. in the west) were included, as were refugees from western Poland and small merchants and craftsmen ('speculative elements').

In keeping with Stalinist views on crime and punishment, responsibility for transgressions against the New Order in the occupied territories fell not only on the individual, but on his whole family. The assumption was that the individual was a product of his environment. This being the case, when a 'criminal' was discovered the course to be adopted was not merely to punish the individual, but to root out the whole family network in which he had been raised and had lived. So, the army officer, mayor or policeman was not alone in his 'guilt'; equally culpable – or at least equally threatening to the communist social and political order – were his parents, his wife and children, and his siblings – especially if they were sharing accommodation. Hence the large number of women and children caught up in the deportations. Few of the deportees had any idea of why they were being deported. Jan Gross has written that the deportees were not given reasons, but were subject to secret decisions of some unidentified organ of Soviet administration. As we have seen above, even among those arrested and imprisoned, many only received notice of their sentences once they had arrived in the Gulag – and relatively few appeared before courts or NKVD tribunals.[52]

The manner in which the deportations were to be carried out was set out in an order by Deputy Commissar for Internal Affairs, Ivan Serov:

> The deportation of anti-Soviet elements is a problem of great political importance. The planning of the deportation must be worked out down to the smallest detail and carried out by 'executive troikas' in each district ('obwod'). It must be carried out with absolute calm so as not to spark resistance or panic among the local populace.[53]

The order, signed by Serov, authorising the deportation of anti-Soviet elements from the Baltic States, fell into German hands at Valka in the summer of 1941. The notorious Serov was to become something of a technical specialist in mass-deportation operations, since he was reputedly involved in the deportations of the Volga Germans and also in the deportations from the Baltic states in the immediate postwar years.[54]

The Polish 'osadniks' who were taken in the earlier (February 1940) deportation were, according to the NKVD administrative order, to be deported simultaneously throughout (western) Ukraine and (western) Byelorussia on a day fixed by the USSR NKVD. They were to be permitted to take clothes, linen, footwear, bedclothes, tablewear, tea and kitchen utensils, food provisions, household and domestic tools, an unlimited amount of money, domestic valuables – and a trunk for packing their effects. The total weight of these objects was not to exceed 500 kg. (This was reduced in the case of the Baltic deportations to 100 kg, but there is no evidence that the weight of goods was ever checked.)

The 'osadniks' were to be transported to their resettlement areas in wagons 'equipped for winter use to transfer humans'. (This indicated that the cattle-trucks should be fitted with bunks and heated, but not all were and, even where small stoves had been supplied, they were usually inadequate.) Naturally, the Commissariat of Transport would supply the necessary rolling stock upon prior application by the NKVD. The wagons were to be organised in columns of 65 wagons – including a first-class carriage for the guards and one equipped as a medical carriage. The Soviet Commissariat of Health was to provide one male nurse and two other nurses per column, plus the necessary medicaments. No more than 30 persons (adults and children) were to be placed in each wagon, while four wagons were to be allotted to the storage of larger implements (agricultural machinery, etc.). Most remarkably, we read in point 7 of this instruction,

> While in rail transit, 'osadnik' special deportees are to be given a free hot meal per day and 800 g. of bread per person. Meals are to be cooked and distributed in accordance with requests presented by the Head of the NKVD columns to the trusts of railway restaurants and refreshment rooms of the USSR People's Commissariat of Food. The food expenses of 'osadnik' special deportees in transit are to be covered by the USSR NKVD.[55]

It seems that here, as in so many other cases, there was a huge gulf between Soviet theory and practice.

THE OPERATIONS

Deportations began in the second half of January 1940 and continued until June 1941, but four 'peaks' of activity can be identified. In the first major deportation, which began during the night of 9–10 February 1940, the largest group of victims were Polish military colonists ('osadniks') as well as forestry workers from the state and private sector. The deportees came from throughout the former Polish territories and in many cases whole families were taken. Ethnic Poles predominated, the number of Jews, Ukrainians or Byelorussians being few.

How the seizures of families appeared in practice we may judge from the following eyewitness account of the arrest of the Zalewski family in the Łomża district. The father was a school janitor in the village of Szumów whose only 'crime' was to have received a parcel of land from the Polish state:

A cart bearing militia and NKVD agents pulled up in front of Zalewski's cottage. The family's modest possessions were thrown on to the cart; bed linen, a small chest and some pots and pans. One of the NKVD men led out a 6-year-old girl in a nightshirt, wrapped in a sheepskin coat and threw her on to the cart. The father brought out his 3-year-old daughter wrapped up in a quilt and put her on to the cart. In front of the vehicle stood an NKVD officer with a revolver in his hand; behind it were Zalewski, his wife and their eldest daughter. At the rear of this funeral procession was a soldier armed with a rifle. To the crying of women and children and Zalewski's defiant words 'Poland is not yet lost' ['Jeszcze Polska nie zginęła', the opening words of the Polish national anthem] they moved off in 35° of frost to the station of Czerwony Bór, some 28 kilometres away.[56]

In many respects, this first mass deportation was the most severe, since it was carried out at a time of the year when temperatures in Eastern Europe can fall very low indeed. Also, being the first, it caught people unprepared. (Later, as the momentum of arrests and disappearances grew, many Poles kept bundles of their possessions ready-packed for just such an eventuality.) Subsequently, during the lengthy train journeys, many children and elderly people were to die. Polish Government sources later estimated that as many as 10 per cent of the deportees may have died from cold, hunger and related illnesses.[57]

Some of those taken began to suffer almost as soon as they set off. Wojciech Morawski, son of a military settler, recalls that the NKVD came at 3 a.m. His family were given three hours to pack a permitted 500 kg of luggage before being moved to another 'oblast'. The family members were reassured by the news that they were being resettled in a *neighbouring* district. (The systematic NKVD disinformation which accompanied individual arrests was also widely practised in the course of these large-scale deportations; no doubt in accordance with their instructions not to alarm or panic the population if it could be avoided.) Having waited at the local village hall until 5 p.m. they were then taken to the railway station in Zdołbunów – some 80 km away. Only small children were allowed to travel in the covered wagons with one woman; the rest travelled in the open with the luggage. On the way, snow began to fall so heavily that some carts were forced to turn back and return the following day. As a result of prolonged exposure to the sub-zero temperatures many people were affected by severe frostbite.[58]

The degree of organisation and planning necessary on the part of the Soviet authorities was considerable, as several authors have observed. Lists of the victims, their precise whereabouts and destinations had to be drawn up.[59] So meticulous and precise was this preparation that cases are recorded of Poles being taken from prison to be reunited with their families at the railway station; also, children taken from school to be reunited with their parents at the station.[60] Trusted personnel had to be mobilised to carry out the operation: the NKVD, local militias, the Army, and even trusted civilians were employed. Herschel Wajnrauch was a Soviet civilian – a journalist brought in to work on a Jewish newspaper in Białystok. He recalled: 'The Soviet police did not have enough people to carry out the mass arrests, so ordinary Soviet citizens were used to help. Our newspaper was asked to provide two people, and I was one of them. We were given weapons and went with the Police to arrest these people and send them to Siberia.'[61] The whole operation was carried out in such secrecy that it came as a complete surprise to most victims.

Finally, there was the question of organising the rolling stock to transport these people to the East. A railway worker has confirmed that all other movement on the railway ceased for the duration of these operations.[62] A number of authors have drawn attention to the rhythm of the movements once they began in February: the two-monthly pause would have given the transports just enough time to disgorge their passengers and turn round to drive to the west again for a further load.[63] The unanswered question, of course, is whether this pattern of two-monthly deportations would have continued, had Hitler's forces not vanquished France so comprehensively.

On the whole, the NKVD troikas carried out their duties with complete efficiency. Sometimes there was brutality but, equally, in some cases, the guards gradually showed a human side, gave advice on which items should be taken and even began to help with packing. It seems also that according to the majority of accounts the deportees were given some two to three hours to pack – longer than provided for in Serov's later order.[64] The transports from this first mass-movement of population were directed to the remote northern and central regions of the Soviet Union – from the Arctic Circle in the north to the Mongolian border in the south – to regions of Archangel, Vołogda, Irkutsk, Sverdlovsk, Kirov, Novosibirsk and Komi.

The second major deportation movement took place two months later, during the night of 12–13 April. Again the victims came from all over the territory annexed to the Ukrainian and Byelorussian Republics. They consisted on this occasion of families of those apprehended by the NKVD during the previous seven months of Soviet rule; police and army officers and NCOs, schoolteachers, industrialists, merchants and traders (including a certain proportion of Jews), people active in community and political life, employees of state and cooperative concerns, the landowning class and wealthier farmers, Ukrainian and Byelorussian nationalists, former members of the Communist Party. Also included were the families of POWs – both those in German captivity as well as those in Soviet hands – and families of those who had escaped abroad. In this wave of transports, there was a preponderance of mothers and children – although some cases occurred where the aged parents and adult siblings of an arrested individual would be taken.

The April operation, as with its predecessor, was planned in complete secrecy. If the idea of deportation to the land of the 'white bears' had lost its capacity to shock, the population was not forewarned about the timing of the operation. It was carried out using the same methods. The April deportees were taken to an area of northern Kazakhstan bordered in the west by the Urals and in the east by the Altai mountains – Aktiubinsk, Kustanay, Petropavlovsk, Karaganda, Pavlodar, Semipalatynsk. In several respects they encountered more favourable conditions than the earlier deportees. They were not dispersed in such remote areas, being employed in rural districts in kolkhozes (collective farms) and sovkhozes (state farms) as well as in the towns.

The third major wave of deportations occurred at the end of June 1940 and involved refugees from the central and western districts of Poland who had fled before the German advance during the military campaign of September 1939. Consequently this group included a high proportion of Jews and, in particular, those who had earlier registered with the Soviet authorities as willing to return to the German-held areas.[65] Candidates for repatriation were informed that if they turned up at the railway station on a given day they would be conveyed to the west. By this ruse not only were the NKVD able to avoid causing panic, but they saved themselves the trouble of conveying their victims to the stations! Having boarded the trains with their luggage, the trains then bore them not to the west, but to the east. The fact that the 'resettled' community of Poles in the USSR was later found to have a large proportion of Jews (estimated by some sources as being 30 per cent – compared with 8 per cent of the population in the prewar eastern territories) can largely be attributed to this third wave of transports.

The final major movement took place between 13 and 22 June 1941 – up to the very day of Hitler's launching of hostilities against Soviet Russia. On this occasion deportations were carried out from the Baltic states, which had been freshly annexed to the USSR. These affected the Vilnius region, which had formed part of the Polish Republic in 1939 and, following the Soviet takeover, had been ceded to Lithuania. There the round-up took place from 15 June onwards. By some estimates ten thousand people were taken from Vilnius alone, of whom the majority were Poles but among whom were Jews and Lithuanians too.[66] These transports travelled east for several days before disgorging their passengers in the Altai district.

THE JOURNEYS

After the trauma of being ejected from their home, the long train journeys to the east were a further terrifying experience for the deportees. Most were transported in freight wagons, packed as many as 50 or 60 to a truck. Transports, or 'eszelons', numbered up to 40–50 trucks, so one 'eszelon' could in theory carry more than 2500 people. But Maria Łęczycka, for example, travelled in a wagon which held 72 people – including 28 children – in a transport of 60 wagons. Assuming that the deportees were evenly distributed between the wagons, this would have meant some 4320 souls taken in just this one transport.[67] The small windows were usually barred and, once the passengers had boarded, the doors were sealed. A tiny hole some 20 cm wide in one corner of the wagon (or sometimes in the centre) was provided for the needs of nature. Makeshift bunks had been constructed at the ends of the wagons. For the first deportation (February 1940) many of the wagons had been provided with small stoves. The deportees travelled in these conditions for three weeks or more.

Those that had brought food with them were fortunate. Relatives who heard about the round-ups came to the stations with food and clothing, but in most cases were turned away by the guards, even though the transports might wait two to three days before moving off. As word spread about the scale of the movement, crowds of sympathetic fellow-countrymen and women appeared at stations *en route* to the frontier and, if they could not approach the wagons, attempted to throw bread, hardboiled eggs and other items of food towards them.

Rations provided by the guards *en route* were meagre and infrequent. In many cases the doors were not opened until the transport was safely on Soviet territory. Then the provisions might consist of black, sour bread, fish soup with heads and entrails in it, or simply hot water (*kipiatok*). Maria Łęczycka's transport in April 1940 received food rations for the first time at Zhitomir in the Soviet Ukraine.[68] Volunteers

from each wagon (called *nosilszciki* – because they acted as 'carriers')
jumped out with jugs, buckets or other containers to bring the millet
porridge and black bread – half a kilogram per person – back to the
train. The travellers were fed in this way on average once every two
or three days. But, on other occasions, guards proved reluctant to supply the prisoners even with water. This was a major problem during
the later deportations (when the weather was warmer), and became
excruciating when the deportees had received salted fish to eat and
developed an overpowering thirst.

Danuta Tęczarowska remembered that, during a halt, Russian soldiers would jump down from the train and walk along the wagons,
offering to sell the passengers tins of crabmeat, ham, fruit and even
sweets. She later learned that the train included a special wagon of provisions for the deportees (as provided for in NKVD instructions; see
above) but that the passengers were being fed on bread alone – 300 g
per person per day, with the option of buying their rations. She writes:

> Theoretically the transport was quite well-provisioned with food. Were
> it not for the fact that some of the food was being 'sold' to us and
> the rest being stolen by the crew, we would have been adequately fed,
> bearing in mind the circumstances and the purpose of the deportation.[69]

Once the initial shock of the prisoners had passed, and the wailing
of women and children had eased, attention had to be turned to making the best of their conditions within the cattle-trucks. A major problem was lack of space. Luggage was rearranged and living space allocated
so as to make life tolerable. For some of the deportees, luck placed
them in a wagon with their neighbours from the town or village. For
others, their fellow-travellers were complete strangers – sometimes of
very different class or ethnic background. The prospect of spending
almost a month, day and night, enclosed in close proximity to people
from outside one's immediate family is daunting. But given the in-
sanitary conditions – the lack of ventilation, the limited opportunity to
wash oneself or one's clothes, the primitive toilet conditions, the rapid
spread of lice and other parasites – conditions must have been unimaginably appalling. There was also the problem of children who, even
in the restricted space available, wanted to play and let off energy.
(Later in the journeys they would become listless and apathetic due to
lack of vitamins.) Babies cried frequently as the journeys progressed,
since there was insufficient milk. Mothers were increasingly unable to
nurse their children, due to their own deteriorating physical condition.
Powdered milk was, of course, unobtainable.

When added to the uncertainty surrounding their ultimate fate, the stresses must have been immense. It is little wonder that disputes broke out. Trivial matters such as the behaviour of a fellow-passenger's children, or a neighbour's malodorous socks might act as the trigger, not to mention social and political differences. Such disputes sometimes resulted in violence, but in some transports a form of social organisation and structure developed, with a leader ('starosta') elected both to moderate in disputes, and to act as representative in dealings with the Soviet guards. (For obvious reasons, the person chosen would often be a Russian-speaker.)

Transports remained sealed until they reached their destination. However, the guards would generally open the doors during scheduled stops (to take on fuel, change train crews) and unscheduled stops. Certainly they were more relaxed once they had reached Soviet territory and having crossed the Urals, in the April transport, the doors remained open for long periods. This enabled the passengers to get out, breathe fresh air, and take some exercise. If the stops were made at small stations, they were sometimes able to buy or barter with the local people for food. Elsewhere the travellers were able to collect firewood in order to boil water. Often, though, the trains would resume their journey without any warning. It was not uncommon for those who had strayed too far from the line to be left behind at a remote station or in the wastes of the tundra or taiga.

Their early encounters with *homo sovieticus* were frequently something of an eye-opener. Many of the railway-workers and other Soviet citizens glimpsed in the proximity of the railway line seemed to be in a worse condition than the deportees themselves. Maria Łęczycka observed a man tending chickens. When she threw the chickens some mouldy pieces of bread, the man threw himself upon them eagerly; a salutary warning about the nature of the regime which had now asumed the power of life or death over them and the value that food would have within this new system.[70] Another Polish woman who, at one halt, asked a passing railway-worker what he possessed, received an answer which she later discovered to be a stock response in Stalin's Soviet Union; 'the sleeves on a waistcoat'.[71]

The Soviet populace in turn were ignorant and ill-informed about the involuntary passengers whose lives came into contact with their own for a brief moment. A woman railway-worker, being asked for boiled milk for the children in one of the wagons, queried why the travellers had brought children with them. When told that they had had no choice, and were being deported, she was astonished. The loco-

motive drawing the train was decked in green, and word had spread
that the 'passengers' on the train were volunteers from the Western
Ukraine who had been unable to find work in capitalist Poland. Only
in the remoter regions east of the Urals were the green vestments on
the locomotive finally discarded.[72]

Occasional halts also meant that contact could be made with Poles
from other transports. Few people caught up in the early deportations
had, at first, any idea of the scale of the undertaking. They had little
conception that it was any more than a local operation. Only when the
trains began to move east, and different transports began to pass one
another, or encounter one another in station halts, were messages shouted
from group to group – 'Where are you from?'; 'Do you know anything of the Lipiński family from . . .?' It was only at this stage that
realisation dawned and, as one survivor recalled vividly, 'it seemed to
us suddenly as though the whole of eastern Poland was on the move'.[73]
The *nosilszczyki* from Maria Łęczycka's transport (which had originated in Lwów) encountered trains from Zborów, Złoczów and
Kołomyja at their first halt in Zhitomir.[74]

Escapes did occur, usually by prising up boarding in the wagon and
making an exit while the train was still in motion. But such escapes
were only worth attempting while the train was on Polish territory, or
within reach of it. Five men from one transport left at Zhitomir. In yet
another, a deportee was dissuaded from escaping – to discover that a
large, steel, scythe-like instrument had been placed below the last wagon,
presumably to end such escapes.[75] In most cases, the household heads
– adult males – had been separated from their families before the journeys
began. This meant that if they had any idea of attempting escape, they
would be abandoning their near ones. They had the comfort of believ-
ing, though, that the families would remain together. (In reality, of
course, this was not always the case. Often the railway trucks were
separated off during the journey, and the males taken off in another
direction.)

Deaths were a frequent occurrence – particularly among the February deportees, who had come unprepared for such an odyssey in the
winter temperatures. But they also occurred among the very young
and the very elderly of the subsequent waves.[76] The starvation diet
weakened resistance to various illnesses. The dead were sometimes
buried beside the railway line, if the guards could be persuaded to
open the doors. But often either the train did not stop or the guard
would not open the door. In such circumstances, the tiny forms of
babies had to be pushed through the window while the carriage was

still in motion. One such case, remembered by a deportee who was a 13-year-old girl at the time, involved a woman who fell into deep shock when her child died, and refused to be parted from it. By the third or fourth day, when the little corpse was beginning to smell, and the other passengers could stand it no longer, a delegation prised the body from her and pushed it through the window. [77]

CATEGORIES AND DESTINATIONS

The fates of civilian Poles imprisoned or forcibly transplanted by the Soviet regime during this period can be summarised under three, or possibly four, headings. The main three categories were outlined by the Soviet Deputy Commissar for foreign affairs, Andrei Vyshinsky, in a conversation with Polish Ambassador, Stanisław Kot on 20 September 1941.[78] Vyshinsky was a professor of Penal Law and therefore could have been expected to have had a first-hand knowledge of Soviet sentencing procedure. He had also been, during 1935–37, Chief State Prosecutor in a number of the notorious Moscow show trials.[79] According to Vyshinsky, the Soviet judicial system allowed for three degrees of administrative restriction of freedom:

1. Confinement in compulsory labour camps, in which the inhabitants work for their living, with total deprivation of liberty.
2. Settlement in special economic units frequently equipped with farming stock and implements, the so-called 'special settlements' (*spetsialnoye posheleniye*), where work is performed under normal conditions and the deportee enjoys complete freedom of movement in the given locality.
3. Individual exile to a definite locality, in which the given person lives quite freely and works entirely as he chooses, but has no right to leave the locality and remains under police (i.e. NKVD) supervision. [80]

There was a fourth possible category which was not mentioned by Vyshinsky: those people considered to be dangerous political opponents of the Soviet regime who were held in prisons or camps under life-sentence and completely deprived of freedom and the right to 'amnesty'. Information about such a category has come from chance conversations with other prisoners. However, because, by definition, such people would not have been released by the Soviet authorities to make their way out of the Soviet Union, it is almost impossible to verify this. Evidence is therefore circumstantial.[81]

The Labour Camps

Large numbers of people of working age – both men and women – were sent to corrective labour camps (ITL – *isprivitelno-trudovye lagerya*) under the administration of the Gulag (*G lavnoye Upravlenie Lagierei*), a sub-section of the NKVD. This was the fate of all those Poles who had been arrested formally and sentenced by NKVD courts – even though many never appeared in person before a court and did not learn of their sentence until they had been in camp for some time. Those who had been arrested on the Polish territories and were taken from NKVD prisons to make the journey east by rail suffered the same fate.

Specially transferred settlers (*Spetspieresedlentsy*)

A further class of deportees had not been arrested or sentenced and were not deemed in need of 'correctional labour' in camp surroundings. These were the so-called 'special settlers'. An individual was assigned to this group if he was considered to be an 'anti-Soviet element' and of some value in terms of manual labour. Their fate might have been expected to be easier, though this was rarely so. They too were despatched to distant regions of the USSR, often far from centres of population – in Archangel, Vologda, Gorky, Molotov, Kirov, Sverdlovsk, Chelyabinsk, Irkutsk, Novosibirsk, Omsk, the Komi Republic, the Marysk Republic, Yakutya, Khaborovsk region, Krasnoyarsk region and Northern Kazakhstan. Often the journeys to their destination did not cease when they left the trains. They travelled onward by cart, lorry, barge, and sometimes on foot. Their surroundings and climatic conditions varied greatly as did their living environment. Such people were directed to *spetsposiolki* (special settlements) and their movements restricted. They were not permitted to leave the *raion*, and were only allowed to leave the settlement for more than 24 hours if they gained permission from the NKVD commandant. Family groups were taken and, although in some cases separated *en route*, were allowed to live and work together as a unit.

'Voluntary Settlers' or 'Free Deportees'

The 'free deportees' (*wolni sylni*) – mainly women and children – were not regarded as suitable for heavy work in forests or mines, but were nevertheless a 'socially dangerous element'. The deportees from the April 1940 and June 1941 movements were chiefly in this category, which consisted of the families of army personnel and police officers, officials and others who had been arrested previously. They were not obliged to work and had relative freedom of movement. However, they risked being denied even the roof over their head and the meagre rations which camp-dwellers enjoyed if they could not find a way of supporting themselves. They were treated more lightly than the 'special settlers', were issued Soviet passports, and were expected to vote.

This group, then, consisted of women with children or elderly relatives. They found themselves suddenly ejected from their trains at isolated stops in the wilderness of northern Kazakhstan or the Altai Krai region. Their journeys usually continued up to a further 50–100 km by other forms of transport to the designated kolkhoz or sowkhoz. There they were either lodged under the same roof as local villagers, or given vacant ramshackle accommodation and told to adapt it.[82]

STATISTICS

How many Poles travelled across the 'Riga Line' into the Soviet Union proper during this period? The statistics of movement, and particularly those relating to the great deportations from Polish territory during the period 1940–41 have been the subject of much debate. There are varying estimates of the numbers taken, broken down according to category (how taken), social or ethnic background, and according to age and sex. Many of the earlier statistics were drawn up on the basis of information collected by the Polish Embassy in the Soviet Union during the period 1941–43. Subsequently different Polish government agencies produced their own estimates. It will doubtless remain impossible to arrive at a firm figure unless the Moscow archives release what must be voluminous documentary evidence relating to these events. Since it seems impossible to claim primacy for any particular set of figures, those given below are for the purpose of general orientation only.

In 1945 the 'Press and Culture Section' of the Polish Second Corps in Italy produced a brochure by P. B. (Bogdan Podoski) which characterised in statistical form the Polish territory taken over by the Soviets in 1939 and the nature of the deported population. Podoski's estimate was that 1 692 000 people had been removed from the region by the Soviets. Of these, 1 114 000 were permanent residents of eastern Poland, 336 000 were refugees from western and central Poland, and 242 000 were soldiers, mobilised in 1939.

Podoski went further in breaking down the figures.

- The 'permanent residents' included 250 000 people imprisoned and sentenced to terms in corrective labour camps; 210 000 conscripted to the Red Army; and a further number subjected to deportation in the mass waves of 1940–41. (Since he estimates the total deported as 990 000 and the refugee population among the deported as 336 000, the number of permanent residents deported must therefore come to 654 000.)
- Of the 'refugee' population, 138 000 were ethnic Poles, while 198 000 were Polish Jews.
- Of the 'soldiers', 230 000 were captured immediately following the September campaign in Poland, while 12 000 had been seized in 1941 following the Soviet takeover of the Baltic States.

Of the overall total, there were thought to be 1 121 000 males and 571 000 females, the age breakdown being as follows:

(i)	younger than 14 years	379 000
(ii)	15–49 years	1 128 500
(iii)	over 50 years	184 000

When classified according to language 58 per cent were Polish speakers, 19.4 per cent Hebrew/Yiddish, 15 per cent Ukrainian and Russian, 3.8 per cent Byelorussian, 2.4 per cent Polesian and 1.4 per cent 'other'. The most numerous category in terms of occupational background were farmers, military colonists, and forestry workers (35 per cent). There were approximately the same number of army and police personnel, while 15 per cent were employed in industry, mining, trade, communications and transport; 10 per cent in education, public and health service. The remainder included the self-employed, and domestic servants.[83]

According to estimates cited by Zbigniew Siemaszko, in the course of the first (February 1940) deportation, 220 000 Polish citizens were deported; in April 1940, 320 000; in June–July of that year, 240 000; and in June 1941, 200–300 000. Siemaszko gives a figure of between 980 000 and 1 080 000 taken in the four major deportation waves alone.[84] The comparable estimate from Professor W. Wielhorski – 1 050 000 – comes within this range. Wielhorski's estimates of the overall movement from eastern Poland is 1 492 000. His breakdown is as follows:

Deportations	1 050 000
Polish troops (POWs)	180 000
Polish troops (from Lithuania)	12 000
Red Army (enforced conscription)	150 000
Prisoners evacuated from jails	100 000

However, Wielhorski, in common with many of the scholars who have worked on these figures, does not give an estimate for the number who moved voluntarily to Soviet territory.[85]

Most estimates from Polish émigré sources range between 1 250 000 and 1 600 000 altogether.[86] The fact that the Soviet authorities only admitted to holding 387 932 Polish citizens at the outbreak of the German–Soviet conflict can be attributed to a number of factors.[87] Firstly, the Soviets' category of 'Polish citizen' may have been restricted to those who were not permanent residents of eastern Poland when the Red Army moved in. The permanent residents of the region were considered by this time to have become Soviet citizens. Secondly, the mortality rate of the Polish deportee population, estimated in some studies to be as high as 30 per cent per year, would have drastically reduced the original number. It is unlikely, however, that Soviet officials had reliable and up-to-date statistics of this kind – still less that they would have taken the trouble to collect them after war broke out. The most probable explanation, as Gross suggests, is that the figures were a guess, a deliberate deception. [88]

2 The Sikorski–Maisky Pact of 1941 and the 'Amnesty' for Poles Confined on Soviet Territory

THE SIGNING OF THE PACT

On 22 June 1941, Hitler launched Operation Barbarossa against the Soviet Union. Five-and-a-half million men, 3500 tanks and 4000 aircraft were hurled at the Reich's unsuspecting ally along a front of some 3000 km. Despite repeated warnings from the British about German designs, the Soviet defences were unprepared for the assault. Stalin had preferred to believe that Churchill was mischievously attempting to foment a German–Soviet conflict, and had discouraged any obvious defensive measures which might have been misconstrued on the German side.[1] Consequently the Wehrmacht raced across eastern Poland and within days had penetrated deep into the Ukraine and Byelorussia. Vilnius was taken on 24 June and Minsk three days later. By mid-July, the Baltic States had been occupied, Smolensk and Kiev captured. The German armies, having covered some hundreds of kilometres in a few weeks, were only some 320 km from Moscow.

At 9 p.m. on the day of the German attack, the British prime minister, Winston Churchill, made a radio broadcast in which he held out the hand of friendship to the Russians:

> Any man or state who fights on against Nazidom will have our aid. Any man or state who marches with Hitler is our foe....That is our policy and that is our declaration. It follows therefore that we shall give whatever help we can to Russia and the Russian people.[2]

The haste with which Churchill chose to make his speech, and the offer of help to Moscow without any conditions attached, met with disbelief and even dismay in some Polish circles. At a meeting of the Polish Cabinet on the following day the view was expressed that Churchill's speech had been precipitate and 'too warm'.[3] But Churchill had emphasised the need for speed of action ('we must speak out now, at once, without a day's delay') and this may have been due, at least in part, to the pessimistic British assessment of Soviet defensive capabilities.

On the following day, General Sikorski made a broadcast of his own to the Polish nation on the new situation which had arisen as a result of the German–Soviet war. His speech, intended also for the ears of the Soviet authorities, was conciliatory towards Moscow. While referring to the recent history of Soviet–German collaboration against Poland, Sikorski signalled that the new turn of events entitled the Poles to assume that Russia would cancel its 1939 Pact (the Molotov–Ribbentrop Pact) with the Germans. This, he continued, should logically bring both parties back to the position governed by the Riga Treaty of March 1921. (In other words, the Soviets would recognise the prewar Polish–Soviet frontier.) He then went further, to ask rhetorically whether the thousands of Polish men and women suffering in Russian prisons should not be restored to their liberty.[4]

A change in the official Soviet position was a few days in coming, but when it did come it was more positive. The initial response could be detected in a radio broadcast by Stalin on 3 July in which the Soviet leader underlined the necessity of helping all the peoples of Europe who suffered under the German yoke.[5] In London, on the following day, Soviet Ambassador Maisky made clear to Anthony Eden that he was prepared to meet with the Polish leader and he outlined the Soviet Government's position regarding relations with the East European states. Moscow had decided to enable Poland, Czechoslovakia and Yugoslavia to form National Committees in the USSR. The Committees would be empowered to recruit national military forces in the Soviet Union, which Moscow undertook to supply and equip. It followed therefore that all Polish prisoners of war held in the USSR would be handed over to this Committee. When this was reported to Sikorski, the Polish leader's response was cool. It seemed, he said, to be a renewed attempt to introduce pan-Slavism, though of a 'red' variety this time. There was, he pointed out, no need for a 'Polish National Committee' since a legal Polish Government already existed in London.[6]

Maisky had continued by saying that Soviet policy was to favour the establishment of an independent national Polish state, the boundaries of which would correspond with ethnographic Poland. This was an early response to Sikorski's 'assumption' in the course of his radio broadcast that Polish–Soviet relations would return to the situation governing under the Treaty of Riga. The Soviet statement displayed considerable diplomatic gamesmanship – regarded by the Poles as

arrogance – in referring to the 'establishment' rather than the 'reestablish-
ment' of the Polish state. If the Soviet side was permitted to present
the matter as starting *ab initio*, then it naturally became easier for
Moscow to treat the frontier issue as being completely open. However, as the Poles pointed out, there was little comparison between the
22-month hiatus during which a legally constituted Polish Government
had been functioning abroad, and the earlier period, following which
Poland's borders had been the subject of discussion and negotiation –
the 123-year period of partition which had ended with the rebirth of
the Polish state in 1918.[7]

By referring to 'ethnographic Poland', however, Stalin was making
it clear that he would not consider a return to the 'Riga Line' (i.e. the
prewar Polish–Soviet frontier). Whether this was merely a bargaining
position, and whether Sikorski could have engineered a Soviet retreat
from their redoubt had he been more determined and less susceptible
to British pressure must remain a matter for conjecture. However, the
political and moral pressures on Sikorski to reach a settlement were
considerable (and he let it be known that he was sensitive to them).
The Polish authorities in London were aware of the plight of the many
hundreds of thousands of Polish deportees on Soviet territory. Sikorski
knew well that for each day he delayed more of his countrymen were
dying. Nevertheless it was politically impossible for him to sign away
a half of Poland, and when both sides eventually sat down and agreed
to cooperate, the frontier question was deliberately left open.

Sikorski and his Foreign Minister, Zaleski, had their first meeting
with Maisky in the presence of British officials on 5 July.[8] While both
parties agreed to set the question of the Polish–Soviet frontier aside,
Sikorski made two telling points. In the first place, he observed, Moscow had no valid claim to the eastern Polish provinces since there had
been practically no ethnic Russians in the regions occupied by the
Red Army in September 1939. Moreover, since the USSR was not a
national state, but a composition of numerous nations ruled by Moscow, she had no grounds to impose strictly ethnographic frontiers on
Poland.[9]

July was taken up with delicate diplomatic manoeuvring, as both
sides sought to gain advantage. Most of the negotiations were carried
on through the mediation of the Foreign Office, and considerable pressure
was exerted on the Poles to reach an accommodation with Moscow in
the interests of Allied harmony. When the Agreement was finally signed
by Sikorski and Maisky on 30 July, it contained five main clauses,
two additional protocols and two secret protocols. It stated that the

Soviet–German treaties of 1939 relative to territorial changes in Poland had lost their validity, and that diplomatic relations between Poland and the USSR would be restored immediately. The Polish and Soviet governments agreed to cooperate ('render one another aid and support of all kinds') in the war against Hitler. This included Stalin's consent to the formation of a Polish army on Soviet territory, under a commander to be appointed by Sikorski. The vexed question of the release of Poles detained in prisons and camps was dealt with in one of the attached protocols. The protocol reads as follows:

> As soon as diplomatic relations are re-established, the Government of the Union of Soviet Socialist Republics will grant amnesty to all Polish citizens who are at present deprived of their freedom on the territory of the USSR either as prisoners of war or on other adequate grounds.[10]

Some five weeks after initial diplomatic approaches had been made, an agreement had been signed which promised to release the captive Poles from their purgatory. But the term 'amnesty', applied to the many hundreds of thousands of civilians carried off by the NKVD, was regarded by most Poles as being both insulting and compromising. It begged the question of the deportees' guilt since, after all, only those who have been convicted of a crime can be given an 'amnesty'.[11] Wherein lay the guilt of the many thousands of mothers and children, the sick and elderly, who had been swept up in the NKVD's maw? Yet their 'culpability' was emphasised by the further wording of the protocol. The 'amnesty'was being granted, it was stressed, 'to all Polish citizens on Soviet territory at present deprived of their freedom as prisoners of war or *on other adequate grounds'*.[12] The Soviet regime was therefore inviting the Polish Government to concur with the view that the mass arrests and deportations and the compulsory call-up to the Red Army had been justifiable. Naturally, for the Poles, it was hardly the time to argue the point or quibble about wording. Their most urgent objective was to free their people and ensure that they were given adequate means of subsistence.

Despite such unpalatable aspects of the diplomatic negotiations, which held warning signs for the future, Sikorski broadcast triumphantly to the homeland. In 1795, he claimed proudly, the signatories of the Treaty of the Third Partition had vowed that Poland and the Polish name were to disappear forever. This Treaty had been cancelled by the judgement of history. In September 1939 a similar Treaty to annihilate Poland 'for ever' had been concluded. This had not even lasted a couple of years. 'Such documents', he maintained, 'are only scraps of paper in the face of the dynamism and vitality of our nation.' Claiming that they stood on the threshhold of a new era in Polish–Soviet relations, Sikorski admitted that the present agreement only provisionally regulated disputes 'which have divided us for centuries. But,' he continued, 'it does not permit even of the suggestion that the 1939 frontiers of the Polish State could ever be in question. It does not allow of any idea that Poland has resigned anything.'[13] This was wishful thinking. Unfortunately there were those in the Kremlin who felt pleased that they too had not 'resigned anything'.

How was the Agreement received? In British circles, unsurprisingly, it was regarded as an act of great statesmanship. *The Times* described it as 'a triumph of diplomatic good sense' that both these allies of Great Britain and 'enemies of Hitlerism' should have settled their differences; the more 'broadminded and statesmanlike views' of the negotiators had prevailed 'over certain partisan objections'. Reporting that henceforward 'Russia' regarded the treaties of 1939, in so far as they concerned territorial changes in Poland, as having lost their validity, the editorial continued, somewhat optimistically, that she 'therefore presumably renounces the gains she made in virtue of them'. *The Times* editorial ended on a high moral tone which must have been read with some irony by those with first-hand knowledge of Soviet justice and the labour camp system:

> With *elementary human rights at stake*, the Soviet and Polish Government have shown their realization of the truth that the need of unity among the States *defending civilization* rises superior to the individual need of any one of them.[14] [my italics]

But, among Sikorski's countrymen, there were divisions. Three of Sikorski's Cabinet – Zaleski, Seyda and Sosnkowski – resigned over the terms of the agreement; namely, over the failure to pin the Soviets down to the Riga frontier. President Raczkiewicz was equally concerned and refused to sign the final document, a task which Sikorski eventually took on himself.[15] There was a widespread feeling of distrust of the Soviet leadership and a sense that they should be tied down now, while they were weak and in need of western help. Most Poles at home, however, like those elsewhere, understood the reasons for the Agreement and signalled their approval.

POLISH–SOVIET COOPERATION

Sikorski had been pondering the choice of a suitable ambassador for Moscow before the talks with Maisky were brought to a conclusion. His eventual choice was partly determined by circumstances, but also in large measure by personal loyalties. His first choice had been the prewar Polish premier, Kazimierz Bartel, who was known to have been in Lwów under the Soviet occupation. However, it proved impossible to establish contact with Bartel. Subsequently it became known that he had been murdered by the Germans after their entry to the city, for alleged collaboration with the Soviet authorities.[16] The post was then offered to General K. Sosnkowski, who was a longtime colleague of Sikorski's, but latterly also something of a rival to the premier. Sosnkowski would have been a disastrous appointment, not only because of his close association with the prewar Sanacja regime, but also because he made little secret of his distrust of, and distaste for, the Russians. Fortunately he turned down the appointment, evidently because he did not believe (in common with many British and Polish military figures at the time) that the Soviet forces would be able to withstand the German onslaught, and therefore that there was any point in his journeying to Moscow. He also objected to Sikorski's failure to press Moscow on the question of borders or who was to be considered a Polish citizen and, as we have seen, he eventually resigned from the Cabinet.[17]

Sikorski then turned to his old friend and confidant, Stanisław Kot, who held the home affairs portfolio in the exiled Polish government. Kot was a member of the Peasant Party and had for many years been a close adviser to the peasant leader, Wincenty Witos. He was an academic historian – Professor of Modern History at the Jagiellonian University in Kraków – and had recently received an honorary doctorate from Oxford University. Yet despite his academic record, the appointment of Kot has been seen as a great mistake on Sikorski's part, who, it is claimed, selected his ambassador more from personal loyalty and the need to have someone in the position that he could trust, than the desire to have an experienced and competent diplomat in place. A number of Polish historians have drawn attention to the fact that Kot knew neither the Russians nor the Soviet Union; he did not speak their language, and had not the slightest experience of diplomatic work. He also lacked the personal qualities – the sense of discretion and tact needed in diplomatic dealings. And he was thrown into a situation which would have proved extremely demanding even for a seasoned diplomat. Certainly the appointment came as a surprise to Kot himself, and it took six weeks for him to arrange his affairs and travel out to Moscow. (He arrived in Moscow on 4 September 1941.)[18] In the meantime, Józef Retinger travelled to Moscow as *chargé d'affaires*, or, to put it more precisely, having travelled to Moscow to represent Polish interests he was subsequently appointed *chargé* – apparently through the intervention of the British Ambassador, Stafford Cripps.

The 'amnesty' decree provided for in the Polish–Soviet Agreement was finally issued by the Soviet authorities (the Presidium of the Supreme Soviet) on 12 August – the day Retinger arrived in Moscow. It was signed by Kalinin as President and Gorkin as Secretary. Two days later, the Deputy Commissar for Foreign Affairs, Andrei Vyshinsky, told Retinger in Moscow that the Soviet Government attached great importance to the Agreement. The Soviet Government would support on a large scale all welfare action undertaken by the Polish authorities for the Polish population. Moreover, the Soviet authorities were anxious that the thousands of Poles residing in the USSR should work and live in adequate conditions and feel at home in the Union; that those fit to fight should fight, and those who wished to work should work. The man entrusted by the Soviet authorities with all day-to-day matters relating to Poles in the USSR was K. N. Novikov, head of the IV Department of the Soviet Foreign Ministry. It was Novikov who assumed responsibility for problems encountered in implementing the Polish–Soviet Agreement – in particular, with problems of individual Poles not freed under the amnesty.[19]

At the end of August a 22-strong delegation left Liverpool by ship to travel to Archangel and thence on to Moscow. The team of officials heading for the Polish Embassy included the writer Ksawery Pruszyński and the artist Feliks Topolski – who captured their vision of wartime Russia in prose and sketches respectively. When the group arrived in the capital, it was to find Retinger already installed in the tall, dark house nestling in a Moscow cul-de-sac that had been rented by the Polish Government before the war. Returning after almost two years, the Poles found the building in a dirty condition. The furniture had vanished and many refugee Poles were already camping in the ground-floor rooms. But a significant discovery was the large quantity of notepaper with embossed headings of the eagle and swastika. Evidently the house had been used by various German agencies (military *attaché*, air *attaché*, purchasing mission, etc.) until their hurried departure on 22 June.[20] The Polish staff had only a matter of weeks in their restored embassy before their work was disrupted by a transfer out of the capital. The proximity of the German forces led to the evacuation of diplomatic missions and many Soviet ministries to Kuibyshev (formerly Samara) on the River Volga. On 15 October a party of seventy people left on a journey that was to last five days. They arrived on the 20th having passed *en route* 'crowds of our wretches sick and hungry, sent off without a plan'.[21]

The moves to establish a Polish diplomatic presence ran in tandem with moves to establish a military presence. On 2 August a Polish military mission headed by General Zygmunt Szyszko-Bohusz travelled to Moscow. The mission was charged with preparing, together with the Soviet military authorities, detailed plans for the formation of a Polish Army in the USSR. The party, which included Major Leon Bortnowski and Wiesław Arlet (later to become first secretary at the Polish Embassy), arrived in Moscow on 6 August, having initially travelled by Royal Navy Catalina flying-boat around the northern coast of Norway to Archangel. Szyszko-Bohusz had been briefed before his departure and entrusted with a number of key tasks. Apart from the signing of a military agreement, he was to secure Soviet agreement to the release of interned soldiers, issue instructions concerning the recruitment of Polish citizens on Soviet territory and select, in liaising with the Soviet military authorities, a suitable site on which to locate camps and to begin the work of organising a Polish Army.

In Moscow the Polish mission was greeted by Andrei Vyshinsky, deputy Foreign Minister, and the Red Army Chief of Staff, Marshal B. Shaposhnikov. The main Soviet representatives in subsequent negotiations with the Poles were Generals G. Zhukov, A. Panfilov and A. Wasilewski. Panfilov was nominally in charge, and Zhukov was to be responsible for NKVD liaison with the Polish commander. But, in reality, Zhukov was the key figure. He was considered a senior expert on Polish affairs; not only had he had dealings with leftist, pro-Soviet Poles in the course of 1940, but he was to resume contacts with figures such as Wasilewska, Berling and the pro-Moscow group in 1943, once diplomatic contacts with the 'London' Polish Government ceased.[22]

The Polish–Soviet Military Agreement was signed on 14 August, only two days after the 'amnesty' decree. Polish military units were to be formed on Soviet territory, and they were to be an integral part of the Polish Armed Forces owing allegiance to the President and Government of the Polish Republic. However, it was anticipated that they would be employed on the Soviet–German front, and would fight alongside the Red Army. The Polish Army on the territory of the USSR would consist of land forces only. Conscripts and volunteers for the

Polish Air Force and Navy would be sent to Great Britain (points 4 and 5). It was agreed (point 7) that Polish units would be sent to the front only when they were fully ready for action and, in principle, they would operate in groups not smaller than divisions and would be used in accord with the operational plans of the Soviet High Command.

The Soviet Government undertook (point 10) to maintain and feed the Polish formations on an equal basis with its own, but it was foreseen (point 12) that some arms and equipment would have to be obtained by the Polish Government from the British and from the Americans through the 'Lend-Lease' scheme. In order to facilitate communication (point 14), a Polish military liaison mission was attached to the supreme command of the Red Army, and a Soviet liaison mission to the Polish High Command in London.[23]

General Władysław Anders was chosen to command the Polish formations. Other senior officers, such as General Stanisław Haller, an early choice for the post, could not be located. Haller, as later became clear, was one of the victims of the Katyn forest massacre, perpetrated by the NKVD. Despite pressure on Sikorski to send an older and more experienced figure out from England, Anders was a good choice. He knew Russia and the Russians, having served (and been decorated) in the Tsarist Army since before the First World War. He had a fine military record and had opposed Piłsudski during the latter's 1926 coup attempt, and so was not tainted by association with the policies of the prewar Polish regime. He had a further important asset: he had experienced at first hand Soviet prison conditions. Although the point was made that Anders, so recently released from prison, would probably harbour strong resentment against the Soviets and find it difficult to work with them, his prison experience was in some respects an asset rather than a hindrance. He had gone through similar tribulations to those of the men and women he was to command.[24] This was important for someone who had to ask his men to cooperate with their former jailers. His personal qualities and achievements subsequently elevated him to near-messianic status among the Polish population in the USSR.

Anders, having been imprisoned in the Lubianka, experienced a remarkable change of fortunes. On 4 August, after 20 months' imprisonment, seven of them spent in solitary confinement, he left the Moscow prison in a limousine driven by an NKVD chauffeur – without shoes but wearing a shirt and pants. He had lost 14 kg in weight. Just prior to his departure he was led through the corridors of the Lubianka to a surprise encounter with NKVD head Beria and his deputy, Merkulev.

Over tea and cigarettes, the NKVD chiefs informed Anders that, with the approval of the Soviet Government, he had been entrusted with the job of commanding the Polish forces to be formed on Soviet soil. They were, they said, very pleased about this, since they had discovered that Anders was the most popular choice for such a position; 96 per cent of Poles supported him. As usual, these figures showing the democratic 'will of the people' had been plucked out of the air; there had been no plebiscite held and the Soviet security chiefs could not have known what degree of support he commanded.[25]

At the beginning of August a number of other senior officers were released from prisons or camps. They included General Michał Tokarzewski, General Michał Boruta-Spiechowicz, Colonel Leopold Okulicki, Colonel Antoni Szymański, Colonel S. Pstrokoński, Lt-Col. Nikodem Sulik and Lt-Col. Kazimierz Wiśniowski. (The 'Małachówka' group of officers, which had been undergoing political reeducation courtesy of the NKVD, was also freed to join up with Anders's forces.) Officers were given a lump-sum payment in order to support themselves until they reached the mobilisation centres; these amounted to 5000 roubles for generals, 3000 roubles for senior officers, and 2000 roubles for junior officers.

Within two days of the signature of the Military Agreement (i.e. on 16 August) a Polish–Soviet Commission met to deal with organisational and supply matters arising from the creation of the Polish divisions. The Commission met five times within 14 days (16, 19, 21, 28 and 29 August) – a measure of the amount of work and the urgency involved.[26] Matters discussed included the registration and recruitment of volunteers, the organisation of recruitment commissions, the selection of a site for the new units to be based, and the issue of uniforms and supply. The Polish side requested that Poles serving in the Red Army be transferred to the new units. A request was also made that the new Polish formations should be served by Polish chaplains; i.e. that the religious freedoms enshrined in the Soviet Constitution should be exercised in deed and not merely in words. Panfilov replied that there were no objections from the Soviet side.[27]

At the second meeting on 19 August, both sides agreed that two infantry divisions would be formed together with reserve units. The sites eventually chosen for the Poles were:

Buzułuk	Command
Totskoye	one infantry division plus reserves
Tatischevo	one infantry division

Soviet representatives agreed that Red Army experts would be seconded to Polish units to instruct in weaponry, artillery and other necessary
skills. Soviet liaison officers were also sent to the Polish units, osten-
sibly to help in easing coordination with the local authorities and with
local military command, but covertly to report back on the morale of
the Poles and their loyalty to their new Soviet ally.

At the initial meeting on 16 August, Anders had requested a list of
Polish officers held as prisoners by the Soviets. In the course of the
second meeting, General Zhukov handed the Polish representatives a
list of the names of some 1658 officers who had been released from
Soviet camps. The list came as a shock to the Poles, who were aware
that a great many more officers had been captured during the period
following the September 1939 defeat in Poland. As early as 5 July, in
London, Sikorski had drawn the attention of Soviet Ambassador Maisky
to the article in *Red Star* (of 17 September 1940) in which the Soviet
Command claimed 181 000 POWs taken – and more than 9000 Polish
officers, including 12 generals and 55 colonels. Thus began the grim
and ultimately fruitless search for the missing Polish officers, a search
which in its initial period met with misinformation and evasion from
the Soviet side.[28]

From the third week of September, Polish military representatives
were placed at key stations on the railway lines leading to the Polish
camps – such as Kuibyshev, Kirov, Gorky, Chelyabinsk, Chkalov,
Novosibirsk. They were to direct Polish refugees travelling to join up
with the Polish forces and they had at their disposal relief supplies to
dispense to the more needy of the refugees.[29]

RELEASE AND FREEDOM

Understandably, the Poles reacted to news of the German attack on
Soviet Russia with excitement. Many felt a sense of satisfaction, feeling that justice had at last been done; the Soviet colossus, which had
attacked them in such a cowardly fashion in 1939, was now receiving
some of the same treatment. There was also a widespread belief that,
if the German–Soviet understanding had now been overturned, the situation of the Poles would improve. Sentiments of this kind, though,
had to be concealed in the presence of fellow-prisoners or 'kolkhozniks',
since any misplaced expression of enthusiasm for this unexpected turn
of events might be wrongly construed and result in a visit from the
NKVD. Furthermore, feelings of optimism on the part of some Poles

were balanced by those who suspected that, with Soviet Russia now at war, their situation would deteriorate. There could be no hope of release since, with the Germans driving towards Moscow, the Soviets could not risk the presence of an alien element – a potential 'fifth column' – behind their own lines.[30] Indeed, many of those in camps and settlements noticed a tightening of their conditions; food rations were reduced and, in the camps, there was greater alertness and rigour among the guards.[31]

Weeks later, when the news of the Polish–Soviet Agreement – and the 'amnesty' – began to reach the Poles, it was received with indescribable relief and joy. Kot reported from Moscow to Mikołajczyk on 10 September that

> almost all those, whom one meets here ... and who are travelling here at our request from the east, cannot find the words to express their appreciation and thanks for the Pact. Today the Kraków socialist, Szumski, arrived, and he recounts how the Poles in Siberia praise Sikorski like a divinity. He was quite astonished when somebody here referred to criticism of the Pact by some of those in England.[32]

While Kot, being a strong supporter of Sikorski, would have been reluctant to relay any criticism of his leader's action, it is true that the general mass of Poles supported Sikorski, and his popularity grew to heroic proportions. Nevertheless some Poles did harbour reservations about the Pact, both about the prospect of fighting shoulder-to-shoulder with the Soviets ('Why together – and how would that be possible?'),[33] and about the unresolved matter of the eastern territories; the potential loss of territory involved was not considered by some to be worth the price of their own lives.[34]

Many of those who were employed in kolkhoz work or in settlements heard almost immediately from Soviet radio broadcasts of 1 August, and were then able to check the news and glean more detail from national or local Soviet newspapers.

> ... we heard the news over the radio that a Polish–Soviet Pact had been concluded and that, on the basis of this Pact, all Polish citizens were to gain their freedom. On the same day we found in a copy of the *Kirov Pravda* the text of this Pact. The effect of this on the Poles in the camp – of whom there were about 400 – was immense. They walked around in groups discussing the turn of events.[35]

Others – especially in some of the camps and 'special settlements' – heard rumours, but for confirmation had to rely on the whims of NKVD personnel; concrete information about the Sikorski–Maisky Pact often reached them considerably later (weeks or sometimes months). Those living more freely as 'settlers' – for example on kolkhozes – heard from the local population, as the news was broadcast through the Soviet media. Others heard in more dramatic circumstances:

> When the Polish national anthem 'Poland has not yet perished' sounded out on the first ship carrying prisoners released from the Polar Sea area along the Pechora River, it caused a tremendous shock among the groups working on the banks and a powerful reaction among those Poles who did not yet know about the Pact, yet felt that their rescue by the Polish Government was imminent.[36]

The news was passed from mouth to mouth excitedly. Janina Kowalska (Hanka Swiderska) recalls how she and her mother in a settlement in the Novosibirsk region, some 600 km from the Mongolian border, heard the news of the Pact over the radio and she went running out into the fields to convey the news to her father. Some time later, Poles gathered outside the House of Culture, raised a makeshift flag and made speeches, sang and cheered. The local residents, she added, looked on as though dumbstruck.[37] The effect on the local Soviet population is reported in many of the Polish accounts. In the camps, the Poles were generally regarded with envy by their fellow-prisoners; their new status often brought lighter conditions and treatment, although they were expected to continue working – even on threat of court proceedings – until the necessary confirmation of release came through from official sources. A certain aura and prestige attached to them not only among the prisoner population, but also among the NKVD staff, since the concept of a general amnesty of this kind for one particular national group was unknown. After all, it was only months since Poles, arriving in camps and settlements had been told by their captors to forget about Poland – that they would not see their homeland again and had to resign themselves to new lives as Soviet citizens. A rather different reaction from the Soviet prisoners, however, was one of envy tinged with resentment. Skrzypek comments that Soviet prisoners freely complained that Poles – 'open enemies' of the Soviet system – were being released while they, Soviet citizens, serving in many cases shorter sentences – were to remain in the camp.[38]

Polish prisoners-of-war were brought from the Komi Republic and concentrated in three camps (Susdal, Juza and Talica) in the Gorky district. The men did not believe the amnesty until the arrival of Colonel Nikodem Sulik, Anders' recruitment emissary. Following Sulik's

attendance and his speech to the men, twelve officers revealed themselves, including Lt-Col. Tadeusz Scheybal, who was entrusted with
command over the camp. But there were still other officers who would
not come out of 'hiding'.[39]

At the time Sulik himself was released (he had been arrested in
Vilnius in June 1941 and spent time in three Moscow prisons, latterly
sharing a cell in the Lubianka with Anders), his wife and daughter
were engaged in railway construction-work at a site some six kilometres from Pavlodar (Kazakhstan). There the camp authorities posted
a notice to the effect that a 'Polish *Red* Division' was being formed
and that volunteers were being sought. Quite clearly, the local Soviet
authorities were unable to believe that a foreign power could be enabled to create military units on Soviet soil. Eighteen-year-old Zofia
Sulik and her mother were the first to leave – having received a letter
from Colonel Sulik informing them about the turn of events. However,
other Poles were suspicious at first, thinking that the recruitment poster
was a ruse to inveigle them into the Red Army. Later, as they gradually gained confidence and applied to leave, the attitude of the local
officials began to change. At first, the camp authorities had sent off
the volunteers with a fanfare, as heroes, but later they appeared less
and less happy to part with the Poles; they had their productivity targets to meet and were losing valuable labour.[40]

Poles released from camps, from prisons or from special settlements
were issued by the NKVD with special release documents – *udostovierenya*. The wording of the documents confirmed that the bearer, as
an 'amnestied' Pole, was free to travel within the Soviet Union. Certain limitations were placed on this freedom: border regions were ruled
out, as were certain forbidden zones and towns considered strategically important. The document was valid for three months, after which
the bearer was expected to exchange it for a passport. Those from
labour camps and prisons received, together with the release document, a travel warrant, and an allowance which amounted to 15 roubles
per day – the total amount to be calculated on the basis of estimated
time of travel to the stated destination.[41] The allowance was of some
value if used at official soup-kitchens and other feeding-points, but
was of no value at all on the open market, where inflated prices put
most foodstuffs out of reach. Those on the *posioleks* (settlements) or
in 'free exile' had to sell their possessions, if they wanted to travel –
or else attempt to obtain cash from the Polish Embassy.

Although the amnesty decree had specified that 'all Polish citizens'
were to be released, accounts indicate that frequently the elderly and

the weak were the first to be released – clearly those who would be least missed in fulfilling plan schedules. Although Poles and Jews seem to have been released in large numbers, there is no indication of whether discrimination was practised against those of Ukrainian or Byelorussian ethnic origin.[42]

On occasion, release from corrective labour camps provided the opportunity for a release of pent-up resentments and a settling of scores. Dr Juliusz Margolin records that among the Polish Jews in his camp at the time of the amnesty, there was one 'who was not a bad fellow' but who began to cooperate wholeheartedly with the camp authorities. Having been put in charge of a neighbouring lagpunkt, he became 'excessively zealous in exercising his right to send people to solitary confinement'. On the first day of freedom he was lynched by his companions: 'strangled to death and thrown from the train'.[43]

MASS MIGRATION

The decision of whether or not to travel was a difficult one for many. Weighing against the difficulties of their present situation was fear of what to expect if they moved. Most Poles had experienced such a dramatic decline in their fortunes that they did not imagine their future could hold anything worse. For some this was true, but for others, with at least rudimentary shelter, perhaps poor but regular food, and a network of Polish and possibly non-Polish acquaintances to turn to in an emergency, the journeys they were to undertake held horrors far worse than those they had endured.

On the whole the men moved, either to travel to join the Polish Army forming at Buzułuk, or, in some cases, to search for their families. Those who were with their families had the choice of leaving them to join the army (and then sending for them), or else risk travelling with them without any knowledge of what provision might be made for them. Perhaps the most difficult choice, though, lay with the families who were separated from their household heads; whether to stay where they were and wait for their menfolk to find them, or move closer to the centres where the army was forming or to the Polish Embassy.

The mass uprooting and migration of Poles that took place in the second half of 1941 as a result of the amnesty from the Soviet leadership was only part of a wider refugee movement taking place in the country at that time. Soviet war-refugees poured eastward from the frontline regions. Estimates of the number of evacuees and refugees flooding eastward from the western territories of the USSR which were overrun or threatened by the German forces vary. Soviet figures indicate that between 7.5 and 10 million people were on the move. But American (US Embassy) estimates were that at least 20 million persons had left the territory overrun by the Wehrmacht. While the Soviet authorities had created a Council for Evacuation as early as 24 June and policy was drawn up in document form a few days later, the evacuation points and feeding points set up could not cope with the overwhelming demand.[44] The rail network was thrown into confusion and was unable to cope with this 'great avalanche of transmigration'. To add to the confusion, factories and industrial plant were being evacuated while military reinforcements and armaments moved west. The Poles were released in an appalling state – half-starved, susceptible to illnesses and infections, very often clad in rags, without proper footwear, and lice-ridden. Consequently, the casualties of this flood of refugees were numerous.

The Poles' situation was complicated since, not only were potential recruits on the move, but also those civilians who hoped that proximity to the forming army – some contact with the representatives of the legal Polish authorities – would ensure their survival. Those heading for Buzułuk in late 1941 began to be directed to the south by the Soviet authorities, since the haphazard movement of thousands of Poles was adding to the already grave problems of the crowded rail network. (Later, it became known that the Polish Army would be transferring to a new area of concentration close to the Persian and Afghan borders.) But some Soviet officials deliberately misdirected the Poles, and were often reluctant to supply them with food at the various station evacuation-points. The attitude 'You have your own authorities now, let them look after you' was frequently encountered. Against this background, General Anders expressed the view towards the end of October that

> the situation of Polish citizens after the signing of the Agreement is considerably worse than it was previously, when they had the organised welfare of the Soviet authorities, such as it was.[45]

One of the displaced wrote in a letter to the Polish Embassy of her odyssey and the plight that she and fellow refugees faced:

> On 10 October 1941 we left our *posiolek* (settlement) Dziabryna on the River Dzwina in the north, for the station of Kotlas. There, in

return for things we were able to sell, we managed to hire a goods wagon for 1558 roubles to make the journey to Buzułuk, where the Polish Army is forming. From Buzuluk, by order of the Polish garrison commander, we were sent free of charge to the station of Vrevskaya in Tashkent, but here too they did not keep us and directed us further to Samarkand, Kagan, Farab and at last to the station of Kitab, Kramowa. There they held us, not allowing us to leave the wagon for two days, and then our transport was sent on to Kazakhstan, to the Ahyrtude station in Dzambul oblast. There we got out and in small groups were dispersed among the kolkhozes lying on the way to Alma-Ata. Our group of 170 people was settled in the Kzyl-ly kolkhoz – in wretched, earthen dug-outs, under snow-capped mountains. Recently we have received 500 gr. of flour per working person and 200 gr. for non-workers, as well as 1 kg. of potatoes per head – and that is all. We need help urgently, above all soap, clothing, fats, sugar for the children, and money. Since, after a journey of almost two months we are completely exhausted and in the conditions in which we find ourselves, we will not be able to hold out for long without help.[46]

By a sad and tragic irony this second, 'voluntary' translocation probably resulted in the deaths of more people than the enforced uprooting which had brought them to the Soviet Union up to two years earlier. A report from Kirov stated that in a transport from the Archangel oblast which has taken three weeks, out of 1850 people, 20 had died (14 children and six adults). In a transport from Kotlas to Kirov, which had travelled between 22 October and 6 November 1941, 16 people had died at the station before the transport set off, and a further four during the journey. This underlines the fact that deaths were occurring before people had even made their way aboard the trains. In the Archangel region, seven people died on the way from Nucht Oziero settlement (Pleshetski raion) to the railway station.[47]

Tashkent was a railway junction through which passed all the transports with Poles travelling north to south – or, in fact, from the south to north – to Buzułuk to join the army. Reports from Tashkent, for the most part undated but relating to the period October – November 1941, state that four people from no. 1017 transport (numbering 1850 Poles) died during a six days' stay at Tiulkibas station. A further five people from no. 321 transport (1600 Poles) died at the same station. During a journey from Buzułuk to Farab, out of 2200 people in the transport, 60 Poles died in the course of two months. Among these, 25 died at

Farab railway station. Another report indicates that nine dead Poles had been found at Tashkent railway station and 'presumably the deaths occurred during the journey from Omsk to Tashkent'. During the one-week period 7–14 November, 70 corpses were found among the people arriving at Tashkent. In another report, we read that not a single child of the group which has recently left Buzułuk lived to reach their destination. Not in all cases, however, were travellers forced to share their journey with the dead:

> On the way to Tashkent, human corpses are thrown out of the trains as if they were carrion. Children die like flies. Typhoid and typhus are decimating them.[48]

Once the journeys were over, the suffering was by no means finished. Guzar, site of one of the recruiting stations for the Polish Army, became 'one of the largest Polish cemeteries in the Soviet Union'. Several thousand Poles died there between January and March 1942, mainly from typhus. Stanisław Skrzypek, who worked at the recruiting station, wrote that whoever could, fled from the place – but not all could. The dead, he continued, were not buried in coffins because there was insufficient wood. Death became such a common occurrence that frequently the funeral bearers would move to the cemetery unaccompanied.[49]

There was no overall plan for the movement of Poles, beyond the expectation that some thousands of able-bodied males would travel to join the Polish Army. Beyond this, no thought had been given to the possibility of the spontaneous movement that might erupt. Indeed, the Polish Embassy's attitude was that if the Poles had tolerable conditions where they were, then they should not leave their current locations.[50] But Poles in the northern camps and settlements, especially, were determined to make their way to the south before a further Arctic winter locked them in – a winter which, in their weakened state, they feared they might not survive. They made their way to the recruitment and reception centres set up by the Polish Army, hopeful that shelter and sustenance would be found for them and their families. There was a firm, mystical faith in the power and justice of the Polish cause, and a belief that once they came under the wing of the Polish authorities, their problems were behind them, their salvation was assured. But first they had to reach their destination. They waited, at times for days on end, for trains which, when they arrived, were often full to bursting. They were directed and misdirected by the Soviet authorities, but frequently fell prey to the rumour and gossip upon which their choice of destination and ultimate survival could depend. Often they were

prevented from making use of the station canteen facilities by the local
NKVD – or even driven from the station precincts. They also fell
victim to bands of Soviet criminals who preyed on the weak and helpless.

The Poles were directed in large numbers to the southern republics,
Kazakhstan and Uzbekistan – in particular towards Tashkent. Once
they reached the south, they were redistributed to kolkhozes and settlements in sparsely-populated areas of population. They were employed
in harvesting, picking cotton, digging irrigation canals. Although they
needed to work, in order to obtain food, they were reluctant to be
dispersed. The further they moved from railway stations and other key
points of communication, the more likelihood there was that they would
become isolated and abandoned.

The Soviet authorities became concerned at the large-scale movement of Polish civilians to the south, and Vyshinsky asked Kot to see
that it was stopped. Exceptional cases were, of course, those individuals and groups travelling to join the Polish Army. Others, claimed
Vyshinsky, should be employed locally in industry or agriculture and
not clog up the transportation system in the way they were doing.
Polish representatives were not impressed with this attitude; on the
one hand, there was evidence that the Soviet authorities themselves
had begun to direct Poles south from the Kuibyshev region; on the
other hand, despite repeated Polish requests, the Soviet authorities had
been dilatory in allocating an area where the Poles could naturally
concentrate and be brought under Embassy care. In any case, although
the Polish Embassy, made attempts to stem the headlong rush, it proved
quite impossible to exercise any significant effect upon it. What action
there was came from the Soviet side. Evidence reached the Poles that
the releases from camps and prisons had begun to slow. Furthermore,
at the beginning of November 1941 the Soviet authorities moved some
45 000 Polish refugees from Uzbekistan north to Kazakhstan, which
relieved pressure on rail communications and welfare services, and also
transferred manpower for agricultural work.[51] The operation was evidently well-planned and in many respects seems to have borne a simi-
larity to the deportation operations from Polish territory during 1940.
Curiously too, as we learn from the following account, those taken
seem to have included Poles engaged in gainful employment:

> On the night of 21 November the operation began in the entire Bukhara
> region. In the kolhozes and sovkhozes the people were given be-
> tween 15 and 60 minutes to prepare for the trip. No food was pro-
> vided for the journey. In a number of districts even the means of

transportation were not supplied. Only after adamant demands were a number of wagons sent to the nearest railroad station. In the city of Bukhara, throughout the night reckonings were made with people for their work, and they were ordered to be ready for immediate transportation.[52]

The spontaneous movement south eased as winter set in. Few Poles were willing to undertake lengthy journeys in unheated trucks, let alone the long delays camped outside stations. At the same time, the flow of Soviet evacuees slowed as the military front stabilised. The Soviet authorities were able to exercise greater control over the transportation movement, and this meant that, although fewer people travelled, those that did move were usually travelling in better conditions (heated wagons, supplied with food, etc.). Refugee convoys during this period were sent to Kazakhstan – primarily to Dzamboul.

THOSE NOT RELEASED – POLISH INTERVENTION

Many thousands of Poles were not released, or found that their release was delayed, despite the continuing protestations, of Polish Embassy representatives and of the Polish military authorities. Józef Drewnowski, held in one of the northern labour camps (at Vietlosian) was not released in 1941–42, and claims that only about one-third of Poles left the camp at this time.[53] Jerzy Głowala too, working in a mining camp 200 km to the south of Vorkuta, recalls that the news that all Polish citizens were going to be freed spread throughout the camp in August 1941. And indeed, releases began. Groups of a few dozen people were gathered and sent to Central Russia. The first to be released, he says, were Jews, Byelorussians and Poles of advanced age. Next followed the Poles of military age who were directed to join Anders' forces. A few remained behind, however, including Głowala himself:

> Our appeals to the camp authorities did not have any effect. It was explained to us quite simply that it did not depend upon them, but upon Moscow.[54]

In Głowala's case, his continued detention may have had something to do with his attempt to escape with a fellow-prisoner in the days following the German attack on Russia. This may seem strange timing for an escape attempt, since the camp inmates had heard of German–Soviet hostilities and might have been expected to sit tight and await

better things. However, they were more influenced by the reduction in
the food rations and the fear that they would be slowly starved to
death if they remained. Like his compatriot Drewnowski, Głowala returned to Poland only in 1955.

The factory, or camp, or kolkhoz supervisors were often reluctant to
allow the Poles to leave at a time of great labour shortage, and employed
various devices – including threats and inducements – to persuade them
to remain. The Polish prisoners at the Kruglica camp had heard about
the 'amnesty' at a relatively early stage but, on 1 September 1941, all
the Polish prisoners from the camp were transferred to a punishment
camp at Osinowka, where they were employed on forestry work.

> As protest and appeals continued to have no effect, there was a hunger
> strike imposed on 29 September. Poles and Polish Jews stood at
> dawn, after the gong for reveille had sounded and sang the old hymn
> 'Kiedy ranne wstają . . .'

The hunger-strike was solid and resulted in a victory for the strikers.
The punishment ordered by the camp authorities was called off and
the strikers were promised that they would be freed within a month,
being immediately moved back to their normal lagpunkt at Osinowka.
However, although groups of prisoners began to be released during
October, not all were set free.[55]

Poles were exhorted to join the Red Army, to take Soviet citizenship. They were persuaded that a reconstituted Poland would in any
case be communist, that the Red flag would fly over Warsaw and that
a future Polish Army would be subject to Red Army control. Many
Poles were subjected to pressure to act as NKVD agents or informers
once they were released, passing back information on the organisation
of the Polish Army or the Polish Embassy and relief effort.[56] It is
impossible to know how many were denied release because of their
refusal to sign such agreements. However, many Poles signed simply
to be able to gain their freedom, without having any intention of carrying
out the spying duties imposed on them under duress.

In some cases, information about the 'amnesty' was deliberately
withheld. When the Poles eventually found out, their letters and telegrams to the Polish embassy were intercepted by local authorities. Others,
living in remote settlements, were denied transport to take them to the
nearest river or rail point. This was the case on the settlement where
Stanisław S. was staying. Earlier, the authorities had withdrawn the
Poles' bread ration, saying 'You are Poles – let Poland feed you.' The
Poles then organised themselves, each family constructing a sledge,

and they left the settlement in a 'convoy,' pulling their sledges through the snowy forests for several days until they reached the nearest station and a train that would take them to Kirov.[57]

Those detained included women. K.S., a sales assistant in her early twenties, writes:

> The amnesty did not embrace all Polish (women) citizens. When we left for freedom from our first collecting point, some dozens of our friends remained behind who had been charged under article 58 of the Soviet penal code. The camp commandant said of them cynically that they would never see freedom.[58]

L.W., a young Polish woman of about the same age, commented after her release from the eastern camps in the Magadan-Kolyma region:

> We left, but not all of us. A few remained behind. I know the name of only one of them: Janina Karpińska. She remained behind because her husband, Tadeusz, an engineer who was at this time in Romania, moved heaven and earth to get her out of the camp and out of Russia. The interest which she aroused in the Bucharest and Moscow embassies did not enchant the NKVD. She was being held illegally as a 'spy' in the camp. In spite of the intervention of the Polish authorities, she remained there. Perhaps because she was the bravest of those who suffered with me in prisons and labour camps.[59]

It is clear that the amnesty was viewed by the Soviet authorities as an act of goodwill, but that their view of the Poles as criminals had not changed. Moreover the authorities reserved for themselves the right not to pardon certain classes of criminals, who were moved to more isolated locations or simply held behind when the others left.[60] Since, in the labour camps, instructions for release came from central authorities, the conclusion is inevitable that cases were examined and decisions taken by the NKVD on the basis of the evidence held in individual files. Many of those detained in the camps were regarded as particularly recalcitrant enemies of the Soviet system, who could not be allowed to go unpunished.

Yet in other cases – in the special settlements and the kolkhozes, as well as labour camps and factories – the implementation of the amnesty was inhibited by local officials. As the orders filtered down through the hierarchy of the NKVD's Gulag empire, they evidently became distorted or adopted to suit local circumstances, and loopholes were introduced. There were a number of reasons for this. Firstly, it has to be appreciated that the Soviet penal system and its functionaries –

accustomed to despatching people in their thousands to the oblivion of the Gulag – knew of no precedent for a general amnesty on such a scale. In the camps and prisons, NKVD guards and interrogators had not taken account of the fact that their victims, and the witnesses to their excesses, might be released *en masse* – and furthermore that the truth about their deeds might be carried abroad to a wider audience. There were personal reasons, therefore, for the NKVD at local level to resist the amnesty call, and seek loopholes in it.

Secondly, there were camps in which Poles – and particularly those Poles of military age – were the most productive element. Camp and factory bosses were reluctant to lose large numbers of their best workers at a time when the Soviet war-economy was striving to make good its massive early losses, and production targets were being raised. This explains why the elderly and less productive elements were often released first. The truth of this was acknowledged by Molotov, who was present at conversations between Stalin and Sikorski on 3 December 1941.[61]

There was a further reason for local NKVD personnel attempting to sabotage the amnesty agreement. In a number of regions the camps had been established on virgin territory and consisted only of Poles and their NKVD guards. Once the Poles were released, the existence of the camps would come into question. If the camps were wound up, it was inevitable that the guards themselves would be earmarked for other duties – including, of course, the possibility of being sent to the front. This was a career move earnestly to be avoided, and therefore local staff had every interest in hanging on to their 'settlers' and maintaining the rationale for their remaining *in situ*.

A further complication over the release of Polish citizens concerned the differing ethnic groups of the interwar Republic. The original amnesty decree had not distinguished between ethnic Poles and Polish citizens of Ukrainian, Byelorussian or Jewish descent. However, on 1 December 1941 the Soviet Government let it be known that, henceforth, it considered Ukrainians, Byelorussians and Jews originating from the 'Western Ukraine' and 'Western Byelorussia' to be Soviet citizens. Although the Polish government protested strongly against this unilateral decision, and continued to issue its citizens of all backgrounds with Polish identity documents, the question of recruitment to the Polish division, or indeed, of the distribution of welfare goods, was ultimately affected by the Soviet standpoint. Also, whereas labour camp authorities had in the early stages released members of the minorities first, from November onwards the NKVD authorities at local level had a pretext for not releasing those Jews, Ukrainians and Byelorussians who had been Polish citizens in 1939, and had been arrested or deported as such. Frequently camp commanders answered complaints by pointing out – especially to Jewish prisoners – that, 'General Sikorski (or: the Polish Government) does not want you.' Soviet policy shows distinct signs of attempting to stir up as much mischief as possible in relations between Polish authorities and the minorities. It served the Soviet ends of confirming to Western opinion that the Poles were unsuitable political masters for a multi-ethnic state.

At a diplomatic level, the effectiveness of the amnesty was the subject of frequent notes and verbal requests. Soviet replies tended to be hedging or purely dismissive, until faced with actual proof of non-release. As early as 28 September 1941, Foreign Minister Molotov claimed that all Poles had been released from captivity. Just over a fortnight later (on 14 October) this information was contradicted by Molotov's deputy, Vyshinsky. Vyshinsky presented figures to Stanisław Kot, indicating that some 345 511 Poles had been freed by 1 October, but that 42 241 were still held by the Soviet penal authorities.[62]

One of the first notes sent by the Embassy querying the non-release of certain Poles was a personal note from Kot to Vyshinsky of 12 October 1941. Kot drew attention to the presence of Polish prisoners in Gorky jail who had been informed that the Polish–Soviet agreement and the amnesty decree of 12 August did not apply to them. Although Gorky lies in central Russia and communications should not have caused too many difficulties (despite the fact that Soviet ministries and central agencies were being evacuated from Moscow at this time), a whole series of notes – including even detailed information regarding the number of the cell in which certain individuals were being kept – had to be submitted in order for the amnesty to be put into effect in this case.[63] Kot sent two further notes to the Foreign Ministry on 25 and 31 October, containing the names and addresses of several hundred Poles being held in Soviet jails or camps. He made it clear to Molotov that before General Sikorski decided on the date of his proposed visit to the Soviet Union, he wanted to be sure that there would be a speedy implementation of the amnesty.[64]

The Polish Embassy was forbidden from intervening directly with Soviet agencies such as the NKVD (although Polish Embassy operatives soon found themselves under close NKVD supervision) and were forced to route all enquiries through the Commissariat for Foreign Affairs. Kot's suggestion during a conversation on 2 November 1941 – that a roving mission including NKVD personnel and Embassy delegates be sent around the camps in which Poles were being held – was frowned on by Vyshinsky and ignored. Vyshinsky did claim that the Soviet authorities had 'name lists of those living and deceased, I promised you figures and I will supply you with them'[65] – but more comprehensive lists, of the kind only the NKVD could have possessed, were never made available to the Embassy.

On 19 November, when the Embassy sent yet another note to the Ministry, repeating its request that the amnesty be applied in full to Polish citizens, it received the reply that 'it is self-evident that the amnesty cannot be extended to people who are serving sentences as common criminals, to Nazi agents or to Germans, Italians, Rumanians, Hungarians and others amongst former Polish citizens'. The Embassy in reply referred to Stalin's declaration of 14 November that the amnesty was 'universal and unconditional' – it could not therefore be restricted or limited in this way. Even common criminals – if they were Polish – should be released. Furthermore, the Embassy had no knowledge of Italians, Rumanians, Hungarians, etc. who had Polish citizenship, and so the question of such cases did not arise.[66]

As a consequence of the Polish Embassy's brief to establish the number and whereabouts of Polish citizens on Soviet territory, it had soon decided to establish an 'Intervention Bureau.' This was to handle cases which came to light of Poles who had not been released from jails and corrective labour camps, or for whatever reason had not got the necessary release certificates and documentation; those Polish citizens imprisoned after the amnesty; POWs from the 1939 September campaign; Polish citizens in the Red Army, its auxiliary formations and labour units. A particular priority were members of the intelligentsia – people who, because of their education and attributes, would be extremely valuable in rebuilding a future Poland, especially in the light of the extermination policies being pursued by the Germans. The Bureau was to appeal to the Soviet authorities both on behalf of Poles about whom concrete information had been received and in following up enquiries regarding Poles of whom all trace had been lost in the camps. It was also to raise the question of the handing-over to the Polish military authorities of Polish citizens detained as prisoners, who had been members of German Army formations (i.e. those drafted into Wehrmacht service by the Germans). There were also private and legal matters to be followed up – such as the reclaiming of property and personal items 'confiscated' by the prison authorities at the time of arrest.[67]

The Intervention Bureau during the period of its activity sent 79 'notes' to the Soviet Foreign Ministry, highlighting the cases of some 5579 imprisoned Poles not freed under the amnesty decree and 1348 'special settlers' who had not been issued with release documents. The Embassy received replies from the Ministry concerning only 3229 – 2950 prisoners and 279 'settlers.' Until the middle of January 1942 no special difficulties or restrictions were introduced on the release of Poles but, after this period, certain categories of prisoner and deportee were regularly excluded from the amnesty provisions. These included prisoners of non-Polish ethnic background as well as those sentenced as common criminals. Further justifications were accusations of 'spying,' or crimes committed after the amnesty had been issued (including cases of starving individuals who had stolen bread). The severity of these restrictions and exclusions began to increase over time. Indeed, after January 1943, as Polish–Soviet relations deteriorated, the Ministry ceased to reply to the Embassy's notes.

On occasion, the Ministry was forced to admit that information sent to it by other branches and lower levels of the Soviet (Gulag) administration was incorrect. Thus, when the Embassy sent the Ministry a note on 12 November 1941, requesting the release of Zdzislaw Łempicki and his wife, it was informed (on 18 January 1942) that those mentioned were not, and had never been, held in a prison or corrective labour camp in the Karaganda oblast. Yet at the end of March the Embassy was able to send the Ministry a copy of the release document, issued by the command of the Karaganda ITL from which Mrs Łempicka had been released. Similar errors occurred in cases where the camp authorities issued certificates – countersigned by the prisoner – but then continued to detain him or her. In some cases Poles were released from camps, only to be told by the NKVD that they could not leave the area. They were not issued with *udostovierenya*, but with another form of release certificate which deprived them of the freedom to travel from their existing place of residence. Moreover, they were required to report to the local NKVD twice a month. This, of course, hardly amounted to release within the terms of the amnesty.

But the replies from the Soviet Foreign Ministry were often so uninformative as to be frustrating. A request for information about a list of named individuals would elicit a reply ending with the words 'the rest have been freed'. The repeated use of this form of words, almost a stock formula, raised doubts both as to whether they were true and as to whether any attempt had been made to ascertain the whereabouts of those listed. In one case (15 February 1942), the Embassy followed up such a reply by asking the Ministry to give the dates on which the remaining listed Poles – 174 in all – had been released, and to provide information about the chosen places of settlement specified by them on their release documents. It was a rather clever attempt to use the Soviet security apparatus's bureaucratic procedures to the Poles' advantage, and embarrass the Soviet officials into action. The Ministry did not reply.[68]

Such lack of information was desperately disappointing to those who were searching for family members. It was even more frustrating when Soviet officials indicated that they were unable to help because they had not been provided by the Embassy with sufficient detail about the location of those Poles being sought.

A considerable number of cases came to light of Poles being imprisoned after the declaration of the amnesty. The Embassy received news of some 344 cases, but this number did not include the arrests of Embassy delegates and other workers during the summer of 1942, and there is little doubt that the true total was much higher. Most of those arrested had 'infringed' the Soviet labour laws. A decree passed by the Supreme Soviet of 26 June, 2 and 19 October 1940 had drastically reduced the freedom of a worker to change his or her employment. The Soviet worker became effectively 'chained' to his existing workplace. The decree overrode the contract freely entered into between employer and employee. Lateness, or not turning up at all, could be punished with short terms of imprisonment.[69] The fact that Poles were prepared to risk being sentenced under these draconian regulations reflects perhaps their frustration, having heard of the amnesty, at not being released from their jobs.

The Intervention Bureau had little success, either, with the Poles called up to the Red Army. It was estimated that between 150 000 and 200 000 young men from the Polish eastern provinces had been called up in the period to May 1941. A further recruitment, thought to be between 12 000 and 20 000, had been drafted in June and July 1941. Furthermore, some Poles had been among those called up in the Baltic States in June 1940 and the spring of 1941. In August–September 1941, Poles in Red Army formations had been withdrawn from the frontline and directed to *stroybataliony*. However, all those drafted in this way, whether to the Red Army, or directly to labour units, were deprived of the identity documents which confirmed their Polish citizenship, and issued with Soviet papers.

In spite of the fact that the agreements concluded between the Polish and Soviet governments contained clauses providing for the release of Polish citizens from the Red Army, the matter had still not been settled by the end of March 1942, the eve of the first evacuation to Persia. There had been numerous approaches made on a diplomatic level, and personally by General Anders.[70] However, the only, meagre results were two groups which arrived at Vrevskaya on 7 and 11 March 1942 (220 and 120 men respectively) and a larger group of more than 500 men which arrived at the 8th Division's headquarters in Chokpak.[71]

THE PROGRESS OF RECRUITMENT

Despite the many difficulties, the Polish Army rapidly attracted recruits and grew in number and strength. On 22 August 1941, General Anders outlined plans to form, the following units:

two infantry divisions	22 000 men
a reserve company	5 000
an officers' reserve	2 000
HQ staff and administration	1 000
total	30 000[72]

On the following day, Anders issued an order informing Poles about the Polish–Soviet Agreements and about the creation of the Polish Army. The first officers began to arrive in Moscow and put themselves at the disposal of the army authorities as early as the end of August. It was decided that the new units would be formed in the southern Urals, the administrative centre, Buzułuk being only some 140 km from Kuibyshev (to which the Soviet ministries and foreign diplomatic missions were evacuated as the Germans threatened Moscow). The 5th Division was to be commanded by General Boruta-Spiechowicz and would be based at Tatishchevo; the 6th Division would be formed at Totskoye under the command of General Karaszewicz-Tokarzewski.

At the beginning of September the whole organisational core of the army left Moscow and was conveyed by air to the Buzułuk region. The first transports of volunteers had already begun to arrive at the recruitment centres from all parts of the Soviet Union. Among the earliest arrivals were former POWs released from camps at Starobielsk, Griazoviets and Suzdal, but the travellers included many categories of people, people of all ages, and women and children – sometimes whole families. The recruitment scheme was to encompass all Polish citizens residing up until 1 September 1939 on the territory of the Polish Republic. (From January 1942 onwards, this instruction had to be modified – at the insistence of the Soviet authorities – to exclude those 'former' Polish citizens who hailed from the western Ukraine and western Byelorussia and were not of Polish ethnic background.) The rank and file would be recruited from those born between 1897 and 1923 inclusive (i.e those of 18–45 years); those volunteers who had been born in 1925, and all those, regardless of age, who had been mobilised in 1939. Officers would be recruited from those former Polish Army officers born in 1892 or later (i.e. under 50 years of age); officers in retirement, in reserve, and those mobilised during the 1939 campaign; and those contract officers up to 60 years of age.[73]

In order to carry out the selection process, mixed recruitment commissions were called into being. These usually consisted of a Polish Army representative, a Polish doctor (on occasion recruited locally), a Red Army officer, and an NKVD representative. Initially the recruitment commissions were based at the Polish Army's concentration-points in the lower Urals, but roving missions were also sent out to areas in which Poles were known to be present in large numbers. Within a matter of weeks, recruitment commissions were established in many of the Soviet republics. Their tasks were to carry out medical examinations, establish the citizenship of candidates (of those, that is, who were suspect to the Soviets), and to compile a report on the recruitment process. On the medical side, categories A to D were regarded as acceptable for army service; category E, however, meant rejection.[74]

A meeting of the Mixed Military Commission on 22 August had fixed the date at which the Polish units would be ready for battle as 1 October 1941 – i.e. less than six weeks away. This was so laughably inadequate as a period for recuperation of the half-starved volunteers, let alone for training and instruction, that Anders did not even at this stage bother to oppose it. Contemporary accounts give a vivid impression of the physical state of the recruits:

> They came exhausted, in rags, impoverished, covered with sores, louse-infected, without hair, having come through typhus, and resembling rather some strange creatures more than human beings. They made their way with the last efforts of their dwindling strength. And it happened on occasion that near the station, or in the yard of the Recruitment Commission, they expired. They died quite simply from exhaustion, from having wasted away, on the very threshold of a new life.[75]

While some of those who arrived at the recruiting stations had military experience, most did not and had to be trained from scratch. But effective training was limited by the poor physical condition of the recruits and the shortage of officers. Barely two-thirds of the required number of officers could be found for the infantry divisions, and many of these were reserve officers. There was a particular shortage of officers with specialist knowledge – for example, of armaments.

Despite such problems, recruitment figures had reached nearly 37 000 by the beginning of December 1941 – the point at which General Sikorski visited Moscow. Sikorski's visit did much to help improve Polish–Soviet relations – particularly his agreement in the joint declaration that 'troops of the Polish Republic located on the territory of the USSR will wage war against the German brigands shoulder to shoulder with the Soviet troops'.[76] Other decisions taken included agreement to increase the size of the Polish forces to 96 000, and that the Soviet side would agree to supply one more division but that Great Britain would have responsibility for arming and supplying the remainder.

Following a request from Sikorski, it was agreed that the area of concentration of the Polish forces would be moved to an area with a milder climate; the southern republics of the USSR (the Uzbek and Kirghiz republics with parts of the Turkmen, Tadzik and Kazakh republics). This would ease the plight of troops who were having to endure temperatures of - 52° in their improvised accommodation under canvas.[77] Being closer to the southern border, it would also be easier for the British to supply the Poles either from Iran or India. This transfer took place between 15 January and 25 February 1942.[78] The dislocation caused by the move did not prevent recruitment figures from rising. They increased by a further 10 000 over the two months to February and then jumped again to reach almost 64 000 by mid-March as recruitment was resumed in the southern republics.[79]

However, the move to the south proved a great mistake. Polish commanders found that their camps were scattered over such a vast area – as much as 900 km apart – that communication was extremely difficult. Although headquarters were at Jangi-Jul (to the south-west of Tashkent), other Polish army centres were situated as far north as Frunze and as far south as Guzar. The rail network was heavily overburdened and alternative transport limited. The army had at its disposal only 69 lorries and 1295 horse-drawn carts. The telephone service was available for only an hour a day and often did not function at all. (It was only from 7 March that radio communication between the units was established.)[80] Furthermore the 'milder climate' that Polish leaders had sought turned out to be murderous for their emaciated countrymen as winter turned into spring and then summer. The climate was subject to great extremes of temperature, and sandstorms were frequent. There was also a profusion of deadly insects. But most dangerous were the illnesses – malaria, typhus, dysentery – to which the Poles fell victim and which, because of the lack of suitable hospital care, qualified medical staff and medicaments, killed them off in hundreds. In February 1942 the number of soldiers sick in the army as a whole was 38.8 per cent of the total, but it amounted to some 73.5 per cent in certain units. The mortality rate was 17.5 per cent of those who fell sick.[81]

The Polish camps attracted thousands of civilians and dependants, whom the Army made efforts to care for. (The transfer to the southern republics had brought the units closer to one area of enforced settlement of Poles – the Kazakh and Uzbek republics – which therefore compounded this problem.) At an early stage a Welfare Office for the families of military recruits had been formed by the Army to help these people. It worked in cooperation with the Embassy. By common agreement, the troops contributed a portion of their food rations to help the civilians. Following the transfer to the south, however, the military requested that the civilian population of the southern republics should not be moved to the Polish Army garrisons as they were already overcrowded.[82]

Although the 'amnesty' had embraced all former Polish citizens, recruitment to the Polish forces was, in practice, limited to those of ethnic Polish background. A note from the Soviet Foreign Ministry to the Polish Embassy (1 December 1941) stated that

> the readiness of the Soviet Government to recognize as Polish citizens, persons of Polish nationality inhabiting the above-named districts (western districts of the Ukraine and Byelorussian republics) till 1–2 November 1939, shows the goodwill and readiness to compromise of the Soviet Government, but in no case serves as a basis for recognition as Polish citizens of other nationalities, in particular, Ukrainian, Byelorussian, and Jewish. . . .[83]

In fact, by the time this pronouncement was made by the Soviet authorities the recruitment commissions had already accepted significant numbers of the minority populations into the army. In the early months of recruitment Polish Jews constituted a large proportion of the deportee population which made its way to the army centres. Such was the number of Jewish recruits in the early stages that there was considerable pressure both from Jewish (Zionist) sources for a separate and semi-independent Jewish brigade to be created. General Anders resisted this proposal strongly, but such evidence of the growing number of Jews in the Polish forces alerted British officials in London, who were unwilling to contemplate large numbers of potential immigrants to Palestine (candidates for the Jewish underground) leaving with the

Polish Army for the Middle East. Although the Polish–Soviet commissions, on the insistence of NKVD officials, were subsequently to block large influxes of 'minority' Poles to the Army, a certain number continued to filter through by passing themselves off as ethnic Poles. The true number is difficult to establish, but Army estimates, which almost certainly understate the minorities' position, give the following percentages:

Poles	92.23
Jews	3.08
Byelorussians	2.72
Ukrainians	1.08
others	0.15[84]

Despite the poor health of the recruits and the unpromising conditions under which they had to work and train, morale was reported to be excellent. Discipline was first-class, with an excellent relationship between officers and men who had all undergone the same privations. In many quarters there was a mystical sense of renaissance, of rebirth from the dead. Having been told so many times by their persecutors that Poland was finished and having seen so many of their fellows die, their own survival, linked with Poland's sudden elevation to a position of prestige in the eyes of the Soviet masses, could be viewed as little less than a miracle.

3 The Evacuation of Poles from the USSR during 1942

DIPLOMATIC MOVES

If the Polish–Soviet Pact of July 1941 and the resulting 'amnesty' had for Poles in Soviet captivity all the hallmarks of divine intervention, many were to experience a further 'miracle' in the course of 1942; evacuation from the USSR, with Soviet acquiescence, to come under British care and control in the Middle East. The origins of the operation, which the British codenamed 'Scalene' – the first evacuation of General Anders' forces from the Soviet Union via Iran to the Middle East – are both confused and controversial.[1] Some historians in postwar Poland sympathetic to the Communist Party line laid the blame for what they saw as a shameful 'back-door retreat' and abandonment of the Soviet ally, on the perfidious British. British politicians and generals, they suggested, needed more manpower to defend their Middle Eastern interests against the growing German threat. The British therefore conspired with General Anders to gain Soviet agreement to the evacuation – thereby confounding General Sikorski's political aim to maintain a significant military presence in the Soviet Union alongside the Red Army.[2] There is an element of truth in this version, although the reality is complex.

Sikorski had made clear at an early stage – indeed, within days of the signing of the Military Agreement with Moscow (14 August) – that the evacuation of Polish units to be formed on Soviet territory was an option under consideration. His General Instructions for the new Polish Ambassador (Kot), dated 28 August 1941, contained the following passage:

> Should the difficulties arising in connection with the formation of Polish forces in the USSR turn out to be insuperable, an evacuation of our soldiers to Near East countries should be envisaged, where new units of the Polish Army could be formed at the side of the British Army. A plan for such an evacuation should be prepared

beforehand by the Military Mission in agreement with the Embassy, choosing the following routes: the Volga, as far as Astrakhan, from thence to Persia, Syria, and Palestine, and also across the Caucasus in the same direction, or through Afghanistan to India.[3]

Evacuation of Polish troops to British Middle East control was very much in Sikorski's mind as a contingency arrangement.

In fact, it appears that Sikorski had already been drawing up plans for the possible evacuation of some Polish troops even before the Polish–Soviet Agreement was signed in London. On 26 June – just four days after the German attack on Soviet Russia – Sikorski sent a telegram to his military attaché in Ankara, Colonel Liebich, with instructions to set up an evacuation post at Teheran. Sikorski was evidently already anticipating some kind of agreement with the Soviet leaders.[4] It may be that he had in mind chiefly the naval and air-force personnel whose transfer to Britain was eventually provided for in the Polish–Soviet military agreement.

As regards Sikorski's reputed eagerness to have Polish troops fighting alongside the Red Army, the evidence is far from incontrovertible. On 1 September 1941, following the signing of the Polish–Soviet Pact and the Military Agreement, Sikorski sent instructions to General Anders in which he specifically *excluded* using Polish troops on the Soviet western front. He considered the use of Polish troops there as undesirable since 'they would be diluted there, broken up and playing a secondary role. These harmful consequences would by no means be compensated for by the possibility of reaching Poland at an earlier date. . . .'[5] Sikorski's words reflected an awareness of the danger facing the Soviet forces as the Wehrmacht continued its lightning advance towards the Don basin and the Caucasus. He did not want to see large numbers of Polish forces concentrated in this one theatre of war, in case the Soviet Union were defeated. Better by far to have forces in three theatres of war – the Soviet Union, Britain and the Middle East. As regards the Soviet–German front, he was determined to see that Polish units were not dispersed among the numerous Red Army formations and destroyed piecemeal, as they had been during the French campaign the previous year; he wanted them concentrated in one sector of the front. Instead of fighting on the 'western front' Sikorski by this stage was expressing a preference to see the Polish units employed in the Caucasus. One important strategic reason for this was to defend the Caucasus oilfields against the growing German threat. But a further consideration was that the British could more easily supply the Poles there and, in the last resort, in the event of a Soviet collapse, they could be evacuated to British care in the Middle East.

Sikorski communicated his nervousness about the precarious military situation on the Soviet–German front to British leaders. These in turn began to exert gentle pressure on the Soviets to 'transfer' some of the Polish troops to the south.[6] Foreign Secretary Anthony Eden met Ambassador Maisky on 13 October in London and suggested that the British could take over responsibility for supplying the Polish units – on condition they were moved to the southern republics.[7] Eden also sent a telegram to Sir Stafford Cripps in Moscow, requesting that the British Ambassador come to some agreement with his Polish opposite number (Stanisław Kot) and General Mason-Macfarlane (head of the British Military Mission to the Soviet Union) as to how to 'secure the agreement' of the Soviet Government to his (Eden's) proposal.[8]

On 24 October, Churchill told Sikorski and Raczyński that the Soviet leadership had been pressing for the British to send divisions to the Soviet–German front.[9] From the British point of view, the best solution to the problem would be the withdrawal of the five Soviet divisions from Iran to the Caucasus, and their replacement in Iran by the Polish divisions from the USSR.[10] The main considerations weighing on both Sikorski's and Anders' minds centred on strategy and supplies. First, would the Red Army be able to hold out, and was it worth aligning oneself with her militarily? Second, did the Soviet Union have the resources and equipment to be able to supply the Polish divisions, and the political will to do so?

The decision to carry out an evacuation was finally reached in a key meeting between Sikorski and Stalin in Moscow on 3 December 1941. Citing the problems of supply and the miserable conditions under which Polish troops were being maintained, the Polish leader proposed that 'the entire army and all the people eligible for military service' should be removed, perhaps to Persia. There, the promised United States and British help would enable the soldiers to recover and in due course, to return to Soviet territory to fight alongside the Red Army. This, he said, had been settled with Churchill.[11]

Stalin's reaction was at first one of displeasure. He could see, he said, that 'England has much to do and needs good soldiers.' He further warned his Polish guests that 'the English may force you to fight against the Germans on Turkish territory, and tomorrow Japan may enter the war'. Anders, who was also present, returned to the subject of the uncertainty and unpunctuality of supplies for the Polish divisions, stressing that this 'is only a miserable existence and months are wasted'. Stalin's emotional reply was, 'If the Poles do not want to fight then let them go. We cannot hold back the Poles. If they want to they may go away.' The Soviet leader had, however, already received appeals from Churchill and Harriman (at Polish prompting) to allow Polish troops to leave Soviet soil for a region where they could be more easily supplied. Accordingly he gave his assent that 'one corps – 2 to 3 divisions may leave'. Recruitment was to continue for a further six divisions which would remain in the Soviet Union.[12]

Stalin had also conceded a request from General Sikorski that Polish recruitment and training should be conducted in a region with a less severe climate. Accordingly, at the beginning of 1942, the Polish forces transferred from the Volga region to camps in Central Asia. The move took place over a five-week period during January and February. The Polish headquarters was reestablished at Yangi-Yul, near Tashkent. However, Polish Army camps were now dispersed over a huge area of Soviet Central Asia, adjoining the Chinese and Afghan borders. Hundreds of miles now separated the various divisional headquarters.[13]

Planning for the evacuation now began in earnest. On the British side it involved intensive communication between London, Middle East Command, No. 30 Military Mission in the Soviet Union (Mason-Macfarlane) and even British Military Command in India. The number of evacuees being planned for in early exchanges was 25 000. Sikorski planned to send up to 15 000 troops, together with another 2500 airmen and sailors to Great Britain, while 10 000 would remain in Egypt. The transfer of the contingents would enable the Poles to form a motorised division in the Middle East and to complete the 1st Army Corps in Great Britain.[14] The British had made clear to Soviet representatives by the end of January that they could handle 2000 evacuees per week at ten days' notice.[15] At this stage British assumptions were that the troops would be moved overland, but it was known that they would cross into Iran initially. Northern Iran had been occupied by Soviet troops since August of the previous year, at which point British formations had established a presence in the south of the country.[16] A series of meetings between General Mason-Macfarlane and the Soviet representative, General Panfilov, convinced the British that the Soviets were stalling.[17] Panfilov maintained that the evacuation would not take place until the six remaining divisions had been formed. General Anders had hoped to undertake the evacuation simultaneously with further recruitment and asked for British help in bringing the Soviets round to this view.[18] A recruitment mission was left in Yangi Yul but was forced by the Soviet authorities to leave.

Why should there have been a desire on the Soviet side to block or slow the exodus? There were early signs that the honeymoon period of Polish–Soviet relations, which had reached a peak with Sikorski's visit to Moscow in December 1941, had rapidly turned sour. There were signs of Kremlin displeasure over the continuing Polish refusal to accept Soviet annexation of the Baltic states and the Polish eastern territories.[19] Soviet irritation may also have been linked with Polish refusal to send their 5th division to the front. Not only was Anders unwilling to use his units in piecemeal fashion, but as yet he considered them insufficiently prepared for battle.[20] There were problems of arming the Polish formations in the Soviet Union – British arms shipments originally destined for the Poles (and one of the reasons they had been transferred to the southern republics) were having to be diverted to the Far East, because of the Japanese threat to British interests there. But Moscow was not only reacting to Polish moves. Broadcasts emitted by Polish communists from Radio 'Kościuszko' were inspired by Moscow and contained material that was highly provocative (for example, slogans such as 'The Red Army is the national army of Poland'). Small wonder, then, that the Poles continued to distrust Soviet motives.[21]

Whatever the cause of the delay, a whole array of problems and excuses were paraded by the Soviets. On 22 January 1942 the reason given for not making any decision on the date of the evacuation was that nothing could be done 'until arrangements have been made locally'. (Subsequently decision-making was moved back to the centre – Moscow.) On 31 January the Soviets suggested an alternative route to that agreed earlier. When it was suggested that the Polish officer responsible, General Wolikowski, should be brought to take part in the talks, no aircraft could be found to bring him, and he eventually arrived *by rail* on 18 February. Frustration was increasing on the British side, and Mason-Macfarlane's impatience showed through at times in his reports to the War Office. Convinced that the Soviets were blocking the evacuation of these troops who were 'badly needed by us,' the British toyed with the idea of applying counter-measures. Yet there seemed little point in threatening to suspend supplies (e.g. of tanks and other military supplies) to the Soviet ally, since the only beneficiary would have been the common enemy – Nazi Germany.[22] In mid-February, in an effort to force the pace of events, an Anglo-Polish advance party from Teheran departed for Pahlevi, having obtained consent from the local (Teheran) Soviet authorities, but not from Moscow. It was summarily ordered out of the Soviet zone.[23]

Yet, when they finally decided to move, the Soviet authorities moved quickly. At the beginning of March a chain of events was set in motion which led within days to the evacuation being carried out. On 8 March, Panfilov informed Wolikowski that SAWO – the Central Asian Military District upon which the Poles had depended for supplies – would in future be able to supply the Poles with only 26 000 rations. The Polish forces already numbered over 60 000, new recruits were trickling in at the rate of 1000–1500 per day, and overall numbers were expected to rise to 100 000. Despite this, the Poles were told that food was very scarce and the Red Army was itself having to cut down ration allocations. In London, a Foreign Office official noted that, if true, this was an indication of the gravity of the food situation in the USSR, and speculated that 'the Russians may be willing now to get rid of these Polish mouths.'[24]

A few days later, Stalin confirmed to General Anders by letter that the food situation was serious and stated that 30 000 Poles could be fed, but only on a reduced scale. The Soviets had expected to be supplied with one million tons of wheat by the Americans, but because of the war with Japan less than 100 000 tons had arrived. Churchill suggested to Sikorski that the surplus – those that Stalin could not feed – might be brought out to Persia where the British would be able to supply them with rations and armaments.[25]

On receiving Stalin's note, Anders asked for, and received, permission to travel to Moscow for direct talks with Stalin. The key conversation between the two men took place on 18 March. There it was established that the Poles would receive reduced rations for 44 000 men – 'three divisions and the reserve regiment' – from 1 April. (The Poles had five to six weeks' emergency reserves of iron rations.) There was agreement that the supernumary elements – including civilian dependants – would be evacuated and that Zhukov would be in charge of the evacuation. Stalin personally marked out a land and sea route which led across the Caspian Sea via Krasnovodsk in Soviet Uzbekistan, with an alternative land route via Aschabad and Meshed pencilled in. He assured Anders that the necessary transport would be made available. Stalin also allayed Anders' fears that the sudden movement of such a large contingent would prove too much for the British. The British, said Stalin, were such good organisers that they could easily grapple with this problem at short notice.[26]

On the evening of the same day, Anders met General Zhukov, who put forward a plan for the evacuation of 30 000 soldiers and 10 000 civilians. On the following day (the 19th) Anders issued an order for the evacuation to be set in motion. He appointed Lt-Col. Zygmunt

Berling to take charge of the Polish Base Unit at Krasnovodsk.[27] In talks with the British Military Mission, Anders confided that he realised the original British plan only provided for 2500 Poles a week at Pahlevi and that 14 days' notice of movement had been requested, but he stressed that the matter was one of life or death for 40 000 Poles, and asked only for bare subsistence for them.[28]

Churchill, when informed of this development, sent a personal note to General Ismay – 'We must make plans to receive and feed these men. Please report.' In fact, of course, the planning had been in progress for some time and was continuing. Subsequently, he wrote to Sikorski (then in the United States):

> The first batch should arrive at Pahlevi on 28 March. You will realise the arrival of such large numbers as the Russians propose to send out at such short notice will throw a very great strain upon our administrative machinery. But you may be sure no effort is being spared by us for the reception of your countrymen. . . .

Churchill continued in his letter to Sikorski by outlining General Auchinleck's proposal to concentrate the Polish forces, together with the Carpathian Brigade, in Palestine, rather than employ valuable shipping to bring detachments to Britain. He asked for Sikorski's agreement to this plan which Sikorski readily gave.[29]

THE FIRST EVACUATION

The executive order from Anders's headquarters for the evacuation to begin was issued on 23 March, but the transport plan was worked out in its entirety by General Zhukov and his NKVD staff. Zhukov had what Polish General Bohusz-Szyszko termed 'almost dictatorial powers' to carry out the evacuation and he set to it energetically, aiming to achieve his goal within two weeks. When Anders expressed the opinion that this was too short a time-period in which to evacuate all the Poles, Zhukov smiled and said, 'You are forgetting that this evacuation will be organised and carried out by the NKVD.' They were indeed effective. Bohusz writes:

> The NKVD showed sparkling organisational skill. Trains were made available almost without any delays, even though wagons and locomotives had to be brought from all over the south-eastern regions of the USSR. On the Caspian Sea all the ships of greater or lesser size

were mobilised and they managed to avoid creating any kind of serious blockage at Krasnovodsk.[30]

The first ship of the sea transport service *Karamin* left Krasnovodsk on 24 March and reached Pahlevi (present-day Bandar Anzali) on the following day. The start of the evacuation caused the British authorities on the Persian side some surprise. As late as 24 March the Soviet authorities in Teheran had professed continuing ignorance of the date of the evacuation. An advance reconnaissance party had returned from Pahlevi on the same day. The sudden change in plan meant that over 40 000 Poles (instead of the original 25 000) were now to be evacuated in just eight days. This meant a daily arrival of between 5000 and 6000 – far higher than the British had originally allowed for. When they arrived in Pahlevi on 25 March, the evacuation staff expected that the first transport from Krasnovodsk was due on the 27th. In fact they found it waiting in harbour; the first Poles were landed the same evening.[31]

The first contingent numbered 1387, almost all of whom were sailors and airmen due for transfer to Great Britain (Operation Scrivener). They were housed in buildings on the west side of the port (Camp no. 1), hired previously by reconnaissance parties. The arrivals found weather conditions cool; snow had fallen in the area a couple of days earlier and patches remained on the ground.[32]

The reception units at the Iranian port were astonished to find civilians travelling with the troops. Neither the British nor the Polish governments had given permission for, nor had they expected, a civilian evacuation. By 31 March some 13 000 Polish dependants had arrived at Pahlevi and were being conveyed to Teheran. There was a feeling in London that the British authorities had been bamboozled. Instead of receiving an army, they had inherited a welfare problem. When this news was brought to Churchill, he wrote impatiently on the telegram from Teheran, 'Foreign Secretary. Are we going to get nothing but women and children? We must have the men.'[33]

His advisers informed the prime minister that London had only been told of General Anders' intention to allow certain families to accompany the Polish troops after the evacuation had already begun. Although instructions were immediately sent by the British and Polish authorities to stop the outflow, it had proved impossible in practice to prevent civilians reaching Pahlevi. 'Once there, we have had to do our best to cope with them.' The Foreign Office minute to Churchill continued:

although we shall have 10,000 to 15,000 civilians on our hands, we shall nevertheless get out of Russia 81,000 to 86,000 troops which is several thousand more than we had originally expected. The morale of these troops could hardly be good had those with wives and children been compelled to leave them behind in the USSR....[34]

The Polish Government discussed the issue of the civilian evacuees at a Cabinet meeting on the morning of 31 March. They, it seemed, were as much in the dark as the British. They had been in constant communication with General Anders over the preceding few days, but 'it was clear that the military authorities on the spot had been totally unable to stop the movement of their civilians'. There was no doubt, claimed the Polish spokesman, that the Soviet Government were putting pressure on them to go, and unfortunately it appeared that the local inhabitants – not unnaturally in view of the food shortage – had adopted a hostile attitude.[35]

There was further confirmation that the evacuation of civilians had come as a surprise to the Polish authorities. From Kuibyshev, British Ambassador Clark Kerr wired that he had spoken to his Polish counterpart (Kot) and found him 'somewhat distressed'. Kot claimed that he had himself been working on an evacuation scheme with the Soviet authorities for some time which would give priority to children and certain selected civilian adults. This had been upset by Anders' agreement to evacuate the troops and dependent civilians from Central Asia. 'The Soviet military authorities had encouraged Anders to ship as many as possible out of the USSR (whether they had visas or not) and not to bring the Polish Ambassador or the Soviet civil authorities into it.'[36] Anders received orders from Polish headquarters in London – under pressure from the British – to prevent the further evacuation of civilians. However, like Nelson, he chose to turn a blind eye. All telegrams from Polish headquarters on the subject were relegated to a bottom drawer of his office desk and not acted upon.[37]

The numbers arriving and the speed of their arrival presented the British and Polish base staffs with a major headache. The main problems facing the British and Polish evacuation staffs in Pahlevi were those of accommodating and feeding the arrivals, isolating and delousing them and arranging transport to move the Poles out of the area. The provision of shelter was a matter of urgency in view of the fact that women and children were accompanying the evacuees, and that the weather was both cold and rainy. The few buildings which had been hired by advance parties were insufficient for the numbers involved. At the height of the influx – on the night of 3/4 April – there were some 30 000 Poles in the port. Polish sappers set about building

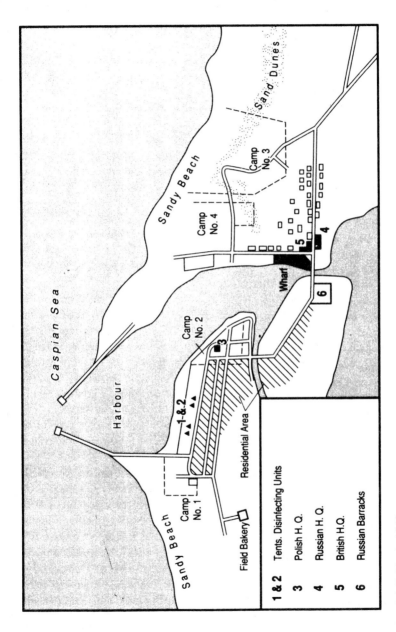

Map 3.1 Pahlevi, 1942

Caspian Sea

Sandy Beach

Sand Dunes

Camp No. 3

Camp No. 4

Camp No. 2

Camp No. 1

Harbour

Sandy Beach

Wharf

Residential Area

Field Bakery

1-& 2

3

4

5

6

1 & 2 Tents. Disinfecting Units

3 Polish H. Q.

4 Russian H. Q.

5 British H.Q.

6 Russian Barracks

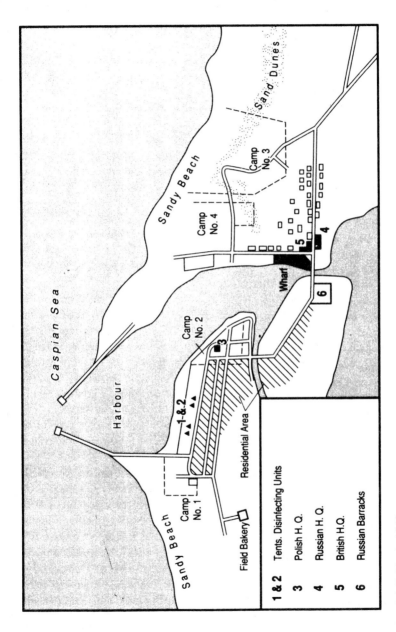

Map 3.1 Pahlevi, 1942

camps but, for most, accommodation meant sleeping under canvas on the beach (tents had been borrowed from the Iranians). The camp areas were eventually to cover more than two square miles, and it was at least possible to ensure that all women and children were under cover.

A further urgent matter, in view of the sickly and diseased state of many of the evacuees, was that of health-care facilities. A Field Ambulance Company and a Field Hygiene Unit arrived at the port at an early stage, and a medical tent was set up at the wharf. Transport was available from the wharf to a small hospital in the port, made available to the evacuation teams by the Iranian authorities. This was staffed by Poles with British assistance. Altogether, in the course of the first evacuation, 1412 people were admitted to the hospital suffering from a variety of illnesses, including typhus (468), dysentry (209), pellagra and other deficiency diseases (171), other fevers (151) and respiratory diseases (97). Thirty-eight people died in the hospital, most (14) dying from typhus. A further 16 Poles had died either on the ships, or else in port before they reached hospital. The deaths did not stop after the refugees left Pahlevi. Some 17 died during the journey by road to Kazvin and more in Teheran and other centres.[38]

Medical arrangements included plans for delousing. Four disinfestation units were set up, including equipment borrowed from both the Iranian and the Soviet authorities. At its height the delousing process was dealing with 4000 cases a day. When senior Polish officers (Szarecki and Okulicki) arrived with a party of evacuees on 27 March, talks were quickly held to discuss general policy. It was decided to form two camps – one on the beach to the west of the port and another on the beach to the east. The intention was to place new arrivals in the first camp (called the 'dirty' camp) before taking them to delousing centres. After having been deloused, they could then be conveyed to the second ('clean') camp.

Despite these arrangements, two problems arose in attempting to isolate the lice-infested newcomers. The civilians were very reluctant to be parted from their baggage; they were desperate to cling to their remaining worldly goods. Although most had few possessions, some had evidently brought a great deal with them. One transport contained 72 tons of civilian baggage, including 'sewing machines, sacks of grain, dogs, fowls and masses of clothing in every state of delapidation'. Once the delousing process was running at full steam it proved possible to pass some items through, but in the early days a great deal was simply burned.[39]

A second problem involved the willingness of the local Iranian population to trade with the evacuees. The Poles, deprived of even the simplest articles for so long, were naturally eager to purchase or exchange. The result was an intermingling of the populations which proved impossible to control, since the Polish guards were not armed. Iranian traders even entered the 'dirty' (i.e. still to be deloused) No. 1 camp. A highly dangerous traffic in old clothes – elsewhere being burned – came to the notice of the authorities.

Arrangements were made for that typically British cure-all, hot tea, to be waiting for arrivals at all hours. Other catering provision was more complex, because of the uncertain numbers involved. British catering staff and stores were brought in (a field bakery and a field butchery), but recourse had to be made to local contractors for some staples, such as bread. In the early days, 2000 lb of government flour was given to local bakers to be baked into bread. When at a later stage bread supplies from Teheran suddenly halted, once again recourse was had to the local bakers. The cooking arrangements in the camps were made by the Poles themselves but on a couple of occasions the weather was so rough that it was impossible to land the evacuees. On these occasions supplies had to be taken out to the transport, lying off shore. One such shipload of civilian refugees had waited for 36 hours, and at least four efforts were made before supplies reached the ship.[40]

The rate of arrival at Pahlevi was as follows:

Date	Number arriving
25 March	1 387
27 March	902
28 March	5 132
29 March	1 587
30 March	3 861
31 March	3 945
1 April	12 241
2 April	1 250
3 April	4 523
4 April	5 148
5 April	3 882
Total	43 858[41]

To control and direct the onward movement of such a large number of people required a major administrative and logistical effort. A variety of military transport was available – up to 100 vehicles – much of which was utilised in bringing supplies up to the Pahlevi area. Indian and Armenian drivers drove around the clock to remove the evacuees

from the port. Moving the soldiers was not a problem; they were organised in units. But it was less easy to mobilise the civilians, who
were not subject to military discipline. The first contingent of 343
refugees was sent to Teheran on 27 March. After this, there was a
regular despatch of convoys to the south. This must have been a terrifying experience for the Poles. The 370 km journey from Pahlevi to
Teheran led over the Ebrus mountains with their multiple hairpin-bends
and deep, chasmic drops. The drivers made few concessions to the
dangerous nature of the terrain. Many refugees must have felt, as they
swept down the mountain passes at breakneck speeds, that they had
cheated death at the hands of the Soviet regime, only to meet it now
in a Persian gorge.[42]

The last transport, carrying 1982 evacuees, arrived in Pahlevi on
Easter Sunday, 5 April. Accompanying this last contingent was General Boruta-Spiechowicz (commander of the 5th Division). The total
number of evacuees, excluding those who had died *en route*, had reached
43 858. This included 10 789 civilian evacuees – 3100 of them children. Of the military evacuees, there were 1603 officers, 28 427 other
ranks, 1159 members of the Women's Voluntary Service (PSK) and
1880 cadets.[43] The end of the evacuation was announced by a Soviet
officer from Krasnovodsk, Captain Samilov, who said that Stalin's orders to have the evacuation (from Soviet territory) completed by
2 April had been carried out and the frontier was now closed. Later
reports indicated that 160 civilians who had not managed to get away
from Krasnovodsk by ship, had been sent back by the Soviet authorities to Tashkent.[44]

If this marked the end of the first phase – the inward movement of
evacuees to Pahlevi – the second phase continued for a further three
weeks. The final convoy of civilians did not leave the port until
17 April. The last convoys taking troops from Pahlevi left after a severe
thunderstorm on 25 April. They took, as the official report details, 'a
few civilians who had emerged from unknown retreats at the last moment'.

> For the first and last time Soviet officers came to view their depar-
> ture. The last lorry to drive off carried a military band which, though
> it had forgotten its instrument cases, left the shores of the Caspian
> playing with abandon that well-known ditty 'The Lambeth Walk'.[45]

The military evacuees were directed south and west by two routes.
One route, taken by road, led via Qazvin and Hamadan to Khanaquin
in Iraq and then onwards to Palestine, where the troops linked up with
Polish Middle Eastern Command. Another group was moved via Teheran

by rail to the Persian Gulf. There, some 1439 were transported by ship to Britain, while the remainder (almost 10 000) were ferried to Palestine by way of the Suez Canal.[46]

The civilians, including 70 orphans between the ages of 6 and 12, were initially more of a problem. As far as the Iranian authorities were concerned, the Poles were merely 'in transit'. In the early stages, the Iranians had pressed for the Poles' speedy removal from their country. Gradually, however, attitudes changed and the Iranians began to cooperate energetically in the provision of accommodation and medical assistance. British officials speculated on the change in attitude. Was it the danger of an epidemic that had galvanised the Iranians? Possibly, but there was a suspicion in British minds that the main objective was propaganda. Not only would Iran appear more generous and hospitable than the Soviet Union, but,

> Russians can no longer upset Persian citizens by singing the glories of the Soviet Union while Teheran is full of Poles who were starving in Russia and admitted that Russians in the same circumstances were starving too.[47]

The civilians were moved directly to Teheran, where they became the responsibility of the Polish Civil Delegation. They were housed in camps in the suburbs of the town, which afforded satisfactory, if not luxurious accommodation. There was a lack of privacy, and most people slept on the floor; only the sick received beds. But kitchens, bakeries, laundries, hospitals and schools, all staffed by Poles, were quickly established. Carpenters' shops and boot-repairers' workshops appeared and women soon busied themselves on sewing-machines making clothes for the community. The Poles set to with an energy and drive which was described by the London *Times* in an article entitled, 'Poles' Eastern Odyssey':

> The arrival in Teheran of thousands of these refugees, destitute though they are and with indescribable adventures behind them, has exerted a marked and quickening influence on the life of the city. Polish notices are seen everywhere; Polish shops have sprung up; and Polish waitresses serve in the cafés and restaurants, where Polish musical and artistic performances have become a regular feature, for the evacuees include a batch of male and female talent from Warsaw theatres and cabarets who took refuge at Lwów during the siege of Warsaw and were caught up in the wave of evacuation. Together they stage an entertainment which for charm and variety would do

credit to any music hall in London or Paris and makes one feel
again the throb of vitality.[48]

MOVES TOWARDS A SECOND EVACUATION

Following the first evacuation of Polish divisions from Soviet Central
Asia, the numbers of troops remaining in the Soviet Union at the
beginning of April 1942 were 40 508, including women soldiers and
cadets ('Junaks'). During his conversation with Anders on 18 March,
Stalin had agreed to further recruitment to the Polish forces. The details of this recruitment had been discussed by members of the Polish–
Soviet military commission at a meeting in Tashkent on 29 March. It
was agreed that three infantry divisions and various ancillary formations would be created within the 44 000 ceiling for the Polish units
set by Stalin.[49]

The Soviet side agreed that a recruiting centre for airmen and sailors
would continue to function, as would the evacuation bases at Krasnovodsk
and Aschabad. Henceforth, potential recruits for the Polish Army would
be directed by the local Soviet military commissars to Guzar, the organising centre of the Polish Army. However, the Soviet representatives demanded the withdrawal of Polish liaison officers from mainline
railway stations, of registration officers and other Polish Army representatives from main towns and cities. The worries about the propaganda effects of well-fed, well-dressed Poles on the Soviet civilian
population – civilian welfare representatives as well as military figures – were growing. An NKVD officer admitted to General Bohusz-
Szyszko quite openly, 'You will leave, but it will take us twenty years
to absorb the mess you have caused by your presence here.'[50]

The implementation of these measures enabled the Soviet authorities to exercise greater control over the flow of volunteers to the
Polish forces – which soon slowed to a trickle. When, nevertheless,
the numbers in the existing Polish units swelled to over 45 000, the
Soviets stepped in to remind the Poles that they had agreed to a 44 000
ceiling and that therefore recruitment should stop. At this stage a major
disagreement developed over interpretations of the Polish–Soviet accord reached between Anders and Stalin. The Poles felt that, while
their units in the USSR were limited by agreement to 44 000, there
was no reason why recruitment should not continue and the surplus
elements be evacuated to reinforce the Polish force in the Middle East
– as had happened in March–April. Although Stalin had seemingly

agreed to this idea earlier, it was now firmly rejected by the Soviet leadership.[51]

Responsibility for evacuating the remainder of the Polish forces from the USSR during 1942 has frequently been laid at the door of General Anders. Certainly Anders was convinced that the Polish forces had little future on Soviet soil. He had little faith in the Soviets' ability to resist the German offensive during 1942.[52] In so far as the Red Army did manage to contain the Wehrmacht by themselves, then he felt their self-confidence would return and any goodwill and preparedness to arm and supply the Poles would evaporate. By contrast, the Polish prime minister, General Sikorski, wanted to retain a sizeable military presence in the Soviet Union to fight alongside the Red Army. He was concerned that Poles loyal to the Government in London should enter combat on the eastern front – the political advantages were significant. If the Polish units were withdrawn in their entirety, it might well prove compromising to the Poles and be exploited by the Soviets, who would be severely embarrassed.

Yet the truth is that Sikorski wavered. During his visit to London in April 1942, Anders found that Sikorski's confidence in Soviet good faith had already been shaken by the dispute over the Polish–Soviet frontier issue. Anders pressed Sikorski to approve the evacuation of Poles from Russia as quickly as possible – while Soviet Russia was still weak. He foresaw Polish forces grouping in the Middle East and eventually re-entering Europe through the Balkans. This, he thought, would be the best solution for Poland, and the quickest route to the homeland for her sons. Sikorski was still not entirely convinced. When he discussed the matter at a Cabinet meeting on 19 May, he stated that in response to General Anders' report on conditions in Russia, he had ordered that the remainder of the army should be evacuated only in the event of a catastrophe (for example, if faced with starvation).[53]

Anders returned to Russia via Cairo, where he talked with General Auchinleck, British commander in the Middle East, about the possibility of evacuating recruits, and even the entire Polish army from the Soviet Union.[54] On his return to Yangi-Yul, on 28 May, Anders was invited by Lt-Col. Tishkov, a Soviet liaison officer, to give his assessment of the general strategic situation, at Stalin's request. Anders emphasised the threat which the German pincer movement posed to the Middle East. With Rommel's forces in North Africa pressing east towards the Suez Canal, there was a danger that British power in the eastern Mediterranean might be extinguished. With the Wehrmacht forces on the Soviet front driving south to the Caucasus, there was a threat

that they would link up with Rommel's forces and cut off completely
the southern routes by which the Western allies had been supplying
the USSR.[55]

In the wake of this gloomy analysis for Stalin, Anders continued to
work upon Sikorski. On 30 June he sent a stark report to London on
the desperate situation the Polish divisions were in:

> The food situation grows worse and worse, in spite of continued
> representations with the Soviet authorities. The local stores are com-
> pletely empty. . . . There are severe shortages and supply difficulties
> in all areas. A general lack of medicines especially in combatting
> malaria, an epidemic of typhus and dysentery. Since February 3600
> soldiers have died. Among the civilian population, around 16,000 of
> whom are located in the vicinity of the army, people have died and
> are dying everyday in large numbers, especially young people and
> children. We are giving them all possible help, in spite of the im-
> mense difficulties which are mounting continually. A depressingly
> large number of tragic letters is flooding in from Polish families,
> especially from those in the northern regions of the USSR.[56]

On receiving Anders's telegram, Sikorski once again turned to Churchill
for help in pressing Stalin to agree to the evacuation of some of the
Polish units from the USSR. (He had already sent a message to Roosevelt
on 17 June.) Churchill in turn raised the matter with Molotov.[57]

The British military authorities had in fact been expecting a further
evacuation since March and had maintained their Evacuation Base Staff
in Pahlevi and Kazvin which, by mid-June, the Soviet authorities were
asking them to remove. Consequently, at the local level, British officials
increased pressure on the Poles to speed up the next stage of the evacuation.[58] British and American pressure brought results. But Stalin's reply,
when it came, was delivered to the British ambassador in Moscow,
Clark Kerr, and relayed by the Foreign Office to the Polish Government.[59] Stalin's offer was couched in face–saving terms. With no reference to the difficulties the Soviets were facing against the Germans
or the problems in supplying the Polish forces, Stalin merely said that
the Soviet Government had been watching with some concern military
developments in Egypt leading to the fall of Mersa Matruh. While the
Soviet Government were loath to weaken their own front, and while
transfer of these Polish troops would present them with some difficulty, nevertheless they were ready to place them at the disposal of
the British Government in order to fill the gaps caused by recent severe fighting.[60] On the day after this telegram from Clark Kerr was

received in London, Sir Alan Brooke (Chief of Imperial General Staff) told the Chief of Staffs Committee that the War Office was very anxious to have these Polish divisions in the Middle East where they would be a useful reinforcement.[61]

The Polish reply, drafted to Clark Kerr in Moscow, expressed gratification at the opportunity to help in defence of the Near East, but drew attention to their duty to Polish citizens in the USSR. In fact the reply amounted to a list of conditions. These included:

(a) Maintenance of a Polish recruiting centre in the USSR after the departure of Polish troops and a resumption of recruiting of all Polish citizens able to bear arms.

(b) The families of troops leaving Russia and the auxiliary military services of women and boy scouts were to leave with the troops. This covered some 20 000 civilians.

(c) Necessary measures were to be taken to begin the evacuation from Russia in collaboration with the Polish Embassy of 50 000 Polish children accompanied by 5000 mothers or guardians.[62]

There was irritation on the British side about these conditions. It was pointed out that the Polish Government had insisted upon conditions (b) and (c) even though they had been asked to do all in their power to *prevent* a large-scale exodus of civilians. (The British had impressed upon the Poles the difficulties of maintaining and transporting civilians in Iran and the Middle East.) Yet, understandably in view of the deteriorating state of Polish–Soviet relations, the Poles were extremely concerned about the fate of their civilians. In June the Soviet authorities had given orders that the civilian personnel located around the remaining Polish units be directed to work on collective farms. Despite the protests of the Polish Embassy, numbers of people were forcibly removed from the environs of camps at Chokpak, Margelan, Guzar and Vrevska.[63] In the course of July, following the departure of Ambassador Kot, the Soviets began to arrest Polish civilian delegates. The widening gulf in Polish–Soviet relations increased the sense of vulnerability and threat felt by the Polish refugee population – including the Polish units remaining on Soviet territory.[64]

Churchill, whose attention was drawn to the Foreign Office reservations, pointed out that the evacuation depended upon the military situation in North Africa. He noted,

The above leaves me in doubt whether you want the three Polish divisions or not, if you have to take with them this mass of women

and children. Personally I want them. If we win the Alamein battle
we ought to be able to handle them even with their encumbrances
[i.e. the civilian dependants – KS]. If we don't win – project impracticable.[65]

A further appeal from the Poles was relayed from Moscow. It pointed
out that there were some 16 000 dependants actually with the troops,
of whom at least half were children and young people. The families
were dependent on the army for food which husbands and fathers shared
with them. If left behind, they would literally starve. Moreover, the
soldiers feared that, given the attitude of the Soviet authorities towards
the Poles, their families would never rejoin them, even if they were
kept alive. From the point of view of the troops therefore, it was essential that the families should go too. The appeal concluded:

> We ask for nothing. Our 44 000 troops in Central Asia each receive
> a ration supposedly equivalent to about 60% of British rations –
> and they do not receive this in full. On this they have to keep them-
> selves and some 16 000 dependants alive. As regards the destina-
> tion and accommodation, the dependants will go anywhere and sleep
> on the bare ground if necessary, as some are doing even now. Even
> if half of them died of hardship outside the USSR, that is better
> than all dying inside. Anything is better than leaving them behind.[66]

The British took the decision to proceed and to include the civilians. On 17 July Churchill sent a message of thanks to Stalin for his
offer of the Polish divisions. He admitted that the civilian relatives
would prove something of a burden for the British Middle East authorities; however, the decision to evacuate the civilians was worthwhile
as a Polish Army was being formed which would serve the general
purpose.[67] Two weeks later, on 31 July, a Polish–Soviet military protocol was signed in Tashkent, providing for the evacuation of the Polish
Army and 'military families' to Persia. The second article of the protocol concerned these military families, and included measures designed
to prevent 'Soviet citizens' from leaving with the Poles. This included
both Soviet wives of Polish soldiers, and also those residents of the
Polish eastern territories who were not of Polish ethnic origin and were
deemed to have acquired Soviet citizenship by the decree of November 1939. Family members who came from eastern Poland and were
Polish by nationality had to have confirmation from their Polish commander that they were indeed close kin of a soldier. This affected
parents, wives, husbands, children and sick brothers and sisters who

were being maintained by the army. The NKVD was to check all documentation and General Anders undertook that the Poles would admit to the transports only those whose names were on the lists.[68]

THE SECOND EVACUATION

On the basis of the Polish–Soviet protocol, the army staff issued the order on 1 August for the second evacuation to be set in motion. As with the first (March–April) evacuation, the Poles were moved by rail to Krasnovodsk and thence by ship across the Caspian Sea to Pahlevi. Before their departure from Krasnovodsk, the Soviet military authorities ordered the Poles to deposit all their holdings of Soviet roubles in a pile and to reduce their personal baggage to 20 kg (44 lb) per person. Some simply left their excess behind, others chose to burn it. The port lay 6 km from the railhead and most of the evacuees had to walk this distance, carrying their possessions in the August heat. In their weakened state many preferred to discard the baggage and cases they had brought with them. It was a decision forced on them by the desperate desire for survival.[69]

A personal memoir of this evacuation is given by Janina Kowalska, who was at the time 12 years old, and had originally been deported in February 1940 to a settlement near Novosibirsk, about 600 km from the Mongolian border. She left Soviet territory with her mother on 18 August 1942.

> We arrived (by train) at Krasnovodsk. At a large station we got down from the carriage and the whole train was led to a canteen for supper. At night, already in Krasnovodsk, we left the train with our belongings. . . . The next morning, we were able to see where we were. It was a large encampment of Poles alongside the railway tracks, in the open air, to which the members of our orphanage had been attached. Before midday everybody began to lug their bundles with great difficulty to some blocks a few hundred metres away. I remained near the lumber while, for over an hour, Mummy and the rest of the group carried luggage to one of the blocks about half a kilometre away. It was midday and the sun was beating down. There was not a drop of water to drink, since it had to be brought from a considerable distance and was very expensive.
> In the shade, in a huge, packed although cool block, there followed a sorting out of the luggage. Mummy's most essential items,

as indeed everybody's, were placed on an open blanket, while the
rest formed a great heap of rags. In the block and outside it there
were huge piles of books, clothes, (holed) footwear, bedclothes. There
was a scrum near the toilets. Some people had fainted and lay there
in the awful stench under the burning rays of the sun at its zenith.

Making use of the proximity of the sea, we went to bathe in it.
But the sea was typical of all things Soviet: dirty, filled with rub-
bish, its surface covered with a layer of grease. From that attempt
to bathe we came out looking like blacks.

In the evening we shared out the supplies: 'Beef', grey sugar,
bread – and that was it. After a fitful sleep lasting some hours,
movement began towards morning and eventually the gathering up
of luggage. As soon as dawn appeared – we moved off to the port
(6 km). The civilian population went on foot with their belongings
on their backs. We, as an orphanage, had only to walk to the train
and were then taken by rail to the port. In the train it was terribly hot
and crowded. From the station again we moved on foot to the port.[70]

The movement began on 9 August and was completed on 1 September, taking 22 days in all. General Anders himself travelled to Teheran on 19 August, after which General Bohusz-Szyszko, who had been
appointed Chief of Staff, remained in charge on the Soviet side. Bohusz
left with the final overland transport which left Aschabad and crossed
the mountains to Teheran. Lt-Col. Berling, head of the Evacuation Staff
at Krasnovodsk, did not leave with the final transport as ordered, but
remained behind in the Soviet Union with a small group of colleagues
who were also sympathetic to the Soviet cause. Berling himself was
no doubt aware that, in view of his past conduct, he did not have
much of a future with the Polish Forces once they were removed from
the Soviet orbit.[71]

The summer evacuation took more than twice as long as the earlier
one and not only because larger numbers of people were involved. As
Berling later pointed out in his memoirs, the second evacuation was
more problematical for the Soviet authorities than the first, since it
coincided with the German push towards the Caucasus and Stalingrad,
which necessitated the evacuation of people, plant, factories, etc. There
were not sufficient means of rail and sea transport and this affected
both the rhythm and the speed of the evacuation. It forced Polish commanders to reduce drastically the weight of equipment and personal
luggage carried by soldiers and civilian personnel.[72]

On the Iranian side, the first transports arrived on 10 August and thereafter ships arrived at all hours for the next three weeks. The last (the twenty-sixth) transport arrived on 1 September. The ships in which evacuees were brought from Krasnovodsk were most frequently tankers which were too big to enter Pahlevi harbour. Consequently, they stood about a mile offshore, and the evacuees had to trans-ship to a smaller vessel, which normally landed the whole contingent in two trips. Conditions on board the transports were beyond description. In a successful effort to get as many Poles away from Krasnovodsk in the shortest possible time, the Russians had packed the evacuees on board until it was almost impossible to move. Sanitary conditions passed all belief – in the largest tankers there were about six lavatories to serve four or five thousand persons. 'Only the fact that the Poles were inured to all kinds of hardships by their two and a half years in the Soviet Union', remarked the author of one British report, 'enabled them to endure this journey.'[73]

The general state of health was poor, and if anything worse than that of the earlier evacuees, owing to the summer climate and the rapid spread of infectious diseases. In general, the military forces were in better physical state than the civilians. But certain localities in Turkestan, where the Poles had collected, were climatically better than others. (The evacuation in Turkestan had been carried out by district, which meant that in general military and civilian Poles from the same locality arrived in the same ship.) The Poles who came from Yangi-Yul were in a reasonable state of health. On the other hand, those who came from Guzar, where they lived in torrid heat with insufficient food, were in a very bad state indeed: 'Civilians from these regions were frequently hardly able to crawl off the ships.'[74]

Of the 69 247 evacuated during this second operation, 25 501 were civilians.[75] Of these, 568 people – chiefly civilians – died in Pahlevi. The peak figure of sick was reached at the port on 8 September when there were 868 in hospital and a further 2000 in the convalescent camp. It was, as one British observer reported, a sad commentary on the conditions under which they had lived in Russia. It was also, one might add, a vindication of the pressure exerted by the Polish authorities to have them evacuated.[76]

Upon landing, the civilian evacuees were registered by the Polish Civil Delegation. The Civil Delegation was also responsible for preparing the civilian parties for convoys onwards. As earlier, the military convoys travelled eastwards into Iraq to Khanaquin, while the civilians were moved down to camps in the Teheran area. By 27 August, 20 000 had been evacuated; by 8 September, 40 000; and by 18 September,

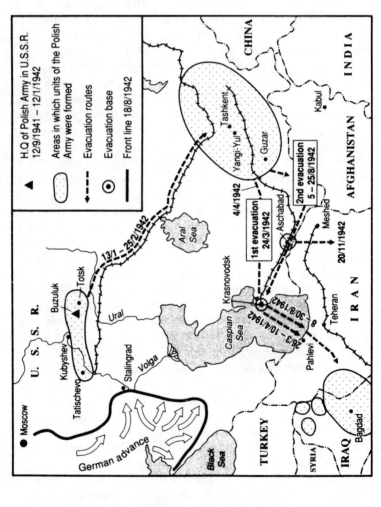

Key:

▲ H.Q of Polish Army in U.S.S.R. 12/9/1941 – 12/1/1942

◯ Areas in which units of the Polish Army were formed

---‣ Evacuation routes

⊙ Evacuation base

▬▬▬ Front line 18/8/1942

Map 3.2 The Polish Army in the USSR and its evacuation, 1941–42

60 000. The last civilians, apart from the sick, left the port on 12 Octob In addition to the seaborne evacuation, a smaller group of Poles (269 made their way in stages overland to Meshed at the end of August.

General Anders visited Pahlevi on 28 August and remained for tw days. During his stay on the 29th, he attended a march-past by 15 000 members of the 5th and 6th Divisions, whose commanders, Generals Rakowski and Tokarzewski, were accompanying Anders. 'His presence', stated British observers, 'had a most heartening effect on all the Poles in Pahlevi and the enthusiasm with which he was acclaimed bore witness to his inspiring leadership.'[78]

The August evacuation was the last major exodus of Poles from Soviet territory, although a few hundred more made their exit over ensuing months. In Aschabad, for instance, the military commission under Lt Perkowicz, charged with winding up the Polish Army's affairs, made its way out of Soviet territory by the land route to Teheran in November, bringing an additional 2637 people.[79] An attempt by Polish authorities in the late summer of 1942 to secure the evacuation of 50 000 Polish children and their mothers or guardians (see above) had come to nothing, despite British and American intervention on their behalf.[80]

Stalin gave an assurance to Roosevelt following the break in Polish–Soviet relations (25 April 1943) that Poles in the USSR would be able to leave the USSR without any difficulty.[81] This assurance seems to have been made only for Western public opinion, since no parties of a size comparable to the earlier (1942) exoduses were allowed to leave. However, small parties of Poles continued to make their way across the frontier until the summer of 1943. Following an appeal by Tadeusz Romer (Polish ambassador in the USSR from October 1942 until the break in diplomatic relations) the Soviet authorities gave departure permission for 110 members of Polish soldiers' families, who had earlier failed to arrive at the evacuation centres in time.[82]

The British evacuation supervisor, Lt-Col. Ross, wrote in his final report for MERRA as follows:

A small Transit Camp has been in existence at Meshed since the summer of 1942. It was originally intended for the reception of Polish orphans released from the Soviet Union and travelling overland to destinations in India via Zahidan, but it has in fact served as a convenient staging post, not only for the orphans, of whom as many as 675 have travelled with their guardians to India by this route, but for other small groups of Poles who have left the Soviet Union by the eastern route via Ashkabad, capital of Turkmenistan, which is only about 20 miles from the Soviet–Persian frontier at Badgiran.

At intervals, small parties of adults and children have arrived at Meshed even since the rupture of diplomatic relations between the Russians and the Poles and it is interesting that, even though Meshed is in the Russian zone of occupation, the Soviet authorities there have not made any attempt to force the Poles to leave.[83]

The second evacuation concentrated the minds of officials on the problem of how to dispose of the evacuees. Anticipating the further exodus during the summer of 1942, the British military authorities in Iran had made arrangements to receive them, and a large site had been chosen for a tented camp (to hold a maximum of 7000 Poles) some eight kilometres north-west of Teheran (there were four camps in Teheran altogether). But the Iran–Iraq theatre was regarded as a potential war-zone, with the approach of the Germans. Furthermore, food-shortages in Iran, exacerbated by the rapacious policies of the Soviet occupiers in carrying off grain stocks, led to public hostility towards the continued settlement of the Poles and pressure from the Iranian Government for their removal. Finally, there was the question of space in the camps; despite provision of new camp accommodation, as the second echelon arrived, it became a matter of urgency for members of the earlier contingent to move out and make space for the newcomers. In the course of 1942 the British Government made exhaustive efforts to find countries which would accept the refugees. The United States and Canadian governments were approached, as were several South American governments. All were either hostile to the idea or else hedged their offers with such conditions that they proved impracticable. In June 1942, the British Government came to an agreement with the East African governments on a policy of temporary settlement in the East African territories (Kenya, Uganda, Tanganyika and Nyasaland). Also included in the plan were North and South Rhodesia and South Africa. India, which had already agreed to take 1000 children, increased its offer in December 1942 to accept 11 000. Finally, the Mexican Government also agreed to take several thousand Poles.[84]

The major problem facing the British authorities was one of transport – how to move these thousands of civilians from their camps in northern and central Iran to the nearest port facilities and thence by ship to their destinations. Although the Poles were given a free choice of destination, many quickly became attached to their camp surroundings after the wanderings of the previous two-to-three years and were reluctant to be uprooted again. This was unsurprising – they had little information on the destinations open to them. The journey to the nearest port on the Persian Gulf, Khorramshar, could only be attempted by rail, yet there were operating difficulties on the line (the Iranian State Railways was short of passenger rolling stock). Furthermore, with the demands of war, there was a chronic shortage of available shipping.

Eventually, a transit camp was established at Ahwaz, some 90 miles short of Khorramshar. Refugees were taken there by passenger-train (which became known as the 'Brimfield' train, after the code-name for the second evacuation of Poles from the USSR) and then required to await the arrival of shipping. The 'Brimfield' train began running on 2 August 1942 and initially carried 800 passengers per journey, making on average one trip every five days. For the remainder of the distance to Khorramshar, the Poles were taken in covered box-cars, which must have reminded them uncomfortably of the cattle-trucks which conveyed them from Poland to the Soviet interior over two years earlier.

By the end of 1943, some 23 788 men, women and children had been evacuated from Iran by this route. They left on 28 transport ships, two of which contained 1653 Polish Jews destined for Palestine. (Unlike other Poles, they were unable to travel overland. The Iraqi authorities, as a matter of policy, refused transit to Jews who intended to settle in Palestine.) Many Christian Poles also exerted quite desperate efforts to make their way overland to Palestine. It was the centre of the Polish Army's Middle East command and was the nearest thing to European civilisation to be found in the area. A British report referred to this drive as amounting at times to 'a kind of mania':

> Many refugees in Persia possessed relatives with the Polish Army in Palestine and everyone with some excuse (and many with none at all) for thinking that he or she ought to be admitted to Palestine has legally or illegally tried to get there. Trouble has even been caused by civilian men and women masquerading as soldiers or ATS and in this way crossing both the Iraqi and Palestine frontiers without the required visas. Severe measures were taken to deal with this. . . .[85]

Others travelled to the United Kingdom if they had family members serving in the Polish forces there. A number of young people also travelled to other destinations. A small group of students, for example, travelled to study at the University of Beirut.

The main recipient countries of these refugees were Uganda (6400), Tanganyika (8000), Northern and Southern Rhodesia (5000) and Kenya

(1500). In addition some 10 000 travelled overland to India. These
were settled at a camp near Balachadi (Kolhapur) and their number
was made up of 5000 orphans and 5000 children with families.[86] The
New Zealand Government invited over 700 Polish orphans together
with their guardians and teachers, and these were settled at Pahiatua,
180 km from Wellington. Although a handful returned to Poland after
the war, most chose to remain in New Zealand.[87] Finally, General Sikorski
had received a promise from the Mexican Government that they would
accept 10 000 Polish refugees. Conditions laid down by the Mexican
government were that they should work in agriculture. At the end of
1943 the transports began to arrive. These refugees were, like all the
contingents, primarily women and children, although with a number of
elderly male relatives. They were settled near Leon, in central Mexico.
However, only 4000 were eventually settled there.[88]

In the Teheran camps where adults were settled, the welfare authorities
encouraged the Poles to set up workshops of various kinds – from
shoe-repairers to cabinet-making. This was a continuation of policy
practised when the refugees had been first received in Teheran; to
persuade them to stand on their own feet, become self-dependent once
again, shake off the lethargy and apathy which had settled upon them,
persuade them to cast off the belief that their lives were being controlled for them. As late as the end of April 1944 (i.e. two years after
the first evacuation) there were still 8200 Poles in Iran. Of these, though
some 5000 were either employed staff, hospitalised, or relatives of these
two categories, a further 1000 were in the Ahwaz transit camp awaiting
shipping; and some 2300 were children and staff of the Isfahan children's
colony destined to remain until they could be moved to India as a group.[89]

The outcome of these two major evacuations and relief operations
was that 74 000 Polish troops were brought out of Soviet Russia and
were armed, trained and prepared to play an important role in the
European war (the Italian campaign). Forty-one thousand Polish civilians were also evacuated and many of them rescued from death by
starvation or a multitude of diseases. The administrative effort involved
in this operation had been immense. It had involved the Polish Legation and Polish Civil Delegation, the Polish Red Cross, a Polish Directorate of Education, the British Legation, the MERRA organisation,
the UK Commercial Corporation (Teheran), British Military GHQ
(Paiforce), the US Foreign Economic Administration, the American Red
Cross, HQ US Persian Gulf Command, the Papal Nuncio, representatives of the Jewish Agency, and representatives of the American Joint
Distribution Committee.[90]

British officials were well pleased with the outcome. In London, one commented on the official report of civilian evacuation arrangements:

> As a working model of a small, but exceptionally difficult piece of displaced persons' organisation, this British–American–Polish (but mainly British) enterprise in Persia deserves study and the report is a very reasonable account of a very creditable piece of work.[91]

In Polish eyes – and above all to the Poles who were rescued from starvation in the Soviet Union, the operation was a miracle. General Anders became a legendary figure long before the military successes of the Polish Corps during the Italian campaign. He was frequently portrayed as a latter-day Moses in the folklore of the Polish émigré community. Contemporary publications showed him parting the Caspian (for which read: Red) Sea and leading his people out of bondage. It was a powerful image and a powerful reputation – one that was to build him up in certain minds as a rival to Sikorski.

4 The Relief Effort on Behalf of 'Amnestied' Poles

POLISH–SOVIET NEGOTIATIONS CONCERNING RELIEF FOR
POLISH CIVILIANS

Securing relief supplies for destitute Poles in the USSR released from
camps, prisons and other places of confinement was a top priority for
the Polish Government following the July 1941 Agreement. General
Sikorski wrote to Stanisław Kot, concerning the latter's appointment
as ambassador,

> the action of protection and assistance to the Polish population will
> be one of the most important branches of activity of the Polish posts
> in the USSR. . . .[1]

A special department was to be created at the new Embassy to handle
welfare questions. This was to be headed by an official from the appropriate branch of the Polish Government – the Ministry of Labour
and Social Welfare. The man chosen for this important task, Emanuel
Freyd, was appointed on 25 August and briefed by his Minister, Jan
Stańczyk, before his departure. His tasks were:

- to establish as quickly as possible the number of Poles freed from
  prisons and camps;
- to ask the Soviet authorities for a list of names of those released;
  to determine whether they were receiving aid – if so, what kind –
  and what kind of additional help should be requested from the
  Soviet authorities;
- to attempt to move as many Polish citizens as possible to areas of
  the most congenial climatic conditions;
- to keep a record of the Polish population in the form of a card
  index;
- to keep London informed about the amount and nature of help
  needed;
- to make use of the International Red Cross to communicate with
  families in Poland;
- to make use of telegraphic and postal services – alternatively to
  use couriers – to maintain contact with those people located.[2]

At the end of August, Freyd travelled out from Liverpool to Archangel, making the journey as one of a 22-strong group of diplomats and officials.

But the Polish–Soviet Agreement of July 1941, which was to lead to the release under 'amnesty' of so many tens of thousands of Poles, had contained no specific provisions for extending relief to the destitute refugees following their release from camps or prisons, or enforced work on state farms. It is true that paragraph 3 of the Agreement stated that the two governments would 'mutually undertake to render one another aid and support of all kinds in the present war against Hitlerite Germany'.[3] However, it is doubtful, given such vague wording, whether the Soviet Government would have understood this to mean diverting resources for non-military purposes, particularly given their desperate strategic situation and massive loss of resources as German divisions streamed towards Moscow.

A more positive, early report on the Soviet attitude towards the Polish diaspora came on 14 August when the Polish chargé, Józef Retinger, arrived in Moscow. In a conversation with Andrei Vyshinsky, deputy commissar for foreign affairs, Retinger was assured that,

> central government organs had already issued instructions to local authorities to ensure employment and accommodation for Poles freed by the amnesty, in particular for women and children. The Soviet authorities were anxious that the thousands of Poles residing in the USSR should work and live in adequate conditions; that those fit to fight should fight and those who wished to work should work.[4]

The Soviet attitude was that the Poles had two options before them – either to serve in military formations or to work. According to communist precepts, only he who worked should eat. The Soviet authorities therefore were reluctant to dispense charity to the thousands of Polish women, children, invalids, elderly, etc. Indeed the attitude towards such relief work was clarified by Vyshinsky earlier in his talk with Retinger, when he stated that 'The Soviet Government would support on a large scale all welfare action *undertaken by the Polish authorities* for the Polish population. . . .'[5] By contrast, the Polish position was that welfare for the deracinated Poles was morally the responsibility of the *Soviet* Government. Sikorski stated in his instructions to newly-appointed Ambassador Stanisław Kot:

> As Polish citizens have been deported to the Soviet Union by order of the Soviet authorities, it is those authorities who are responsible for the present position of those people. They must consequently

provide for the maintenance of those among them who have no adequate means.[6]

The subject of Polish welfare and relief was also, some weeks later, the subject of an exchange between British Ambassador Stafford Cripps, and Vyshinsky. On the question of feeding the Poles, Vyshinsky asked whether Cripps intended to imply that all those who did not work were to be maintained?

> C. No, but those who cannot work – the aged, infirm, invalids – must be maintained.
> V. Why not by the Polish Government?
> C. Because the Soviet Government has removed them from their homes and they are in the USSR, not in Poland. Moreover the Polish Government has not got the necessary supplies.

Cripps' unwonted frankness in his exchange with Vyshinsky may have owed something to the fact that a few days earlier 16 corpses had been among a transport of Poles arriving in Moscow.[7]

Nevertheless the Soviet Government did not accept such responsibility. It could not be brought to admit that it had violated international law or was morally in the wrong by forcibly deporting thousands of Polish citizens during 1940–41. Conversations between Polish and Soviet diplomats during the ensuing weeks became at times sharp, as the former lamented the conditions their citizens were forced to endure, while the latter stated blandly that released Poles enjoyed the same rights as Soviet citizens. The Soviet authorities were reluctant to extend to the Poles preferential treatment over their own citizens – especially where this concerned people not fit for work or military service. But the Polish argument (backed by the British) was that it was the very young, the elderly and the infirm who were in particular need of help. Furthermore, comparisons with Soviet citizens were inappropriate, since (a) the Poles had been torn from their homes and had been forced to leave most of their belongings behind; and (b) they were not as familiar with the realities of life in the Soviet Union.

The Polish Government was driven to create its own relief network, but the procedure was not without problems. Sikorski had asked Kot at an early stage to ensure that the protection of all Polish citizens be ensured by consular posts. Consulates, or consular agencies, depending on the number of Polish citizens living in a given area, should be established for as long as was needed to care for the concentrations of destitute Poles. Afterwards they could be wound up. Kot was to ask for the immediate restoration of the Polish–Soviet Consular Convention of 15 July 1924. This had provided the basis for the functioning of the Polish Republic's consular posts in the USSR before the war, and would guarantee the diplomatic immunity of members of consular staff.[8] It should be pointed out, though, that the 1924 Convention had not helped the Polish consul in Kiev, Matuszyński, who, together with two of his chauffeurs, was seized by the NKVD in September 1939 and subsequently disappeared.[9]

Kot quickly discovered, in any case, that the plan to establish consular posts was not one which the Soviets favoured. As he wrote a month later to Foreign Minister Raczyński in London, things were not going easily:

> As for a network of consular posts, there is no hope of achieving this. In this direction not even Cripps has managed to obtain anything. In the eyes of the Soviet people a consular service is identical with espionage.[10]

This comment emphasises the degree to which, from the Soviet standpoint, the undertaking was almost unprecedented. Under Stalinist rule both paranoid and xenophobic tendencies had been fostered – to the extent that Soviet citizens preferred to avoid even going near foreign diplomatic outposts. The Soviet Ambassador in Washington, Umanski, in conversation with his Polish counterpart, openly admitted Moscow's exaggerated suspicion of outsiders:

> Up till now all requests on the part of foreign welfare institutions have always been flatly refused by our Government because, unfortunately, we suspect them of wanting to investigate internal problems, to control our politics, to pry into our affairs.[11]

For similar reasons the Soviets objected to the presence of the Polish Red Cross.

The security situation, as German armies penetrated deeper into Soviet territory, was more threatening than it had ever been under Stalinist rule. Yet the Soviet authorities were being asked to authorise the establishment of a welfare distribution network, comprising representatives of a foreign power, to spread out over Soviet territory and act with relative freedom – proceeding under orders received from the Embassy of the 'London' Polish Government. It was a wholly unfamiliar situation for the Soviet Government, and one that made them feel distinctly uneasy. Nevertheless, it was a situation which eventually they were forced to tolerate – at least for as long as they felt threatened

by the Germans and dependent upon supplies of war materiel from
their Western allies.[12]

Further problems for Polish officials were created by the heavily
centralised nature of Soviet government, and the increasing paralysis
of the decision-making process in late 1941, as German forces approached Moscow. Kot wrote (to Stanisław Mikołajczyk, the Peasant
Party leader and chairman of the National Council):

> I have not yet advanced a single step in the search for our people
> despite my persistence. [13]

On the following day he wrote in greater detail to Sikorski:

> Here there is an everlasting lack of decision. Today Cripps com-
> plains that he cannot even extract the signature for an agreement in
> which Britain gives Russia everything for nothing. . . .[14]

And, later still:

> The (Soviet) government is absorbed in defence and evacuation and
> has no time for anything else.[15]

At an early stage in the Embassy's work, a Mixed (Polish–Soviet)
Commission was created on the Embassy's initiative to smooth issues
relating to welfare provision. It included a representative of the
Narkomindiel (Soviet Foreign Ministry), Novikov, and a commissar
from the NKVD, as well as two representatives from the Polish Embassy. The Commission was, in some senses, a civilian counterpart to
the Polish – Soviet Mixed Military Commission, but it worked less
well – reflecting, perhaps, the lower priority of civilian welfare in
Soviet eyes. It had its first meeting on 9 September, when the Polish
side put forward a number of requests. The vagueness of the Soviet
replies indicated that the representatives lacked the authority to take
decisions, and the Commission eventually stopped meeting. Even the
smallest details relating to welfare were thenceforth pursued through
the normal diplomatic channels.[16]

The most positive and fruitful early step towards creating a relief
network was made by the Polish chargé, Józef Retinger, before Kot's
belated arrival in Moscow. Retinger, on 22 August, had sent a note to
the Soviet Foreign Ministry requesting that telegraphic directives be
sent to administrative authorities in localities and regions where Poles
resided. His suggestion was that respectable and trustworthy Polish
citizens living in the localities should notify the Polish Embassy in
Moscow and send in personal details and information on the approxi-

mate number of their compatriots in the locality. From those names the Embassy would select an 'homme de confiance', whose duty it would be to approach both the Embassy and the local Soviet authorities concerning matters affecting Polish nationals.[17] Retinger's approach to the problem was clever, since he projected the appointment of 'hommes de confiance' firstly as a means of ensuring cooperation between the competent Soviet authorities, the Embassy and interested Polish nationals; secondly as a means of avoiding burdening the Soviet administrative organs. Vyshinsky informed Kot on 10 September (three weeks later!) that the list of candidates for 'men of trust', in the sense of Retinger's note, had been forwarded. The appointment of men of trust went ahead, subject to certain provisos. The Soviets made it clear that they did not want 'committees' formed by Poles. The reason was that the term smacked too much of unauthorised and illegal political organisations.[18] Furthermore, the Soviets had stated that they did not want former prisoners or camp inmates being appointed to positions of responsibility within the Embassy structure. Perhaps they were aware that a residue of resentment towards the Soviet authorities might make such people difficult to work with.

On 15 October, while the desperate defence of Moscow continued, the staff of the Polish Embassy and other diplomatic missions began evacuation to Kuibyshev (Samara) on the River Volga. According to Kot, 70 Poles took part in the rail transfer, which lasted five days and, as he reported to Sikorski, 'En route I saw crowds of our wretches, sick and hungry, sent off with no planning.'[19] The evacuation caused further disruption in the relief effort, at a time when it was in the process of establishing itself. Indeed, according to one version of these events, the Social Welfare Department of the Embassy was directed first to Buzuluk, site of the Polish Army's headquarters, before arriving at Kuibyshev in late November.[20]

A major breakthrough in relations with the Soviet Government occurred at the beginning of December 1941, when General Sikorski made a trip to Moscow which had been in the offing for several months. Stalin cannot fail to have been impressed by Sikorski's nerve in agreeing to meet in Moscow, at a time when German troops were only a few dozen kilometres away from the capital. Perhaps because of this, and aware that the Soviet chances of defying the German advance were being written off in other quarters, he was more than usually indulgent in his talks with the Polish leader. Sikorski took advantage to impress upon Stalin the importance of giving due weight to the question of civilian relief, despite the desperate wartime conditions.

In Kuibyshev I saw a transport of our people which made a terrible
impression on me. It is necessary to give them speedy relief. . . .
People even die because of the terrible conditions. These conditions
will heavily influence our future relations. . . .[21]

The result was immediate. Stalin promised a loan of 100 million roubles
– in addition to military loans already promised – for the Polish Embassy's work with destitute civilians. Sikorski also managed to cir-
cumvent the Soviet objection to Polish 'consular officials' being
appointed. He obtained permission for a number of Polish Embassy
'delegates' to be sent to key areas where large numbers of Poles were
concentrated. The 'delegates' – twenty in number – would monitor the
arrival of relief supplies from outside the Soviet Union, supervise their
storage and distribution to centres of Polish settlement throughout the
vast spaces of the Soviet interior.[22] At last, with the promise of such
resources and of officially approved representatives in the provinces, it
was possible to get the relief operation moving.

HOW RELIEF SUPPLIES WERE OBTAINED

At the time the relief operation was being mounted, the Polish population in the USSR was in the last stages of exhaustion. Large numbers
of Poles were facing their second winter without means of support,
having traded most of the portable wealth they had been able to bring
with them from their homes. The large-scale movement following their
release firstly to Buzułuk and then to the southern republics, was a
natural and spontaneous attempt to make contact with the Polish forces.
Unfortunately, not only were most of the deportees in no condition to
undertake such lengthy and arduous journeys; for many it meant abandoning employment, shelter and sources of food and sustenance for
the unknown. Thousands of Poles began to arrive in areas of Uzbekistan,
Kazakhstan, Tadzikistan and Turkmenistan at a time when summer work
on the kolkhozes had finished and there was no work for them. In
their weakened state, they fell victim to illness and disease; dysentery,
pneumonia, typhoid and scarlet fever all claiming victims. Faced with
an emergency on this scale, the main priorities of the relief organisers
were to deliver food supplies, clothing, blankets and medical supplies
with urgency. Virtually all such goods had to be acquired outside the
Soviet Union, transported into the country and then distributed to the
points where they were most needed. It was a huge logistical under-

taking under any circumstances, but one made more difficult by war-conditions and the events which had impelled the Polish authorities into an enforced exile.

The Polish Government in London did not possess its own financial resources. It relied upon credits from the British Treasury to finance its operations. In seeking therefore to obtain relief supplies for its citizens in the USSR, it was dependent upon the good offices of its British hosts, whose Middle East presence and shipping resources were to play a large part in the ferrying of the supplies. In Britain, although there was considerable sympathy for the tragic plight of the Poles, official responses to Polish Government appeals were guarded. Britain had been at war for two years already. Her trade-lifeline to the rest of the world was under continual threat by U-boats, and food-rationing was in force. The British Government was unwilling to allow sterling credits to be used for purchasing outside the UK (e.g. rice in Persia), but at the same time was concerned about the effect of large-scale purchases on the depleted home market. It became necessary to coordinate large orders with British civilian departments and shipping lines. A private firm (The Poland Supply Company Ltd) was established by the Polish Government to liaise with the Ministry of Supply in supervising sterling purchases.[23]

British voluntary agencies also helped in raising funds although, under conditions of wartime austerity, the British public was not in a position to give substantial amounts. Appeals were made to the British public (by the Anglo-Polish Relief Fund) over BBC radio and through the press.[24] The Polish–Jewish Relief Committee also launched an appeal for Poles in the Soviet Union endorsed by, among others, Ignacy Schwarzbart (a Jewish member of the Polish National Council). In backing the initiative on behalf of Polish refugees, it directed its own appeal to the Anglo-Jewish community. Assurances were given to potential contributors that relief in Russia would be distributed according to need among all Polish nationals without any distinction of race or creed.[25] As the scale of the problem became clearer, members of the Polish Government and administration in London decided that their own individual contributions towards the relief of their compatriots should be levied more systematically. In February 1942 it was decided that regular donations amounting to 2 per cent of pay would be made by all government workers, except in cases where there was (a) illness in the family or, (b) a numerous family to support. Several senior figures offered to contribute 10 per cent of their income.[26]

By far the largest contribution to the relief effort, in terms both of

money and supplies, came from North America. Energetic efforts on
the part of Jan Ciechanowski, the Polish Ambassador in Washington,
and Sylwin Strakacz, the Consul-General, brought considerable success. Most American supplies came from the US Government itself
under the 'Lend-Lease' scheme.[27] The proportion of aid supplied from
this source began to arrive at Soviet ports only in February 1942, but
it grew rapidly, soon outstripping the volume of supplies arriving from
other (mostly private voluntary) sources.[28] Independent voluntary agencies, especially those in the United States, nevertheless played an important role. These included Polish emigrant organisations, the US
Catholic Bishops' Committee, and the American Red Cross which, in
December 1941, offered the Poles its entire stock of blankets, condensed milk, canned foodstuffs and medicines from local stores in the
Middle East.[29] On 2 October, Kot had spent a good deal of time in
Moscow convincing American Red Cross delegates Wardwell and
Nicholson, of the Poles' need for aid. To drive the message home to
the Americans, Eugeniusz Lubomirski acted as translator for the ses-
sion; he had just arrived from a labour camp and, in Kot's words 'was
still in his ragamuffin attire'.[30] The part played by Jewish organisations in the US was also significant, the three largest donors being the
Jewish Labour Committee (New York), the American Jewish Joint
Distribution Committee, and the American Federation for Polish Jews.[31]

The acquisition of relief supplies was, however, only the first hurdle.
The next problem faced by the Polish authorities was to have the goods
transported to Soviet ports, or else to states bordering the Soviet Union,
from which they could be taken into Soviet territory overland. Given
the acute difficulties faced by the Allies in trying to keep their supply-
lines open – particularly the losses due to U-boat operations – this
was not an easy task. (The United States was a neutral state until
December 1941 and domestic legislation prevented goods being transported to warring states on board American ships.) The earliest relief
supplies were brought into the northern Russian ports on British and
Soviet vessels. The first 50 tons of food sent by the Polish Ministry of
Social Welfare arrived at Archangel as early as 1 September 1941.[32]
Since, at that time, there was no Embassy representative in the port to
receive the goods (Józef Gruja was despatched to Archangel some weeks
later), the relief supplies were sent south to Buzułuk, together with
military supplies they accompanied. A second convoy arrived in the
port on 11 October, and was followed by further convoys on 31 October, 21 November and 15 December. Goods arriving by ship included
dried soups, flour, beans, oatmeal, corned beef, semolina, lentils,

powdered milk, vegetable oil and dried fruit.[33] But clothing also arrived – men's shirts, overcoats, trousers, sweaters, skirts, headgear, socks, children's clothes and blankets.[34]

Almost inevitably, losses occurred. Some of these were due to enemy action. In July 1942, the Polish Embassy in London was informed that two consignments – on the SS *Barrdale* and SS *Cape of Good Hope* – were 'casualties' and were unlikely to arrive (i.e. it was feared that they had been sunk).[35] Earlier, in January 1942, the SS *Harmitris* arrived in Murmansk carrying 202 tons of supplies. The ship was torpedoed as it was entering port and 25 tons of goods fell into the sea. These were recovered from the water, however, and dried. On the basis of an agreement between the Polish Embassy representative in Murmansk and the port-workers, the latter were given 25 per cent of the dried goods as a reward for their efforts in rescuing the cargo.[36] Not so fortunate was the American ship, *Steel Worker* – one of three ships arriving at Murmansk between 15 and 22 June 1942. She was sunk in port during an enemy air-raid almost as soon as she had dropped anchor. Her entire cargo was lost.[37]

The sea route to the northern ports was far from ideal; besides being a favourite haunt of U-boats, the elements made it even more hazardous in winter. Furthermore, although there was a large colony of Poles in the Archangel region, the main concentrations were now in the southern republics, where the army was forming under General Anders' command.[38] An alternative route via the Persian Gulf meant a lengthier journey for transports coming from Great Britain or from the eastern seaboard of North America (they had to come around the Cape of Good Hope), but it was the one preferred by the Polish Government. The first relief shipment sent by this route on the SS *City of Elwood* arrived at Basra in February 1942. Relief supplies transported by this route included food bought in Iran and India, as well as gifts from voluntary agencies in New Zealand.[39]

Once landed in Iran, the supplies came under the UK Commercial Corporation. The UKCC conveyed most of them overland to the ports of Pahlevi and Babol Sar on the Caspian Sea. At the Persian ports, responsibility for conveying the goods to the Soviet side (Krasnovodsk) was contracted to a Persian company, Sovtrans. The first shipment to arrive via this southern route were moved across Iran to cross the Soviet frontier near Aschabad at the end of December 1941. Indeed, Aschabad became a distribution-point for goods which were redirected to the various delegates and 'men of confidence' in the localities. Wagons of goods were sent on to Samarkand, Yangi-Yul, Bukhara, Chymkent,

Djambul, Kirov, Semipalatynsk, Stalinabad, Djalal Abad, Pavlodar, Barnaul, Krasnovodsk, Krasnoyarsk, Aktiubinsk, Petropavlovsk, Novosibirsk, Akmolinsk, Chelyabinsk, Kustanay, Frunze, Chkalov, Fergana, Omsk, Tomsk, Tobolsk, Alma-Ata, Nankent, Salvgorod, Turkiestan, Taishet and other centres.[40]

As the relief operation in the United States gathered momentum, American and Soviet shipping was used, and it proved easier to develop other routes. Supplies could be moved direct from ports on the US west coast to Vladivostok. The first transports to arrive at Vladivostok in early 1942 were from American Jewish organisations and were shipped from San Francisco. Supplies arriving in the Pacific Coast (Sea of Japan) ports could be more easily directed to the many colonies of Poles in the Far East. This same route was used for goods (medicines, powdered milk, vitamins) purchased in China by the Polish Embassy in Tokyo.[41] As an emergency measure, air transport was also used to ferry in supplies – primarily much-needed medical items. In April 1942, for example, a consignment of anti-typhoid vaccines and tetanus anti-toxins was sent by air from Miami to Kuibyshev by the American Jewish Joint Distribution Committee.[42]

The Polish Government's energetic attempts to secure relief and welfare supplies for its citizens in the USSR resulted in supplies being brought from several countries including Great Britain, North and South America, China, India, Australia and New Zealand and Persia. The largest donor was the United States. In the course of 1942 alone some 7414 tons of goods were sent from the US to the value of \$4 728 000.[43] The volume of supplies was modest in relation to the scale of the need, and transport problems (the difficulty of obtaining shipping) exacerbated the situation. Within the USSR there were further difficulties to overcome – particularly with regard to transport. On occasion problems were caused by a reluctance on the part of the Soviet authorities to supply wagons. There were other cases where transports were 'lost', travelling around the USSR for up to three-and-a-half months before intervention with the authorities resulted in their being located. Pilfering from stores and warehouses was also a problem.[44]

THE DISTRIBUTION OF RELIEF SUPPLIES

In the aftermath of General Sikorski's visit, on 24 December, the Polish Embassy secured Soviet agreement to the establishment of 20 Delegates' offices. These were to be located in Archangel, Akmolinsk, Alma-Ata,

Aktiubinsk, Aschabad, Aldan-Jakutski, Barnaul, Chkalov, Chelabyinsk, Chymkent, Djambul, Krasnoyarsk, Kustanay, Kirov, Pavlodar, Petropavlovsk, Samarkand, Saratov, Syktyvkar and Vladivostok. Due to the length of continuing negotiations, most of the Delegates only began to carry out their functions effectively in mid-February. Only one Delegature – that in Saratov – remained unfulfilled, while nine positions were filled by officials who possessed diplomatic titles (i.e. they were secretaries or attachés of the Embassy). Of the remaining ten, one was headed by an Embassy official who had no diplomatic immunity, and the other nine were headed by representatives of the deported Polish population.[45]

The Delegates' tasks were clearly set out in an agreement reached in December 1941 between the Embassy and the Peoples' Commissariat for Foreign Affairs. They were to

1. Inform the Embassy of the requirements and situation of Polish citizens.
2. Supply Polish citizens with information and guide them according to the spirit of the Polish–Soviet Agreement of 30 July 1941.
3. Register Polish citizens in a given area, to record their movements, fitness for military service, for work, and their professional qualifications; also to search for missing family members or relatives.
4. Cooperate with local Soviet authorities in directing Polish citizens to suitable work in accordance with the labour legislation in force in the USSR.
5. Exercise due care that Polish citizens unfit for work are assured the minimum means of subsistence, by distributing among them aid in the form of money or in kind.
6. Organise cultural aid for adults and education for youth.
7. Supply Polish citizens with essential documents (passports, certificates, etc.)
8. Receive, despatch, store, and distribute shipments of aid in kind from abroad for the relief of the Polish population.
9. Seek out representatives for regions or localities where Polish citizens are resident (i.e. the 'men of confidence').
10. Finally, where there were no permanent Delegates, their duties would be performed by travelling Embassy Delegates.[46]

The 'men of confidence', recruited from among the local Polish population, had a scope of activities which was considerably narrower than that of the Delegates. They were expected to carry out the Delegates'

requests in the localities and they were answerable to the Delegates.
(The Delegates were directly answerable to the Embassy.) By August
1942 there were 351 'men of confidence' about whom the Soviet Foreign
Commissariat had been informed; however, only 131 of these had been
recognised by the Soviet authorities.[47]

There were essentially three stages in the work of the Embassy's
Relief Programme. The first stage, from October 1941 to February
1942, was a period of disorganised and uncoordinated work, at a time
when the first overseas supplies were only arriving at Soviet ports.
During this period the initiative of individual Polish citizens, aided by
limited financial help from the Embassy and the Army, played an
important role. It was a period of genuine cooperation from the Soviet
central authorities, crowned by the goodwill which resulted from General
Sikorski's December visit. It was also a period of exceptionally friendly
treatment by the local Soviet authorities in some districts (e.g.
Kazakhstan).

The second period, from February to July 1942, began with the establishment of the Government Delegatures and the issuing of instructions for relief workers. The first relief supplies began to be distributed
to the regions. The third period began with the closing down of the
Delegates' offices, mass arrests of their personnel and seizure of files
and documents. Institutions set up by the Poles (schools, orphanages,
etc.) were also closed down without explanation. It marked a growing
hostility and suspicion on the part of the Soviet authorities towards
the relief operation, although there was a marked hiatus in the last
months of 1942, when some of those arrested were released and new
officials were approved by the Soviet authorities.

The letters begging for help which flooded into the Embassy proved
too voluminous for its slim resources of manpower.[48] Stanisław Skrzypek
recalled that in the early days following his release he sent several
telegrams to Moscow requesting help from the Polish Embassy. He
did not receive a reply. Only later, when he was working at the Embassy himself (which by that time had been moved to Kuibyshev), did
he realise that the Embassy received daily boxes full of letters and
telegrams, which no one read, since there was insufficient manpower.
His own telegrams were not opened until January 1942.[49]

There was also the problem of how to address the needs of the refugees. Cash payments were sent out to the destitute – both indirectly,
via the Embassy's representatives, for distribution, and direct to sup-
plicants. It was a speedy way of sending aid while awaiting the much
tardier distribution of goods, and particularly useful in reaching the

more remote settlements of Poles, isolated by distance or by climatic conditions. Over a million roubles were dispensed in this way by the end of September 1941, and some five-and-a-half million between 1941 and 1943.[50] Several reports of the relief operation emphasise that, although cash was relatively easy to send, it was no substitute for the essential articles such as clothing, footwear, bedding, and the higher-value food items, which could not be purchased at any price in local Soviet markets. Money indeed was often of limited value, particularly where the Soviet authorities refused to allow the Poles to buy at subsidised 'official' prices. Prices in markets and bazaars (under deteriorating war-conditions) were wildly inflationary and the purchasing power of the rouble as a consequence was much reduced. Hence the most important form of relief aid was aid in kind.

The Soviet authorities did not feel comfortable with the inflow of overseas goods for civilian relief – especially once the relief operation gained momentum (in the spring of 1942). There were obvious reasons; goods were distributed widely, within sight of Soviet citizens, and the distribution of such largesse both called into question Soviet propaganda about conditions in capitalist states and highlighted the failure of the Soviet regime to adequately feed and supply its own people. Moscow could not question the existence of warehouses at ports of entry, but worked to limit the number of personnel involved in their running. At transfer points, such as Aschabad, the local tax officials carefully checked incoming consignments and demanded the appropriate documentation. At first, such goods were brought into the country free of customs charges and conveyed by rail at a reduced tariff. However, with time, the Soviet authorities began to limit the customs concession to individual relief parcels and gifts; the concessionary rail tariff was withdrawn completely.

After prolonged negotiations, the number and location of the Embassy's stores or depots were established. They were sited at Archangel, Kirov, Mamlutka (near Pietropavlovsk), Vladivostok, Samarkand and Aschabad. In addition, each Embassy Delegature had its own depot from which the 'men of confidence' in the region could be supplied. When the Embassy's Delegatures were closed by the Soviet authorities in July 1942, only the Vladivostok depot closed permanently. The Archangel store closed for a few months only, while the remainder continued to operate, some under new leadership. At the end of 1942 there were ten depots operating, but this modest network was insufficient to supply almost 400 'men of confidence', and so an unofficial network of 44 'unloading points' developed.[51]

This system worked in the following way: the Embassy directed a sizeable aid transport to one of the 'men of confidence' via the rail network. The 'man of confidence' to whom this task had been entrusted received a statement from the Embassy, detailing how the supplies were to be reallocated. In this way one transport could be divided between several – sometimes a dozen or more – 'men of confidence'. The supplies were conveyed on to them by other means of transport. Regional representatives ('men of confidence') often had to depend upon more primitive means of transportation – oxen, donkeys and even camels – to convey goods from railway-points to more remote communities. Although this procedure exceeded the competence agreed for the 'men of confidence' and was frowned on by the Soviet authorities, it was a way of simplifying the procedure involved in liaising with the representatives individually. Furthermore, given the circumstances – the desperate need of the Poles, and the restricted ability of the depots to cater for these needs – it was an essential measure.

The division or allocation of goods, both by the Embassy among its local representatives, and, at local level, by the representatives among their dependent population, presented inevitable difficulties. Firstly, the amount of relief in kind was insufficient. The normal amount needed to supply all the centres with which the Embassy was in touch was around 2500 tons per month. Meanwhile, in October–November 1942, the aid which it was possible to distribute varied between 1200 and 1400 tons per month. The Welfare Department (Dział Opieki) of the Embassy was therefore forced to decide on priorities each time it carried out an allocation from the Embassy's stores. At the beginning of December 1942 the division provided for between one-and-a-half and two kg of foodstuffs per person.[52]

As a result of this shortfall, the local representatives were often faced with a dilemma. In keeping with the instructions issued to them by the Embassy, they were to supply in the first place the welfare institutions, and then divide the rest between the categories most in need – children without support, those incapable of working, families with a large number of children, etc. There were several such categories and the Embassy's 'men of confidence' had to decide priorities on the spot. Inevitably, disputes and disagreements broke out and numerous letters arrived at the Embassy with complaints or accusations against particular individuals responsible for distribution of supplies. Accusations were made that the representatives discriminated on ethnic or religious grounds (for example, that they discriminated against Jews or, conversely if the representative was Jewish, that he discriminated against non-Jews) or that discrimination occurred for political reasons. One woman, the wife of a general, wrote that army wives and families (in the vicinity of Semipalatynsk) were being discriminated against. Whether this was because the Army was felt to have put up a poor showing during the 1939 September campaign, or because those of senior rank were associated with the prewar Sanacja regime, or because they were not regarded as 'civilians' – and should look to the Polish Army for support – is unclear. Other letters complained of open abuse, in some cases favouritism – representatives looking after their friends – or else the sale of relief goods on the black market.[53]

There is little doubt that some of these accusations were well-founded. The Embassy was working in difficult circumstances and, despite its attempts to recruit people of standing and principle, did not, at the end of 1942, have personal details on all its 'men of confidence'. There were several reasons for this. Embassy welfare representatives in the south had left their posts and made their way out of Soviet territory with both the evacuations which took place from Soviet territory during 1942.[54] New ones had to be appointed quickly to carry on the essential work, and there was insufficient time to carry out checks properly. A further point was that in many regions the 'men of confidence' had been appointed by the local Delegates, without formal agreement from the Embassy (which in many cases did not have even their names and – most importantly – could not establish the territorial limits of their competence). After the arrest of the Delegates, the network was rebuilt at local level based on these 'men of confidence' – thus compounding the scope for abuse. Finally, although many of the 'men of confidence' (some 30 per cent) worked alone, others had between one and twelve assistants, of whom the Polish authorities had little knowledge and even less control.[55] Although the Embassy demanded that accounts be kept of the goods and monies distributed, it admitted that these could have only a purely formal (symbolic) value:

The numerous complaints which the Embassy's Welfare Department receives testify to the fact that the welfare network has serious shortcomings. Unfortunately there is no way of checking all these accusations, complaints and outright charges of corruption, favouritism and similar abuses. The central Soviet authorities have rejected however all the Embassy's proposals aimed at establishing any form of control, which perhaps raises justified fears that at the right time they may use such abuses to compromise the whole of the Embassy's relief apparatus.[56]

The Polish relief effort went beyond distributing food, clothing and medicines. The Embassy began to organise from January 1942 (and in some localities such initiatives were taken spontaneously at an earlier stage) a series of institutions to care for distressed Poles. These included orphanages, nursery schools and 'punkty dożywiania' (feeding points) for children; invalids' homes and old people's hostels; canteens and various workshops or units. The orphanages were set up throughout Soviet territory, but especially in the southern regions (Uzbek SSR, Kirghiz SSR and the southern regions of Kazakhstan), since it was here that most orphans were found. The mass trek of Poles to the south and the new, unforeseen obstacles that they encountered – heat, lack of food, primitive living conditions, continual epidemics, together with exhausting work in cotton-fields, harvesting crops, digging canals – caused a high level of mortality. Other 'semi-orphans' were thrust into the arms of the relief workers by mothers who could not feed them or else needed the freedom to be able to work to survive. Yet others were brought in by fathers travelling to join the Army. There was therefore a large number of unaccompanied children and the need for welfare institutions to care for them. (A large number of orphanages were also created by the Army – and many were evacuated with the Army in the course of 1942.)

The Soviet Government had given its agreement (on 24 December 1941) to the organisation of institutions for children without parents. However, local authorities varied in the degree of cooperation they offered. In most cases, the Poles had to rent a building to establish an orphanage. Indeed this was the pattern for almost all the care institutions established by the Poles; not one institution established in Kazakhstan was free from the need to pay rent, only 2.6 per cent in European Russia and 3.8 per cent in the south. The Soviet authorities tended to direct Polish children into *dietdomy* (Soviet children's homes) – sometimes by force. Republic and oblast authorities openly expressed the view that Polish orphanages were pointless, since (they argued) the equivalent Soviet institutions could carry out the same task. It became clear that the Soviet authorities were either deliberately bent on 'expunging' all traces of Polish national awareness from the children and rearing them in the communist ethic; or else that this would be a not-unwanted side-effect of other policies. Some children ran away from the *dietdomy*, and made their way alone to Polish agencies.[57] Towards the end of the period of welfare operations, during the winter of 1942–43, the Embassy was still receiving letters from Polish children 'imprisoned' in Soviet homes – and desperately beseeching their compatriots for help.[58]

Education was another area in which the Embassy relief workers and local members of Polish settlement felt impelled to act. Children had often forgotten their Polish or spoke in a mixed jargon of Polish, Russian and whatever local dialect or language prevailed. Illiteracy was a common problem. Religious and cultural knowledge had to be fostered. Furthermore, there was a frequently-expressed concern to remove children from the coarsening influence of their Russian counterparts. However, education was a problem area, since the question of schooling had never been definitely settled with the Narkomindiel. Although it was included in point 6 of the Regulations agreed upon for the guidance of Embassy delegates, the lack of a clear policy from the central Soviet authorities meant that officials at lower levels of administration (republic and oblast) interpreted the instructions in their own way. Some banned Polish teaching and courses altogether, while others showed tolerance and even encouragement towards such activity.[59]

The attitudes of the authorities in European Russia towards attempts to set up Polish schools were 'negative'. The Poles were usually prevented from organising normal school courses in orphanages, and 64 per cent of children in such orphanages had to attend Russian schools. (Nevertheless they were taught to read and write in Polish.) In Siberia, the authorities were 'decidedly negative' towards the idea of Polish education. However, in the Semipalatynsk region, permission was freely given for courses to begin and cooperation with the authorities went well. Indeed, cooperation seems to have lasted until the end of 1942 in some areas. One 'man of confidence', named Pieczko, writing to the Embassy, stated:

> Material help from the Embassy has so far been insignificant and has resulted barely in small amounts of flour, rice, sugar, cocoa. Thanks only to the Soviet authorities, and namely to Kraytorg, which agreed to allocate special products to the preschool, we managed to rescue the children from hunger and starvation. [60]

Another 'man of confidence', Koronowicz, from the Troytskoye raion, Novosibirsk oblast, reported that

> the nursery school's canteen receives supplies (*fonds*) from Lesprodtorg, which gives us bread (200 grammes per person) and other products in large amounts under the same conditions as for Soviet nursery schools.[61]

This highlights the fact that some Poles at least were being supplied with food from Soviet sources – although it is not clear whether these

supplies were being paid for out of the Soviet 100 million rouble credit.
Nor is it clear from Polish sources how substantial these Soviet supplies were.

THE DETERIORATION OF POLISH–SOVIET RELATIONS AND
THE WINDING-UP OF THE RELIEF APPARATUS

The period from the re-establishment of Polish–Soviet diplomatic relations in July 1941 to their rupture in April 1943 was some 21 months.
However, the period of the Polish Embassy's effective work in carrying
welfare supplies to its citizens was very much less than this – really
from October 1941 to January 1943, or 15 months. The 'honeymoon'
period of cooperation between the Poles and the Soviet authorities lasted
only until January or February 1942, by which time a number of issues had begun to sour relations.

In the period following his arrival in Moscow, Polish Ambassador
Stanisław Kot was able to cable Sikorski (on 16 October) that the
atmosphere towards the Poles was cordial (*przychylny*) although few
concrete promises had been given. He therefore judged that the projected visit by the Polish premier was essential.[62] Sikorski made efforts to cement that relationship during his visit at the beginning of
December, although there were signs already at this point that Soviet
policy was beginning to harden. This was due in part to the success of
the Soviet military operations outside Moscow; the German advance
had been halted and was being for the first time pushed back.[63] The
Saratov conference of 'Polish patriots' led by Wanda Wasilewska was
bruited loudly in the Soviet press and had been drawn to Sikorski's
attention during his Moscow visit, evoking an irritated response. Furthermore the Soviet authorities had attempted as early as 1 December
to place curbs and restrictions on those whom it regarded as Polish
citizens, thus resurrecting the thorny issue of the Polish–Soviet border.[64] A further fly in the ointment was the Soviet refusal to allow
'special treatment' (i.e. their recruitment to the Polish divisions) for
Poles taken into captivity in Wehrmacht uniforms.[65] At the same time
a dispute arose over an article by Polish Foreign Minister Edward
Raczyński, in the London *Sunday Times*, relating to the status of the
territories annexed by the USSR in 1939.[66]

Concurrently discussions and disagreements were taking place concerning the supplying of the Polish military formations and the date at
which they should be put into frontline action. The Poles' persistent

enquiries about the fate of thousands of their missing officers were eliciting ever more fantastic theories. Repeated Polish interventions, which proved an irritation to Soviet officials, were being made on behalf of thousands of men and women not freed under the 'amnesty.' Agonised appeals were being made to Vyshinsky and Molotov to permit the evacuation of 50 000 Polish children. These led to a heated exchange on the true conditions under which Polish civilians were living and their mortality rate.[67] Finally, in March–April 1942, came the first evacuation of Polish units from the USSR – which Stalin himself had intimated earlier would be a great humiliation for the Soviet authorities if it should take place.

In the spring of 1942, when the relief effort on the ground really began to show results, Poles in some districts detected a hardening in the attitudes of local authorities. Nursery schools and other institutions were closed down in some localities.[68] But the main assault against the welfare network came in the summer months and when it began, was clearly coordinated by the central authorities. On 9 June, the Narkomindiel directed a note to the Polish Embassy regarding the issue of Polish passports. It stated that, in order to 'regulate matters properly', the Embassy should present alphabetical lists of Polish citizens to whom it proposed to issue national passports. These lists, made out separately for each district inhabited by Polish citizens, were to be presented in four copies, with a Russian translation attached, to the Ministry. Clearly this was a step designed to ensure that Embassy staff were not issuing documents to Jews, Ukrainians and Byelorussians from eastern Poland whom Moscow regarded as Soviet citizens. Two weeks later, the Embassy issued a rebuff; it did not consider it possible that 'the Soviet authorities should decide the citizenship of Polish citizens . . . who between 1939–1941 found themselves . . . not of their own free will on the territory of the Soviet Union'.[69]

This was an understandable and justified, but perhaps unfortunate response from the Polish Embassy, in the light of events. On 25 May the Embassy Delegate for Akmolinsk, Rola-Janicki, had been called to Kuibyshev to report on his activities. In his hotel room he had left a brief-case containing secret papers from his office. These were 'lifted' by the NKVD. The papers included courier's instructions, political instructions, lists of names of Lithuanian and Soviet citizens of Polish extraction and other materials which, from the NKVD's point of view, were 'suspicious'. This matter provided the Soviet authorities with the pretext they needed. Pressure on the Poles was increased. The Embassy buildings were surrounded, callers had their papers routinely checked, and arrests began to occur where the regulations laid down for the conduct of Embassy representatives were not strictly observed.[70]

On 2 July, Sikorski sent a cable to Kot in Kuibyshev, informing him that Stalin had agreed to the second evacuation. Sikorski had earlier, faced with the prospect of the second military evacuation, expressed concern to Anders about the fate of the Poles being left behind:

> It appears from (your telegram) that the position of the Army, which is better than that of the civilian population, is catastrophic. What conclusions am I to draw from it about the position of hundreds of thousands of civilian refugees?[71]

Concern over whether the care of civilians would be continued after a further evacuation of Polish troops were voiced by Foreign Minister, Raczyński, on 4 July in the course of a conversation with British official Alexander Cadogan.[72]

The main blow fell on 6 July, when the Soviet authorities announced the withdrawal of diplomatic immunity from the Embassy delegates, justifying this step with the argument that

> they do not in fact carry out any diplomatic activity, being engaged in work which has nothing to do with their official diplomatic duties; moreover they retain their diplomatic rights and privileges. This position is improper.[73]

However, a first move towards winding up the network of Delegates had been taken four days earlier. On the afternoon of 2 July, the offices of the Delegate in Archangel, Józef Gruja, were entered by five Soviet officials. (Gruja himself had just left to travel to Murmansk.) The four officials present – including Gruja's deputy Waldemar Kuczyński – were arrested and taken from the premises by the NKVD. The Soviet officials also took archival materials, official correspondence, seals and money belonging to the Delegate's office.[74] On 3 July a Soviet aide-mémoire was sent to the Polish Embassy, indicating that the delegate's offices in Aldan, Vladivostok and Archangel were to be closed.[75]

In the course of the following ten days, further arrests took place in Barnaul, Samarkand, Kirov, Syktyvkar and Petropavlovsk. The property of Delegates' offices was confiscated, and accounts with the State Bank were closed. In its protest note, the Polish Embassy complained that 45 per cent of the Delegates' offices had been paralysed and the issue of food-aid and clothing to tens of thousands of Polish citizens had had to be stopped.[76] The arrests, however, continued. A characteristic move was the arrest of Mr Słowikowski, who had been called from Chelyabinsk to work at the Embassy. His arrival at Kuibyshev on 16 July, and his status had been announced to the Narkomindiel on the same day. On 20 July, though, he was arrested in front of the entrance to the Embassy. Other arrests included those of Kosciałkowski, Delegate in Chymkent, and Glogowski, Delegate for Aschabad, one of the principal receiving depots for all relief shipments. By the third week in July all the Delegates had been arrested, detained or expelled.[77] Polish protests elicited an initial reaction from Vyshinsky that he did not know about the arrests, and that the Poles 'should not draw general conclusions from the fact of a diplomat's arrest' (a significant acknowledgement that the two held diplomatic status!).[78] In a conversation some time later, he maintained that,

> The cessation of further activities of the regional Delegates does not justify the implication that the Soviet Government intends to hamper or to liquidate the welfare work for Poles in the USSR.[79]

These sentiments were echoed by Bogomolov in London two days later to Raczyński.[80] This was a cynical statement, in view of the fact that nurseries, orphanages, old people's homes, medical centres and other institutions continued to be closed down during August.

The Embassy's welfare activities were thrown into confusion – the Embassy was uncertain to whom it should direct correspondence or money remittances at any one time – and the Polish population was thrown into panic at the prospect of being 'abandoned' not only by the Army, but also by the Polish civilian representatives. Morale was not improved at this crucial juncture by the departure of Ambassador Kot, who took leave of Vyshinsky on 8 July, leaving Soviet territory some 12 days later for Persia. Kot explained that he was leaving for health reasons – he was completely exhausted.[81] This was understandable in view of the extremely difficult physical conditions (cramped, lack of privacy, etc.) in the Embassy and the frustrating, nerve-racking process of day-to-day dealings with Soviet bureaucracy. However, he left his position at the worst possible moment, and once again (as in the late summer of 1941 before his arrival) the Embassy was left in the hands of a chargé; Henryk Sokolnicki ran the Embassy for the next three months, until Kot's successor, Tadeusz Romer, arrived in October.[82]

Initial Soviet responses to Polish protests were that the Delegates and their assistants had been guilty of carrying out intelligence work.[83] However, a detailed Soviet account of why the arrests had taken place was not made available until the end of October (by which time the new Ambassador had arrived!). The Soviet authorities alleged that an espionage ring had been controlled and instructed from within the Embassy. But this accusation seems to have referred to the efforts of the Embassy and the Delegates to collect information concerning the numbers of Poles, their whereabouts and situation. The arrested were also supposed to have 'spread all kinds of slanderous allegations and lies detrimental to the USSR with a view to discrediting the Soviet authorities and the Soviet regime'. Furthermore, they had 'spread false information depicting the situation of the Polish population in the USSR in the gloomiest colours.' An especially popular provocation. . . . was '*the spreading of false rumours on the allegedly high mortality rate among the Polish population*' (my italics – K. S.).[84]

This whole operation can only have been an attempt to bring the turbulent Poles to heel – a warning to the Embassy that the patience of the Soviet authorities had reached its limit; that Soviet statesmen were not prepared to listen to further litanies on the appalling plight of the Poles or homilies on the Soviet leadership's responsibility for it. The irritation on the part of Soviet officials is evident from a number of exchanges, but particularly from Vyshinsky's encounter with Kot over the mortality rate among Polish children and requests for their evacuation.[85] Furthermore, accusations from the Soviet side that Polish officials had been involved in stealing welfare goods intended for the Polish population were an attempt to counter Polish allegations of theft made against Soviet personnel and to sow doubt and dissension in Polish ranks.[86]

It is true that at a time of tension and greater than usual wariness on the part of the Soviet authorities and people, some Polish representatives behaved in a less than discreet manner.[87] Tadeusz Romer himself questioned the quality of some of the welfare representatives – and the way in which they set about gathering information. There were some 'men of confidence' who, having been released from prisons and camps, were filled with hatred against the Russians and did little to conceal their feelings, or their contempt for the Soviet system. Moreover, Stanisław Świaniewicz, who had the good fortune to avoid the Katyn massacre and later write of his experiences in the Soviet Union at this time, suggests that some of the delegates brought into the USSR from Britain may indeed have been involved in gathering information on the Soviet war effort and defensive capability – for British Intelligence.[88]

General Anders cabled to Sikorski on 23 July that 'undoubtedly Embassy officials and attachés have taken some unwise steps which had all the appearances of intelligence work'. This work had been carried out 'by various Embassy Delegates or members of the Delegatures; people who had no idea of how to organise intelligence gathering operations, were unfamiliar with the technical side of such matters, and were doomed sooner or later to be compromised – without producing any significant results'. 'The Soviet authorities,' he continued, 'who have suspected the existence of such a network for a long time, obtained irrefutable proof in the form of letters of instruction for Delegates and carriers, issued by the Embassy, reports by Delegates about the state of Soviet industry, the army and the movement of units from the interior of the country to the rear, as well as other compromising documents.'[89]

But there were other factors which must have alarmed the Soviet leadership at local and national level. The propaganda effect of the arrival of Western welfare goods for the Poles – at a time when the Soviet population was in a similarly wretched condition – aroused both resentments and envy among Soviet citizens. Aleksander Wat wrote:

> Relations were already tense. And understandably, since before this during the first months, Poles behaved a little like their forefathers had done in the Kremlin. The strong do not arm, but with earthly goods demoralise the population. Poles were dispersed over the whole of Central Asia, of Siberia and suddenly the population sees that the bourgeois state is pouring fabulous riches, an excess of goods, free. Such goods as they had never in their lives seen. It was politically demoralising. They could not tolerate that for long, really they couldn't.[90]

In the autumn, on the intervention of the British Government and of the Americans (Wendell Wilkie, President Roosevelt's special envoy) the NKVD refrained from further arrests and court cases. Most of the arrested diplomats had already been released by the NKVD with the proviso that they should leave Soviet territory. Of 109 people arrested by the Soviets to October 1942, 93 were released and as many as 16 were unaccounted for. Sikorski stated on 19 November that 94 had been released and that the Polish Government were still attempting to secure the release of the remaining 15.[91] A number, however, were reported to have died in jail.[92]

In November 1942 the Polish Embassy proposed that welfare activity be resumed via a network of local officials, who would limit themselves to 'control functions only'. In order to allay any remaining suspicions harboured by the Soviet Government, Ambassador Romer suggested that the Poles be accompanied by Soviet officials who would

both act as a form of liaison and also 'supervise' the welfare activities.[93] This last throw was rejected by Molotov. Although his deputy
Vyshinsky signalled agreement to decisions concerning the activities
of the 'men of confidence' and the goods stores, on 16 January 1943
the Narkomindiel informed the Embassy that the Supreme Soviet had
issued an order for local authorities to take over all Polish welfare
institutions.[94] With this order, the efforts of the Polish Embassy to
seek a resumption of welfare activity on behalf of its citizens effectively ceased. On 16 January there followed an NKVD order regarding the compulsory issuing of (Soviet) passports to Polish citizens.[95]

The Polish warehouses and stores thus fell into Soviet hands. The
goods within them – and those that were still in transit – were subsequently to be used when the Polish Communists (ZPP) began to adopt
a welfare role on behalf of Poles later in 1943. In the meantime, on 25
April there occurred a break in Polish–Soviet relations. Immediately
following this break, the interests of the Polish Embassy were taken
over by the Australian Legation.[96]

5 The Role of Polish Communists in the USSR, 1943–45

THE CREATION OF THE UNION OF POLISH PATRIOTS

Following the evacuation of General Anders' forces in 1942 and the 'suspension' – effectively, a complete break – of Soviet diplomatic relations with the Polish Government in April of the following year, the situation of the deported Polish population remaining in the Soviet Union was bleak. There was little hope of their being able to leave Soviet territory in the immediate future. Furthermore the departure of the Embassy staff and dismantling of the relief apparatus reduced the prospects that welfare supplies would continue to be distributed. Attitudes of the Soviet public too had become less friendly, showing the effect of official propaganda that Anders and his troops had abandoned the Soviet people to their fate, at the crucial moment when German troops were approaching Stalingrad.

Historians have debated as to whether, in dealing with Polish affairs during this period, Stalin had some long-term aims, or whether he was simply reacting to circumstances, seeking advantage as the opportunities occurred. It seems clear, however, that in the spring of 1943, not only was Stalin keen to engineer a break in relations with the Polish Government in London, but he had prepared the ground. He was not taking a leap in the dark. He had other cards to play and had indicated earlier that it might prove necessary to play them.[1] The first 'card' was the small group of communists in Warsaw, the core of which had been parachuted into Poland by the Soviets at the end of 1941. This group created the Polish Workers' Party in Warsaw in January 1942. The use of the word 'communist' was pointedly avoided in the party's name. Stalin and the Communist International (Comintern) were aware that a party which was openly communist would have little support – even among the working population in Poland. The communists had not been widely supported in the interwar period; what support could they hope for now, when memory of the Nazi–Soviet Pact and the Soviet annexation of Polish territory were so fresh?

The second 'card' consisted of a somewhat larger group of Polish communists and socialists who had made their way to the east following the German invasion in 1939, and had subsequently come under Soviet protection and control. Some of the Party faithful might have been excused for having misgivings about throwing themselves upon Stalin's mercy. Only two years earlier (1937–38) the Soviet leader had disbanded the Polish Communist Party (KPP) for its 'Trotskyist and nationalist tendencies' and had consigned the majority of its leaders and many of the rank-and-file to the firing-squad or to labour camps.[2] Those that survived owed their survival in most cases to the fact that they were languishing in Polish jails when the summons to Moscow arrived; names such as W. Gomułka. B. Bierut, S. Jędrychowski, F. Jóźwiak, E. Ochab, S. Wierbłowski and A. Zawadzki. Out of 26 members of the KPP listed in postwar editions of the Polish *Encyclopedia Powszechna*, 23 were victims of Stalin's purge. The remaining three – J. Brun, F. Fiedler and A. Lampe – survived because they were outside the USSR. Yet, either ignorant of their comrades' fate, or feeling that circumstances had changed, or perhaps fearing worse treatment at the hands of the Gestapo, several hundred communists and other Poles of left-wing persuasion had flocked to the eastern provinces occupied by the Red Army and were later – in the summer of 1941 – evacuated deeper into the Soviet Union with Soviet officials and their families.[3]

During the period of Soviet rule in eastern Poland large numbers of these Polish communists had been concentrated in three main centres – Lwów, Białystok and Minsk. They found themselves in a strange situation. The Polish Communist Party had not been rehabilitated by Stalin, and suggestions that it be revived were muted, in the face of official disapproval.[4] Indeed, some former Party-members suspected of Trotskyism or other deviationist tendencies, were liquidated by the NKVD. By contrast, others, and some radical socialists who had never formally been Communist Party members but were ideologically in sympathy with the communists' aims, were used to mobilise the new authorities' cultural propaganda campaign. Some were employed in the Polish-language radio and press. In autumn 1940 a leading member of this group, Wanda Wasilewska, wrote to Stalin, suggesting that some former members of the KPP be admitted to the Soviet (Bolshevik) Communist Party. The possibility was admitted by Stalin, and Wasilewska – although not herself a KPP member previously – was one of the first to join.[5]

A particularly influential group had gathered in Lwów. There, apart from the Polish-language newspaper called *Czerwony Sztandar* (Red

Banner), which was issued from the autumn of 1939, a literary journal called *Nowe Widnokręgi* (New Horizons) began to appear in January 1941.[6] The editorial board included Wanda Wasilewska, Janina Broniewska, university professor and literary critic Tadeusz Boy–Zelenski, and the poet Julian Przyboś. The editors also included Zofia Dzierżyńska, the widow of Feliks Dzierżyński, founder of Lenin's secret police, and Helena Usiejewicz, daughter of Feliks Kon, another of Lenin's collaborators, who had spent the years 1920–39 in Russia. Their appointment marked a direct link with the more cosmopolitan of the Polish communists who had sought to establish Bolshevik rule in Poland some two decades earlier.[7]

Seven issues of the journal appeared by the time the Germans attacked in June 1941. When the Wehrmacht overrran Lwów and other towns in the east of Poland, publication of the journal was suspended and its editorial team evacuated. They moved first to Moscow, where the editorial board was strengthened by the addition of activists Alfred Lampe, Stefan Jędrychowski and Leon Pasternak. Then, as the Germans approached Moscow in the autumn, a further evacuation took place to Kuibyshev. There, they were employed in compiling Polish-language radio broadcasts for transmission to the homeland (at the same time, ironically, as the Polish Embassy, in the same city, was attempting to mount a relief operation for Poles). Other Polish communists in the Soviet Union at this time included those grouped around the Comintern. Early on, these included the members of the 'Initiative Groups' being trained as agents for parachuting back into Poland. Bolesław Mołojec, Paweł Finder and Marceli Nowotko were among the members of the first group which travelled at the end of December 1941.[8] During the first months of 1942 the remaining members of the 'Comintern group' were based in Ufa. There was a further group of Polish communists based in Saratov, working for the 'Taras Szewczenko' Ukrainian radio service and in the Publishing House for Foreign Literature. The members included Jerzy Putrament, Adam Ważyk, Zygmunt Modzelewski and Edward Ochab.[9]

In the honeymoon period following the signing of the 1941 Sikorski–Maisky Pact, the Polish radicals had been under warning to maintain a low profile and, in their writing, to deal lightly with General Sikorski and the London Polish authorities. One of their number, Janina Broniewska, was later to complain that they were not allowed to criticize the operations of the Polish Embassy and were even barred from contact with the Polish community on Soviet soil.[10] Nevertheless, the Polish Government was left in no doubt as to their existence. During

Sikorski's visit to Moscow in December 1941, the Soviet press carried a report of a gathering of these Polish 'progressive elements' in the town of Saratov. Sikorski was said to have been furious with the news, but determined nevertheless to continue with his mission.[11] The conclusion seems inescapable that Stalin wished Sikorski to know that he had other, more compliant Polish cards to play, if the need should arise.[12] Indeed a further blow at Sikorski's prestige was struck while he and Stalin were engaged in talks at the Kremlin on the night of 3/4 December, with the arrest of the Jewish Bund members Ehrlich and Alter.[13]

In April 1942, Alfred Lampe and Wasilewska set about bringing together an editorial team with the aim of reviving the cultural journal *Nowe Widnokręgi* in Kuibyshev. They quickly gained the approval of the Soviet authorities and the first issue of the journal in its revived form appeared on 5 May 1942.[14] From its very first issue the editors made no secret of the fact that there was a group of Poles in the Soviet Union, who shared common convictions and were sufficiently committed politically to take over leadership of the Polish interests. Unsurprisingly, the Polish Embassy in Kuibyshev did not look on these activities favourably, and reportedly made attempts to block distribution of the journal.[15]

In late autumn 1942, some two months after the second evacuation of General Anders's forces, a conversation took place between senior members of the Polish 'democratic camp' – Wasilewska, Bolesław Drobner, Wiktor Grosz, Hilary Minc – in the presence of the Ukrainian writer and politician (and third husband of Wasilewska), Alexander Kornieczuk. They discussed the possibility of creating a formal grouping of all Polish activists on Soviet soil.[16] On 4 January the group associated with *Nowe Widnokręgi* sent a letter to Molotov proposing the organisation of the Polish left into a body which could help to resolve Polish questions as they arose and, in the short term, could carry out educational work (including, of course, political re-education) among those Poles in Wehrmacht service captured on the eastern front. The letter also included two further appeals. The first was a renewed plea that former members of the KPP be admitted into the ranks of the Soviet Communist Party. This request was curious not only because it indicated either that the petitioners did not expect to return to Poland, or perhaps more likely, that they expected Poland to become completely Sovietised once the Red Army had liberated the country. It also completely ignored the fact that the Polish Workers' Party (Polska Partia Robotnicza) had been formed in Poland almost exactly a year earlier by Paweł Finder (1904–44) and Marceli Nowotko

(1893–1942), two of the Polish communists who had been parachuted into Poland. The second appeal was that Poles should have the right to fight in the Red Army. Poles from the Soviet-occupied territories had been subject to recruitment to Red Army service since 1940, but for the first time it seems the idea was being put forward of Polish units serving within the Red Army.[17]

Although there was no immediate response from the Soviet authorities, a number of factors were working in favour of the Polish communists. The first was that the Comintern, headed by George Dimitrov, was reputedly in favour of the move, as were many figures of authority in the Soviet government and Party.[18] The second was the situation on the military front. The Red Army had gone on the offensive in the third week of November, and within a matter of days had trapped the German 6th Army at Stalingrad. The titanic struggle which ensued ended with the capitulation of the German garrison of over a quarter of a million men on 2 February 1943. This reversal of military fortunes affected the political arena profoundly. Once Stalin felt the tide had turned and the Germans were being forced into retreat, he was no longer in such desperate need of Western support. Accordingly, he had less need to bend to the will of the Western allies and to pretend to cooperate with a Polish Government which he felt to be a 'client' of the British.

During late January and February 1943 a series of conversations took place between Stalin and Molotov, on the one hand, and Wasilewska and Zygmunt Berling, on the other. Wasilewska had to be summoned from the Stalingrad front, where she was being employed as propaganda and education officer. It was during one of these meetings that the idea of a formal grouping of Polish left-wing elements was approved by Stalin. However, it appears from Wasilewska's account of these meetings that the idea of a Polish newspaper or journal – *Wolna Polska* (Free Poland) – came first and the concept of a formal organisation to support it was something of an afterthought! This sounds a rather strange order of events, but it was in this context that the 'Union of Polish Patriots' (Związek Patriotów Polskich – ZPP) came into being towards the end of February 1943.

I then talked with Stalin and Molotov. On the subject of *Free Poland* there had to be two sessions. We discussed who was to head the journal and that it would not be good if it looked as though it was the initiative of a tiny group of people. In order that the journal expressed people's mood and did not repel, but drew in all Poles, we had to give it the name of some organisation. At this point Stalin himself suggested the name Union of Polish Patriots. At first the name did not appeal to me at all and I said that the word 'patriot' was fairly compromised in Poland. He told me by way of answer that each word can be given new meaning and it depends on you what meaning you give it.[19]

Two important points are clear from this passage. The first is that the name of the organisation was suggested by Stalin himself. Second, there is the implicit acknowledgement that pro-Moscow Poles were a tiny group; only by choosing such a neutral and all-embracing name could the mass of Poles be attracted and drawn in. The movement was superficially to be an 'anti-fascist' popular front which it was hoped would eventually embrace not only communists, but socialists, Peasant Party activists, and others whose patriotic inclinations could be harnessed to the general purpose.[20] For the moment, however, there was no organisation – only a name. This was still the case a few days later on 1 March 1943 when the new weekly, *Wolna Polska*, made its appearance.[21]

The articles in early issues of *Wolna Polska*, which described itself as the organ of the Union of Polish Patriots (ZPP), were written in the main by Wasilewska, Hilary Minc and Wiktor Grosz. These three, together with Alfred Lampe, were all later to join the organising committee of the ZPP. The journal contained a statement outlining the general aims of the Union – aims which were later to be set out more fully in the Union's 'Ideological Declaration'. We can derive the tenor of subsequent pronouncements from the following extracts:

We have started to publish this journal in an attempt to attract the attention of all those who are living on Soviet territory and with weapons in hand, by their work or their writing, struggle for an independent Poland freed from the Nazi yoke. For a democratic Poland. For a Poland in which the peasant receives land and both white- and blue-collar workers receive employment, state welfare, and civilized living conditions. For a just Poland without racial and ethnic hatred. For a Poland which is strong externally, not by the seizure of others' territory, but through neighbourly relations. For a Poland strong internally, not by the strength of the fist and the police truncheon, but through the unity of its people, its economic and cultural development. For a Poland which allows freedom of conscience, in which no one will be persecuted for his beliefs and views.[22]

Furthermore,

> in the future Poland can only be really independent and strong if
> she is linked by brotherly, neighbourly relations with the Soviet Union.[23]

There is little here that would have been objectionable to Polish democrats
– no outright statement of communist views. Instead the reader is promised tolerance, social justice, employment, decent living conditions and
freedom from the arbitrary application of force. Indeed, the passage is
skilfully written, in that, while it seems to be directed against conditions prevailing in Poland under German occupation, there are sufficient clues to indicate that it also contains an oblique attack on the
prewar 'Sanacja' regime in Poland.

Certainly, though, the journal did not shirk from attacking the policies of General Sikorski's government. In the first issue an article by
Wasilewska ('O cześć narodu' – 'Concerning the honour of the nation')
developed into a polemic with Sikorski over the extent and degree of
resistance activity in Poland. The underground Home Army, which
owed allegiance to the London Government, was under orders to refrain from widespread military activity until the time was ripe for a
general uprising against the Germans. They were instead to concentrate on intelligence-gathering, sabotage and diversion. The aim was
to spare the civilian population as far as was possible, from German
reprisals. However, this policy contrasted with that of the Soviet partisans, parachuted into Poland, whose aim was to inflict the utmost
damage on the Germans irrespective of the cost to the civilian population. Wasilewska wrote:

> The prime minister is afraid of battle-cries which might encourage
> the struggle with the Germans. But he is not afraid of words and
> phrases which can germinate there, at home, a harvest of fratricidal
> murders.[24]

In the second issue of the journal, in an article entitled 'The Apostles
of Passivity', Wasilewska developed this theme further. She poured
scorn on those who advocated caution in the struggle with the Germans. The first to die, she suggested, were those who sat and waited.
There was a need for a 'second front' in Poland – for military activity
on a large scale from the partisans.[25] The journal also supported Soviet
calls for a shift of Polish borders – for a return of Poland to the Oder
and the Baltic and a redrawing of the eastern frontier in keeping with
'ethnographic principles'.

One Polish historian of the ZPP has claimed that it is impossible to chart accurately and chronologically the early activities of the ZPP's organising committee, since it had a largely informal character and many (perhaps the majority) of issues were settled through direct intervention with the Soviet officials and agencies concerned.[26] Here Wanda Wasilewska, who enjoyed a relationship of some confidence with Stalin (he referred to her as 'Wanda Lwowna') was certainly a key figure. Indeed Stalin must have been amused by the irony of finding the daughter of one of Marshal Piłsudski's close political allies collaborating with him.[27] Wasilewska claims to have sorted out many of the key issues facing the Polish left on a personal basis, without any formal approach to the Soviet authorities being made by the ZPP. If her account is to be believed, she seems to have managed to cut through much of the red tape of Soviet bureaucracy.[28] It is important to repeat that, certainly until 1939, Wasilewska had not been a member of the Polish Communist Party, however sympathetic she may have been to their aims and programme. But her influence was such that one Polish historian has written, 'From the summer of 1940, Wanda Wasilewska became the *de facto* representative of the interests of the Polish community in the Soviet Union, including the communists. . . .'[29] While one must question the date mentioned in the above extract, she certainly seems to have adopted this role from the spring of 1943.

THE FORMATION OF A SECOND POLISH ARMY

The establishment of another Polish Army on Soviet soil, to replace and possibly rival the force that had left with Anders, went in tandem with the formation and growth of the ZPP. The idea of a Polish Army under communist control had been conceived at an early stage in the war. In the autumn of 1940 Stalin had directed Wasilewska to approach captive Polish officers and sound out their views on serving in 'Red' Polish formations.[30] A later scheme, in the summer of 1941, was devised by Polish communists from Minsk and Białystok, who had moved into the Soviet Union in 1939 or thereafter. Chief movers in the scheme were Paweł Finder and Czesław Skoniecki. At Mohylew, in eastern Byelorussia, they set about forming a Polish battalion, which it was intended should fight alongside the Red Army. The formation was to be drawn from refugees from Białystok, Pińsk, Baranowicze and Brześć. It was to be commanded by Polish veterans of the civil war in Spain (i.e. from the International Brigades), and Polish communists in the USSR.[31] Uniforms and emblems were to be Polish, as was the system of ranks. An appeal for volunteers was broadcast by the Staff of the new formation, before the project collapsed in August. The signing of Sikorski–Maisky Pact and the agreement to form a Polish Army in the USSR under the auspices of the London Polish Government meant that, for the time being at least, such plans had to be shelved.

They were revived some eighteen months later at the beginning of 1943. On 4 February the revitalised journal *Nowe Widnokręgi* published an appeal to Poles to form their own military units to fight alongside the Red Army. This statement appeared in print almost three months before the break in Polish–Soviet relations occurred.[32] There were considerable reserves available for such a force. As early as 1940 General Sikorski had anticipated creating a force of some 300 000 from the manpower trapped in the USSR.[33] Barely a third of this number, though, had left with General Anders, and following the two evacuations of 1942, the 'London' Poles had been refused permission to carry out further recruitment. With the formal break in Polish–Soviet diplomatic relations, the ground was cleared for Moscow's Polish followers to make their move. On 28 April, a mere three days after the break, Wanda Wasilewska made a radio speech in which she argued:

> To Poland, to our homeland, to our families' homes there is only one road – the road of struggle and work towards victory. And the shortest route home is from here, from the Soviet Union. . . . We believe that in the near future we will be able to prove our love for Poland, our right to Poland – shoulder to shoulder with the Red Army under Polish banners. . . .[34]

At the same time she sent Stalin a letter suggesting the creation of a further Polish Army on Soviet territory, citing the Czech battalion of Ludvik Svoboda as a precedent.[35] The creation of a Polish division would be possible, she suggested, by mobilising those ethnic Poles who were prewar citizens of the Soviet Union, those who had come from the western districts of the Soviet Union (i.e. the deportees from regions of Poland annexed in 1939) and those who had already been directed to labour battalions of the Red Army. She also drew attention to the need to carry out educational work among Polish prisoners captured in Wehrmacht uniforms, and suggested that these people might be recruited into the new Polish Division. Finally, in view of the shortage of Polish officers, the majority of whom had left the Soviet Union with Anders,[36] she acknowledged that it would be necessary to draft in some qualified Red Army personnel in order to help train the new unit.[37]

It seems that the possibility of a further Polish formation had been discussed informally with Stalin already. Certainly the idea of forming a Polish army 'independent of the Polish Government in London' had been put to the Soviet authorities in September 1942 – immediately following the second and final evacuation of Anders' troops – by Colonel Zygmunt Berling.[38] Berling and Wasilewska had a series of conversations with Stalin during the early weeks of 1943, and it seems likely that the subject was broached. But Stalin did not give a formal reply until April 1943, when it must have been quite clear to him that relations with the Polish Government in London would soon be ruptured. Berling was promised that his request, 'if directed to the appropriate Party and State authorities', would be supported by Stalin.[39]

The Soviet Committee for State Defence approved the establishment of a Polish Division on 6 May, the day after Polish ambassador Tadeusz Romer left Soviet territory. The news was reported in *Wolna Polska* two days later, together with the information that Berling had been appointed to command the new force.[40] He had already informed Stalin that in his view there were sufficient Poles in the Soviet Union to form an army of 100 000 men, but that initially, because of organisational problems, he foresaw the creation of a single division with reserve units.[41] It was decided to create an infantry division along the lines of a Red Army Guards Division; this would allow certain advantages with regard to supply and equipment.

At a meeting with General Zhukov towards the end of April, a group of Poles (including Wasilewska, Lampe, Minc, Grosz and Berling) had discussed details of the new force.[42] It had been agreed that the new division would be at the disposal of the Red Army High Command as regards operational matters, but it would be under the political guidance of the ZPP, which would cooperate with the Soviet authorities in appointing political officers (*politruks*). The division was to be named after the Polish patriot, Tadeusz Kościuszko – apparently to emphasise the Polish national character of the unit and its liberating goals (although the irony must have occurred to many that Kościuszko's patriotic efforts in the 1790s had been aimed at liberating Poland from Russian rule.) The emphasis upon the Polish national characteristics of the division were doubtless both for reasons of morale and for long-term political goals. If this unit were to form the backbone of the armed forces of the Polish Republic at some indeterminate point in the future, it would not be politic for it to be seen as merely another unit of the Red Army. Uniforms therefore were to be the Polish Army uniforms of 1939, and the symbol of the division would be the Piast

eagle (i.e. an eagle without the royal crown). The language of communication in the division was to be Polish, and there was even to be
a regular Sunday mass! Photographs from the period show that a Polish
priest was put on display along with Wasilewska, Berling and other
notables when occasion demanded.[43] The flag would be Polish, as would
the national anthem. As regards the oath of allegiance, this too would
resemble the prewar oath, although brotherhood with the Red Army
and the loyalty of an ally towards the Soviet Union were also included
in the wording.[44]

Following formal Soviet approval to the creation of the 'Kościuszko
Division', the radio and press announced that recruitment was taking
place. Significantly, the recruitment appeal was directed to volunteers
among 'former Polish citizens of non-Polish background' and Poles
who were permanent residents and citizens of the USSR.[45] In Britain,
Soviet Monitor announced that the 'newly-formed' Polish division in
the USSR would not form part of the Red Army, but would be under
the operational direction of the Supreme C-in-C of Soviet Armed Forces.
It quoted the stirring propaganda of Radio Moscow:

> This Division is the foundation of a truly fighting Polish army which
> by force of arms will destroy the enemy. The battle-cry of the Divi-
> sion is 'Fight the Germans'.[46]

This information, which was also conveyed to the British public through
the columns of *Soviet War News*, aroused ire within the Polish political establishment in London. Sikorski immediately considered sending
a protest to members of the United Nations against the formation of a
Polish division by the Soviets, since he regarded this as an infringement of Polish sovereign rights. However, he was persuaded by Eden
to delay the protest until clarification of the issue had been sought
from Moscow.[47] In the British Foreign Office it was observed with
cynicism that,

> this new division in Russia will be recruited from precisely those
> categories of Poles who, according to the Soviet note to the Polish
> Government of January 16 last, were in future to be regarded as
> Soviet citizens. Nevertheless, the division is to be essentially Polish,
> using the Polish national anthem and flag, and not part of the Red
> Army.[48]

Indeed, when questioned in Moscow by British Ambassador Clark Kerr,
Molotov confirmed that the recruits for the Polish legion would be
drawn from men who, although Polish by nationality and formerly

living in the Western Ukraine and Western Byelorussia, were now Soviet citizens. At the same time he seemed to confirm previous assurances by Soviet spokesmen that the Union of Polish Patriots would not be treated by the Soviet authorities as a future Polish Government.[49]

The Poles were allocated a camp in the Moscow military district for recruitment and training. The camp, at Sielce on the River Oka (50 km north-east of Riazan), quickly became a magnet for Polish volunteers, in the same way that their compatriots had flooded to join Anders' divisions at Buzułuk almost two years earlier. The first six recruits for the Polish division arrived at the Sielce camp on 13 May. On the following day, its commander, Colonel Berling, arrived and he was followed into the camp during the following weeks by a flood of willing recruits.[50] By the beginning of July, in just over six weeks, the number had reached 14 000. Many years later Berling gave his own impressions of the new recruits as they crossed the River Oka from the nearest railway station at Divovo, and stepped off the ferry to walk the last kilometre to the camp:

> When these people came closer, we saw the material from which this Division had to be created. The picture was extraordinary. People whose appearance bore witness to the fact that they had come through extremely hard times. . . . There were people in rags which had once been jackets, with bundles, or with some kinds of boxes which had once been suitcases, in shoes, moccasins, and felt boots. . . . These were the people we had to make into soldiers.[51]

It seems, then, that the appearance of the new recruits to Berling's division was just as unpromising as that of the recruits to Anders' forces had been in 1941.[52]

At this point, the question arises of why these people did not make the earlier journey to join the Polish Army being formed by General Anders? Why did some wait almost a further two years before deciding to join up? There are numerous answers to this question – and we can only list a few of the possibilities here. As we know, many Poles in 1941–42 did not hear about the 'amnesty', or perhaps the news was concealed from them by the workplace or factory management. Others were told that the amnesty did not apply to them. By contrast, some Poles talk of being 'called up' to the Berling division (i.e. issued with recruitment papers), or being virtually given an ultimatum by the Soviet authorities. There had been no official call-up to Anders' forces, however; Poles had merely been released from camps and kolkhozes and given a free choice of where they wished to take up residence.[53] It should also be remembered that some Poles would have been too young for army service in 1941, but old enough two years later. Some were hospitalised either before, or even after they had made contact with Anders's forces and, by the time they recovered, it was too late; the army had been evacuated.

Even for those who had the freedom to join Anders' forces during 1941–42, there was a frequently-stated reluctance to abandon families to their fate, especially where the head of the household was sole bread-winner. Karol Ozimek, for example, having fought in the September 1939 campaign, had returned to his family in Soviet-held territory and from there was deported in February 1940 to the Chkalov oblast. Despite the declaration of the 'amnesty' for Poles in August 1941, however, he did not leave the commune on which he was working:

> Many people from our settlement, and especially officers and NCOs, travelled to join the Polish Army. A few families travelled too. But because of my family I stayed put and continued to work in the mine.[54]

There were also some, no doubt, who were not at all enthralled by the idea of going to war. When they gained their freedom following the 1941 amnesty, they may have moved to work in more congenial conditions.[55] Indeed some prospered. One Pole, working on a kolkhoz, was paid his wages in peas, by the kilo. These he was able to exchange for bread which, in turn, he sold on the black market. Thanks to these peas, as he writes, he was able to arrive at the Sielce recruitment camp with 10 000 roubles in his pocket.[56]

There is an insinuation in the above quotation – which reinforces Party propaganda of the time – that it was the officers and capitalists (and their families) who made their exit with Anders and the workers and peasants who remained behind. Indeed, the accusation has on occasion been levelled quite openly that both Anders's recruitment officers and the Embassy officials who dispensed Polish identity documents discriminated against the common people, the *lud*.[57] This line has been frequently reproduced in the historical literature on the subject produced in communist Poland. Although it is true that soldiers of working-class and peasant background predominated in the first and second Polish divisions formed under Berling's command,[58] it is far from true that they were not present in large numbers in the earlier formations. Many of the people who made their exit in 1942 were from farming backgrounds – particularly the *osadnicy wojskowi* (military settlers). However, there is a clear reason why people who had been toughened by years of manual work, and therefore found it easier to adjust to harsh conditions in wartime Russia, would not have been as desperate perhaps to leave their places of forced residence. If they had a roof over their heads and a job which brought in a sufficient income, they were taking a huge risk in leaving, unless it was to be directed to paying work elsewhere.

On 15 July 1943, the anniversary of the Battle of Grunwald, the 1st Polish Divisions's oath-taking ceremony took place at the Sielce camp. Representatives of the ZPP were present and indeed, as the sponsors of the Division, they formally presented the Division with its new standard. A small group of Western journalists were invited to attend and to review the Polish units, their accommodation and equipment. Among the observations which they brought back with them, and which were later communicated to the Polish Government, were that some 600 women, including the teenage daughter of Wanda Wasilewska, were serving in the camp as cooks, nurses, etc. A women's battalion was created as a part of the Berling forces, although the number of women serving in uniform at its height was under a thousand.[59] The journalists (admittedly civilians and not necessarily expert in military matters) were impressed by the weaponry held by the division, which included T34 tanks. All the armaments appeared to be new, as though they had only just arrived from the Soviet factories, and indeed, all the equipment was of Soviet manufacture, apart from American Dodge trucks used to haul the heavy artillery pieces, and Jeeps (the American vehicles had been supplied to the Soviets under Lend-Lease arrangements). The proportion of automatic arms to each company was very high, more than 80 per cent in some cases, and there was a plentiful supply of anti-tank weaponry. The journalists were also treated to a review of mortars and artillery, all of which appeared modern and fresh from the factory.[60]

The progress of recruitment to Berling's forces was speedy during the summer months and on 10 August the Soviets agreed to transform the 1st Polish Division into a Polish Corps. A 2nd Division, under the command of Colonel Antoni Siwicki, began formation on 19 August from the reserve units of the 1st Division and from new recruits. Although the flow of new recruits began to level off towards the end of the year, the Polish units continued to grow in size until there were four Divisions, and the Corps had become a full Army Group.[61]

The number of Soviet officers and technical specialists loaned to Berling's Polish forces has been a topic of controversy among historians, being seen as something of an indicator of the true 'Polishness' or otherwise of the divisions. The number was certainly considerable, and seems to have been, at the beginning, more than half the officer cadre.[62] The ratio of officers to men in Red Army divisions was in any case high, but when we consider that command and staff posts, quartermasters, down to some platoon commanders and even drivers, mechanics and electricians (as 'technical specialists') were brought in from the Red Army, it can be seen how pervasive their influence was. Initially most wore Soviet army uniforms. Many of these officers, especially the instructors, were of Polish descent. Some were descendants of the political exiles of the 1863 Rising in Poland, of left-wing (SDKPiL) revolutionaries who had remained in Russia after the Revolution, or members of Polish 'Red' formations who had fought in the civil war. While a number spoke some Polish, many did not – especially those who were not of Polish, but of Ukrainian, Russian or Byelorussian descent. The number of such officers grew markedly as the Polish forces increased in number and moved across the Riga frontier, recruitment continuing as they did so. It is not clear, however, how many of these Soviet officers remained behind in Poland after the war, either as permanent settlers (those of Polish descent) or as 'advisers' in the ranks of the People's Army.[63]

The recruit element joining the Polish forces were, as has been indicated, varied in their backgrounds, as regards education, military experience and political views and affiliations. It is far from true that soldiers joining Berling's ranks did so out of political idealism, and that these same political convictions had prevented them earlier from joining the 'reactionary' forces of General Anders. Considerations of this kind can have affected only a minority. Most of the troops in the 'Kościuszko' Division were not in the least politically active or aware, although patriotic feelings seem to have been strong. Indeed, there was a certain concern about the political reliability of people who had been themselves forcibly deported, in some cases with their families, had had their way to join Anders' forces blocked and been arbitrarily deprived of their Polish citizenship by the Soviet authorities. Wanda Wasilewska recalls that there was some concern from the Soviet intelligence and security apparatus about whether she should visit the Division in the summer of 1943 – they were concerned about her safety![64] This indicates worries that many of the Poles arriving at Sielce were still hostile towards the Soviets for the earlier treatment they had suffered, and might be 'unreliable'. Furthermore it indicates that the more patriotic elements, far from being taken in by the ZPP propaganda, may have regarded Wasilewska as a traitor for her criticism of Sikorski and for having collaborated with the Soviets.

So the organisation of political education, a component of all Red Army formations, was considered to be essential. But political education within the Polish divisions was not a subject which could be handled by Soviet personnel for a whole range of reasons, ranging from that of linguistic competence – the need to establish a close personal bond with the troops – to that of national feelings and aspirations. From the communists' point of view, the soldiers had to be convinced of the ZPP's political aims; that the shortest route to the homeland was from Soviet territory, by fighting on the Soviet front; that friendship with the Soviet people and its forces had to be an important cornerstone of future Polish policy; that Polish military traditions and a historical sense had to be cultivated (especially the Piast traditions of Polish expansion to the west); finally, the troops had to be instilled with confidence in the role of the ZPP and weaned away from the influence of the 'London' Polish Government. To carry out this work, the ZPP allocated many of its best people, accounting eventually for two-fifths of the total employed on such work. There were insufficient Polish communists to be able to fill all the posts, and so candidates were chosen from among the non-communist Polish element. Most of these were of a left-wing orientation and were in any case subjected to intensive training before assuming their duties.[65]

Combat training for the Division began on 1 June, less than a month after recruitment had commenced. Soviet practice was that each division received a three-month programme of special training before it was sent to the front – although the Polish Division was only in the process of being formed and had not yet undergone its basic training. On 30 August, a Special Commission with Polish representatives attached arrived from Moscow and declared that the 1st Polish Division was ready for combat.[66] On the next day, 1 September, with almost indecent haste (indeed, preparations for departure must have anticipated the Commission's decision) the Division began to move westwards by rail in the direction of Smolensk, eventually travelling via Moscow to Wiazma, some 220 km behind the front. From there the Division was directed to the Soviet 33rd Army. Between 11 and 13 October the Division engaged the Germans on the fields of the Byelorussian villages of Polzuchy and Trygubowo (south-east of Orsha) – although for propaganda purposes the battle was named after the nearby town of Lenino.

The engagement was a disaster for the Poles. The German defences were strong and they had the benefit of aerial support. By contrast, the Poles' tanks became bogged down in marshy terrain, there was a lack of communication between infantry and artillery and there were chronic supply problems – frontline troops at one stage ran out of ammunition! Crucially also, the neighbouring Soviet divisions were slow to advance, leaving the Poles exposed on the flanks. According to official figures, 493 of the Division's soldiers died and 1776 were wounded. A further 600 'disappeared' (i.e. were presumably taken prisoner).[67] German sources subsequently claimed, by means of radio in occupied Poland, that the 600 Poles had 'deserted from the Bolsheviks' and had come over to them.[68] When Wasilewska was informed of the level of casualties, she immediately asked Stalin to withdraw the Division from the front:

> After the Lenino battle Zhukov telephoned me. I at once contacted Molotov and asked him what the level of losses had been.
> – Normal – he said – 30 per cent.
> I immediately rang Stalin. I said that I had found out that there had been 30 per cent losses, that Molotov had told me the losses were normal and I added that, where the Red Army numbering many millions was concerned, this may be acceptable, but when it applied to the small units of the Polish Army, it meant that within the next three days we would not have a Division left.
> Stalin replied: I will immediately give the order to have them withdrawn to the rear.[69]

It became sadly apparent that the Division had been sent to the front prematurely. For this, much of the blame must rest with Wanda Wasilewska and her political ambitions.

According to Wasilewska's own account of events, she herself had asked Stalin to send the Division to the front,

> When the Division was ready and I asked that it should be sent to the front, so that the story of Anders' army should not be repeated, Stalin asked me: Are you telling me that they will fight properly? To that question I answered with a one thousand per cent conviction that they would. And I stated it in such a way that the question would not be repeated. The Division received permission to move to the front.[70]

K. Sobczak, however, states that the Division was not ready; it had not completed its training, but was sent to the front anyway. Wasilewska, he writes,

> came to the conclusion that the 'Kościuszko' Division, although it

had not yet completed its second period of training, was ready for combat and should move to the front. . . .[71]

and further:

In conversation with the Commander in Chief of the Soviet Army, M. Stalin, she received provisional agreement to the Division moving to the front earlier than originally planned.[72]

It seems then inescapable that Wasilewska was so eager for the Poles to establish their credentials with Stalin, to persuade him of their loyalty as allies, that despite her limited competence in military affairs she nevertheless overrode agreed training requirements.

Yet if the Lenino battle was a military disaster, the communists regarded its political significance as being considerable. One historian has written that the Poles' participation in the Battle of Lenino, 'lost, badly commanded and obtained at the cost of high losses', was an important event for the Polish communists in Russia, since it established their political legitimacy in the eyes of the Kremlin.[73] It had been shown that Poles were prepared to fight the Germans, and moreover that they had fought and shed blood in a brotherhood of arms alongside the Red Army. Even if in strategic terms this contribution had been largely meaningless, in symbolic and propaganda terms its significance was huge. In postwar Poland, the general trend was for Party historians to claim the Lenino battle as a great success.[74] Only with time came a more realistic admission that the Kościuszko Division was 'primarily a political and propaganda unit' and that the Division 'carried out its political tasks very well'.[75]

In the aftermath of the Lenino battle, the Polish Government in London received intelligence that soldiers of the Kościuszko Division were not only being awarded Soviet decorations, but also Polish decorations such as the Virtuti Militari and the Krzyż Walecznych. These, of course, neither the ZPP nor the military leadership had any right to bestow, and the event marked a further usurpation of the rights of the legal Polish Government.[76]

THE ZPP CONFERENCE: AIMS AND IDEOLOGY

A little more than a month after formal permission was given to begin recruitment to Berling's forces, on 9–10 June, the ZPP held its first Congress in Moscow. Sixty-six delegates took part, 30 per cent of whom were soldiers' representatives from the 1st Polish Division forming at Sielce. The rest had been summoned from all corners of the Soviet Union to take part. These included Andrzej Witos, brother of the legendary Peasant Party leader Wincenty Witos. Andrzej Witos had been deported by the Soviet authorities in 1940 to the distant Komi Republic. When the ZPP leadership heard that 'Witos' was in the Soviet Union, they immediately assumed that it was the illustrious Wincenty. It was self-evident that they had to do all in their power to bring him to join them. Only when Witos arrived in Moscow did it become clear that they had the wrong brother. Nevertheless, as Wasilewska admitted with cynicism, they decided to make use of the family name and 'od razu zaczęlismy robić z niego wielkiego działacza' (we at once began to make a great activist of him).[77] In fact, Witos became Chairman of the Union of Polish Patriots, following Molotov's advice that it would not be advisable to have someone as closely identified with the communist cause as Wasilewska in such a prominent position. It was important, Molotov stressed, to persuade people that the ZPP was not a communist set-up but a broadly-based national organisation.[78]

The Presidium of the Congress consisted of the following members: W. Wasilewska, Colonel Z. Berling, Father F. Kubsz, Professor J. Parnas, Dr B. Drobner, Colonel A. Siwicki, Dr S. Jędrychowski, A. Klos and K. Witaszewski. At least two of these people, Wasilewska and Jędrychowski, in addition to being Soviet citizens, had earlier been admitted to the Soviet Communist Party, and their qualifications as 'Polish Patriots' were therefore very much in question. Nevertheless it was Wasilewska who gave the opening speech to the Congress. She emphasised that the formation of the ZPP was not an accident, but a 'historical necessity'. Its origins should be sought, she claimed, in the events of 1939 and what had gone before. She attacked the 1939 Polish leadership for abandoning the Polish nation to its fate in the face of the German threat. With the Nazi attack on Soviet Russia and the signing of the Polish–Soviet Agreement, it had appeared that Poland would once again take part in the fight. Unfortunately, it quickly became evident that the Polish Government was in the hands of the same elements that had control in 1939. Although there had been widespread enthusiasm when news spread that Anders was forming an army, 'because people thought that they would be fighting shoulder to shoulder with the Red Army', Anders had declined to fight on the eastern front and had led his forces out to Iran. 'It had ceased to be an army and had been transformed into an unorganised émigré group.'[79]

The Union's ideological principles were expounded at every opportunity, and the formal 'Ideological Declaration' is probably the fullest expression of these principles and aims.[80] From this and other statements made by the ZPP leadership, it can be seen how the communists attempted to steer a narrow course between criticising Sikorski's government and yet maintaining brotherhood in arms with Poles in the West (and in Poland) who felt allegiance towards that government. Care was taken not to antagonise Poles at home or in the West by labelling all those who were serving under the London Government's banner as fools or knaves.

In the course of the Conference, Wasilewska appealed for more volunteers to the new Polish Division being formed under the aegis of the ZPP. She stressed that while the Germans oppressed Poland, 'we' (i.e. Poles in the USSR) stood on the sidelines:

> We number hundreds of thousands. We want to work and to fight. It would be shameful if we waited until they [i.e. the Red Army and Soviet government] handed a liberated Poland to us.[81]

It seems evident even at this early stage that Wasilewska and other Poles of a left-wing persuasion in the USSR saw the Kościuszko Division not only as a military force with which to confront the Germans, but as a weapon with which to determine the political complexion of liberated Poland.[82] The formation of the army was therefore a top priority for the ZPP. Subsequently, Berling reported to the Congress on the progress of recruitment; almost 10 000 people had been accepted and the division had already begun training.[83]

A further priority indentified at the Congress was the assumption of responsibility for distributing relief supplies to Polish refugees – a task previously carried out by the Polish Embassy. There was recognition too that cultural and educational work was important – particularly among children and young people. However, there was one issue that needed to be clarified before questions of military recruitment or distribution of aid, or setting up of schools and orphanages was discussed; this was the question of citizenship. Who was to be eligible both for service in the army's ranks and to receive relief supplies? Who was to be considered a Pole for the purposes of the ZPP's activities?

The question of citizenship had been a source of conflict and irritation in relations between the Soviet Government and the London Polish authorities. Indeed, it is fair to say that the definition of Polish citizenship was manipulated shamelessly by the Soviet authorities in order to exert pressure or to demonstrate their displeasure at the London Poles' actions. It is perhaps worth reviewing the situation from the restoration of Polish–Soviet diplomatic relations in July 1941:

1. From the signing of the Polish–Soviet Agreement until 1 December 1941 *all* those living within the 1939 frontiers of the Polish Republic, including those from the eastern provinces annexed by the USSR in October–November 1939, were recognised as Polish citizens. They were eligible for release from the prisons and labour camps, recruitment to the Polish Army, and to receive relief supplies.
2. From 1 December 1941 until 16 January 1943, those Polish citizens of Jewish, Ukrainian and Byelorussian descent formally resident in the areas of eastern Poland annexed by the Soviets were excluded from this arrangement. It was claimed that they had become Soviet citizens as a result of the incorporation of Western Ukraine and Western Byelorussia in October–November 1939. They could not therefore be considered candidates for the Polish Army of General Anders, nor could they be eligible for relief distributed by the Polish Embassy.
3. From 16 January 1943, in a further turn of the screw, the Kremlin determined that only those Poles who could prove that they originated from the *central* districts of Poland could be considered Polish citizens. That is, even ethnic Poles from the former eastern provinces were deemed now to be Soviet citizens!

It was estimated that, if this prescription were to be applied rigorously, the restrictions would provide grave problems not only in recruitment to the Kościuszko Division and to the ZPP, but also in determining who should be eligible to receive relief supplies. Only 25 000 people of those remaining in the Soviet Union had been given identity papers by the Polish Embassy before the break in Polish–Soviet relations.[84] Understandably, then, it was a burning issue for delegates to the ZPP Congress, and many raised the issue. Wasilewska's answer was unequivocal: by 'Poles' the Soviet authorities included all those who had been Polish citizens until 1939 and who felt themselves to be Poles – irrespective of their ethnic background or the documents they possessed. The Soviet leadership was therefore signalling a return to the situation in late 1941 – the 'honeymoon' period in relations with General Sikorski's government – when the *paszportizacja* process of bestowing Soviet citizenship on residents of the annexed territories was ignored and in theory even members of the national minorities (Jews, Ukrainians, Byelorussians) could be regarded as Polish citizens – if they so wished. In practice, however, the ZPP, since they acknowledged the Soviet claim to the Western Ukraine and Western Byelorussia and the 'unification' of the two peoples, did not make great efforts to enlist mem-

bers of these Slavic 'minority' communities (and, indeed, it is doubtful that they would have been accepted).[85]

News of the ZPP Congress was received coolly in the West. The
Pravda report of the Congress was brought to the attention of the
Foreign Office in London, which was already aware that the 'Kościuszko'
radio station was making a good deal of the event.[86] However, when
the prime minister, Winston Churchill, received a telegram of greeting
from the ZPP signed by Wasilewska, Foreign Office advice was that
the telegram should not be answered. The Union of Polish Patriots, it
advised, was 'in no way representative of Poles and its President, Madame
Wasilewska, is the wife of the Soviet Vice-Commissar for Foreign
Affairs. It has openly attacked the Polish Government in this country
and accused them of collaborating with Hitler.'[87]

The Polish Government in London also refrained from acknowledg-
ing the event. However, an article in the émigré Polish press a week
after news of the Congress had reached the West probably contained
the Polish Government's reply to the ZPP's declaration:

> The so-called 'Union of Polish Patriots' constitutes a fiction, the
> maintenance of which impedes the restoration of Polish–Soviet col-
> laboration. It impairs the unity of the Allied front – a unity which is
> more indispensable now than it has ever been.[88]

This was a particularly barbed comment, since the break in Polish–
Soviet relations in April had been justified by Soviet accusations that
the Polish Government was destroying the unity of the Allied front by
appealing to the Red Cross to investigate the Katyn affair.

THE ZPP's WELFARE ROLE

The problem of supplying material relief to Polish families – in other
words, continuing the work undertaken by the Polish Embassy and its
network of delegates between 1941 and 1943 – was the most urgent
task that faced the ZPP. It was a problem which grew in importance
and was closely linked to the recruitment programme and the morale
of the troops in Berling's units. As soldiers were mobilised, the men
who made their way to Sielce were in most cases the sole breadwinner
for the family. Frequently, those who remained behind – elderly parents or wives with young children – were not capable of supporting
themselves by working. News of the difficult situation that their families were in was brought most forcibly to the attention of officers and

was passed on to unit commanders and eventually to the Main Council of the ZPP. Almost all Polish unit commanders were referring to the problem in their reports during 1943: 'Feelings are darkened by a deep and widespread concern for their families'; 'help for the families is an important political issue and is the main . . . theme of hostile agitation'.[89]

The delegates from the Kościuszko Division raised the matter at the ZPP Congress in June. The point was made that use could be made of foreign supplies brought in during the earlier period to be distributed to Poles via the London Polish Embassy's relief apparatus. Vast quantities of these supplies were still being held in stores around the country, since the Polish authorities had been forbidden to take them out, and there was no mechanism for distributing them to their intended recipients. Wasilewska, however, anxious to play down the role of the London authorities and the importance of foreign supplies, moved a vote of thanks at Congress for the one-million-rouble gift from the Soviet Government advanced in December 1941 for Polish relief.[90] She also argued that families of military personnel deserved to receive state welfare benefits from the Soviet authorities on the same basis as those extended to the families of Red Army soldiers.[91] It was accepted as a principle that 'aid should be dispensed without regard to the background or the political views of the recipient – nor whether he or she possessed documents' confirming Polish or Soviet citizenship'.[92]

The ZPP Congress therefore approved a Resolution that aid should be distributed to the families of combatants. This included families not only of those who were serving in Polish formations in the USSR, but of those who were serving in Britain and in the Middle East, of soldiers who had fallen during the 1939 campaign in Poland, of those who were in German captivity and of those who had fallen on the Soviet–German front (presumably those who had been forced into Red Army service earlier).[93]

The lack of discrimination between the different formations was important to the ZPP, since it was one of their ideological tenets that they did not feel any hostility at all towards the ordinary soldiers – merely towards the politicians and senior commanders of the 'London' camp who were leading them. However, such fine-sounding sentiments were extremely difficult to put into practice, given the nature of Soviet bureaucracy. In the first place, the degree of family relationship or kinship was carefully drawn up by the authorities. It referred to immediate family such as parents, wives and offspring, but the relationship had to be proved with documentation! (The families of war invalids or those who fell in battle came within the scheme, but not relatives of those who were serving in labour battalions.) Secondly, proof had to be provided of an individual's combatant status in the form of an appropriate signed document from the military authorities. Leaving aside the work such requests must have involved for the military authorities at such a busy time, it must have been next to impossible for relatives of those in German captivity in the West, or who had fallen in 1939, to obtain such a document. However, statements by witnesses and decisions of local ZPP boards would sometimes suffice.[94]

In June 1943 moves began within the Kościuszko Division to draw up lists of families who were in particularly difficult circumstances. In July 1943, during one of her visits to the Division at Sielce, Wasilewska noted,

> I collect. . . . a package of mail. A thick envelope for Welfare. Anxiety for the fate of families oppresses the men even on the most successful day on the exercise grounds and firing ranges. We will lift this weight from their shoulders.[95]

A Social Welfare Department (Wydział Opieki Społecznej) was established to carry out the work of distributing the food supplies, medicines and clothing which had been provided by foreign governments, Western charitable organisations and, in part, by the Soviet authorities themselves.[96] The ZPP Congress was told that a priority in the Department's work would be to aid military families – especially those with children and those whose members were unable to work. The Social Welfare Department (WOS) was not to work alone, however. At a 'briefing' of ZPP delegates a few days before the June 1943 Congress, it emerged that because of the wide distribution of the Polish population on Soviet territory, and the ZPP's lack of equipment (particularly transport) it would have been impossible to carry out the relief work without Soviet help. Hence a parallel organisation, Uprosobtorg, was created within the People's Commissariat for Trade.[97] There is some confusion about the date of its creation, but little doubt as to its aims. Within a short space of time the Uprosobtorg had established 14 widely-dispersed bases for the distribution of relief supplies and, from the warehouses it established, goods were despatched to the local ZPP organisations. Polish liaison personnel were attached to these outposts.[98]

The question arises of why the Poles themselves were not entrusted with the task of distribution, since most of the supplies from outside the country had been sent for their use. If they lacked equipment, why were the Soviet authorities not prepared to supply them with it? The obvious answer is that the Soviets, having been alarmed by the activities of the London Polish Embassy's network of delegates, did not wish to see a repeat performance, even though the relief enterprise was now being undertaken by a much more compliant group of Poles. They quite simply did not trust the ZPP – understandably, since the number of committed communists among the Union's members was tiny – and were determined to keep a tighter hold on Polish activities.

Most of the goods distributed by this organisation came from the relief convoys which had continued to bring in goods from government and private charitable sources in the West until March 1943 – i.e. immediately preceding the break in Polish–Soviet relations. This supply could not last for ever, though, and a year later, by the spring of 1944, it is clear that the ZPP was desperately looking for new sources of supply. It is interesting to note therefore that six months earlier, in September 1943, the Soviet Vice-Commissar for Foreign Affairs, Kornieczuk, mentioned to the Australian chargé, that since the Polish Embassy had left the Soviet Union, consignments of stores for Polish relief had stopped coming. He made it clear that the resumption of such consignments was not being asked for by the Soviet Government, but that if shipments were started again, the action would be welcomed. Since Kornieczuk was Wanda Wasilewska's husband, however, it is difficult not to believe that this 'hint' was inspired by her. If so, it indicates that the true picture as regards relief was more desperate than postwar communist accounts have painted it.[99]

The first Director of the Welfare Department was Bolesław Drobner. But Drobner, together with Andrzej Witos, was also delegated to the organising committee of Uprosobtorg as 'inspector general'. This was not a happy arrangement. For a competent person to have filled one position, let alone two, would have been difficult. But Drobner was far from efficient, as Wanda Wasilewska herself, who knew him from her grammar-school days, later admitted:

> Drobner was a superb speaker and an exceptionally interesting fellow, but as an organiser. . . . in a given situation he was hopeless.[100]

The Welfare Department remained an organisation in name only, and crucial weeks were lost until September 1943, when Drobner was replaced by Jan Grubecki, who had been seconded from the Kościuszko Division. Grubecki set about the task more energetically and, by all accounts, against considerable odds, did a good job, creating an extensive and efficient network of helpers. The odds, though, were formidable; the factors he had to contend with included staff shortages and lack of equipment.[101]

In the course of 1943–44 the ZPP Welfare Department sent out food and clothing to destitute Poles, mainly through the offices of Uprosobtorg. It also sent out some cash payments. Efforts were made to publicise these moves, both for propaganda reasons and to boost the morale of the troops. Apart from coverage in the Polish press of the welfare effort, families who received aid were encouraged to write to their menfolk in uniform with news of such gifts. Relief of this kind began to wane, however, by the middle of 1944, owing both to the exhaustion of foreign aid supplies and the growth of demand from an increasing number of local ZPP groups.[102]

ZPP requests for help were also sent to local Soviet authorities. In the autumn of 1943 it became easier to intervene with Soviet agencies, since families of members of the Polish Corps in the USSR were put on the same legal footing as those of Red Army personnel.[103] The Soviet authorities took the important step in spring 1944 of transferring a number of Polish military families from regions with an unfavourable climate.[104] At the same time, efforts were made to give additional help to displaced Poles. A two-month ration of food and clothing was allocated to military families, while a limited amount of footwear and knitted garments were made available to children.[105]

Much of this aid was made available to especially needy families and those related to members of the Polish Corps in the USSR. But, despite the efforts of the ZPP and the legal measures adopted by the Soviet authorities, the welfare provision theoretically available in law was often not (in fact, was rarely) carried out in an effective manner, certainly until the middle of 1944. This was because (a) several Soviet agencies were involved, involving overlap, omission and general confusion; (b) Poles were generally ignorant of the provisions that had been made for them and their entitlements.[106] A good example of this gap between official statements and the situation on the ground is the information that, by 20 March 1944, all Poles 'evacuated' to the USSR should have received an allotment of ground to cultivate. No figures are given for the actual allocation, but in any case there would have been problems in using such an allocation given the difficulties of obtaining seed.[107]

Poles who had survived were now facing their fourth year on Soviet territory, and it was felt to be important that the children should receive teaching in their own language before they forgot it entirely. But equally important from the ZPP point of view was the need to educate them in the 'democratic' values which would prevail under the New Order in a renascent Poland. On 30 June 1943 the Kompoldiet

(Committee for Polish Children in the USSR) was formed by decree within the People's Commissariat of Education. Its particular aim was to organise, in cooperation with the ZPP, schooling and institutions of welfare for Polish children.[108]

The ZPP had set out to develop and extend its organisational network, in order both to distribute relief and to establish the number of Poles on Soviet territory. It began with the central regions, but soon branched further afield with local outposts being established in Eastern Siberia, Kazakhstan, the Komi Republic and Central Asia. Organisation of branches took place on a hierarchical level according to the numbers in any one settlement. A 'local group' (*koło*) could be formed where there were upwards of five people; a 'regional' or 'district' committee could be formed where there were more than a hundred people; and a 'district' committee (*zarząd obwodowy*) could be established where there were more than three hundred people. Between June and September 1943 some 26 provincial committees had come into being.[109] At the end of 1943 the ZPP completed a register of members in 72 'obwods' (administrative districts). Of the 223 806 people registered, 114 209 (51 per cent) were of Polish ethnic background, 98 071 (44 per cent) were Jewish, and 11 526 (5 per cent) were from the Ukrainian and Byelorussian 'minorities'.[110]

By April 1944 there were 51 and by October 1944, 88. The pattern of growth was very uneven, however. In some areas – such as Altai Krai, the Saratov region, Irkutsk, Chkalov and Omsk – the level of organisation had not made appreciable progress by the beginning of 1944. It seems clear that a large proportion of the Polish deportees, despite their poor material situation, looked on the activities of the ZPP with suspicion. The ZPP also seems to have had great difficulty in recruiting good organisers at the regional level – again possibly due to the fact that many members of the Polish intelligentsia made their exit with Anders in 1942, and those that remained were wary of cooperating. Some reports from the period are critical of the poor work of local bodies, claiming in mid-1945 that there were many Poles who were not aware of what the ZPP stood for. In the province committee in Altai Krai, changes in the leadership were carried out.[111]

There was an increase in affiliation and organisation of ZPP local cells from the beginning of 1945 – and particularly after the conclusion of the war in Europe. This may have been due to a spreading awareness of the ZPP's activities in the remoter areas of the Soviet Union. But perhaps a more plausible reason is that, by this point, many Poles saw involvement with the ZPP as their best hope of making an

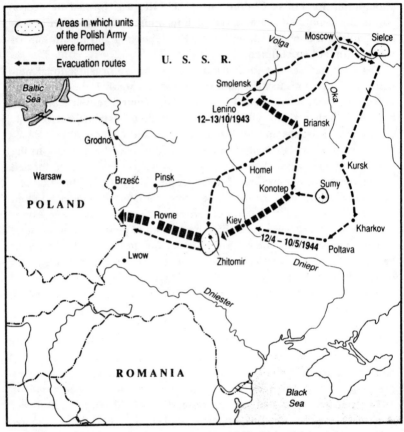

Map 5.1　The Polish Army in the USSR, 1943–44, and its return
to Poland

early return to Poland. The ZPP continued in existence until 1946,
when the organisation was wound up. Until that time, it continued
relief work and played a large part in the administration of the repatriation scheme. But its political significance had long since ceased.
In July 1944, political power had moved to the KRN (Homeland National
Council) which had assumed authority over both the ZPP and the units
of Berling's army, prior to the latter's impending move into Polish
territory.

　　Berling's forces, withdrawn following the Lenino battle, had continued to increase in number with the arrival of new recruits at the Sielce camp. The Kościuszko Division had been transformed into a Corps on 10 August 1943, and on 18 March 1944 it had undergone a further transformation, becoming the 1st Polish Army. In the spring the 1st Corps of the Army moved in stages via Kiev to the Berdichev–Zhitomir region of the Ukraine, where it was augmented with an army staff, staff services, supply and specialist services. Berling, now a Brigadier-General, was still in overall command, with Swierczewski his deputy in operational matters, and Zawadzki deputy with responsibility for political affairs. On 29 April the formation, now officially designated the 1st Polish Army, was put at the operational disposal of Rokossovsky's 1st Byelorussian Front. Meanwhile, at Sumy, further recruitment and organisation towards the consolidation of the Polish Army continued.

On 21 July Rokossovsky's Army Group crossed the River Bug – the frontier of what the Soviet authorities regarded as 'ethnographic Poland'. At this point Berling's Army numbered some 78 000 men on the Byelorussian Front, with a further 40 000 still training in the USSR. With the extra reserves of Polish manpower now at their disposal, there were ambitious plans to expand the army, which, with its heavy complement of Red Army officers and 'political officers', would be sufficiently reliable, or so the communists thought, to carry out the policies of the Lublin Committee (PKWN). Aims to expand the Berling forces by 400 000 men had, though, to be abandoned in the face of widespread hostility from the population towards the policies of the NKVD on Polish soil and a common perception of the Berling forces as 'lackeys'.

Rokossovsky's Army Group had reached the outskirts of the Polish capital by August, but, when the Warsaw Rising broke out on 1 August, Rokossovsky scrupulously observed Stalin's orders that the Red Army was not to intervene. During the seventh week of the Rising (on 15 September) however, Berling sent a group of his men across the Vistula to establish contact with the insurgents. When Rokossovsky's Byelorussian Front resumed its advance in January 1945, Berling had been removed from command of the 1st Army. His successor was General S. Popławski. The 1st Army, now comprising some five infantry divisions, continued in the direction of Bydgoszcz and the Baltic coast (Kołobrzeg, Szczecin) eventually taking part in the final drive on Berlin. In the final weeks of the war a 2nd Polish Army of five divisions (numbering eventually 90 000 men) took part in Ukrainian Front operations to the south, including the liberation of Prague.

In the postwar period, the army of the Polish People's Republic was largely created by former 'Berling Army' officers, several of whom rose to positions of prominence. The best-known is General Wojciech Jaruzelski, the architect of Martial Law in Poland in 1981.[112]

6 Renewed Deportations from Polish Territory, 1944–45

THE RED ARMY ENTERS POLISH TERRITORY

When, in January 1944, the Red Army resumed its winter offensive in the push for Berlin, to the north, Soviet units moved west from Leningrad, occupying some eastern districts of Latvia. But the speediest advance was made further to the south on the Byelorussian–Ukrainian border, where the left wing of the 1st Byelorussian Front sped west and north. In Volhynia, during the night of 3–4 January, units of the 1st Ukrainian Front crossed the prewar Polish border in pursuit of the retreating Germans. The town of Łuck was taken on 2 February. Further south the advance was somewhat slower. It was not until 26 March that Kamieniets Podolski fell.[1]

The entry of Soviet forces into the territory of the prewar Polish Republic had been anticipated by two Polish camps; the small minority in Poland and in the Soviet Union who held extreme left-wing and pro-Moscow views and those who looked for leadership to the Polish Government in London. The Polish communists anticipated that, once the Red Army occupied territory on which there was a large Polish population, the opportunity would present itself to recruit more manpower for the Berling army. The Union of Polish Patriots (ZPP) requested that the Soviet authorities approve recruitment from the numerous Polish elements in the former 'eastern borderlands' of the Polish Republic. A Soviet decree confirming approval for such measures was issued on 16 March. Some days earlier – on 10 March – Berling's forces (the First Polish Corps) had transferred to the Zhitomir-Berdichev region of the Ukraine and a recruiting and training camp was soon established at Sumy.[2]

Despite the prospect of an end to the five-year occupation of their country, the Red Army's coming was viewed with foreboding by many Poles, especially by those who had experienced the earlier period of Soviet occupation which followed the Nazi–Soviet Pacts of 1939. The Polish Government in London was faced with a dilemma too. As from

April 1943 – with the rupture of Polish–Soviet diplomatic relations – it had had no direct means of communicating with Moscow. There was therefore no way of negotiating an agreement regarding the administration of Polish territory liberated by the Red Army. Worse still, from the Poles' point of view, was the continuing gulf between the two sides over the frontier question – over precisely what constituted Polish territory. The Soviet regime obstinately continued to regard the results of the October 1939 'plebiscite' carried out in Soviet-occupied eastern Poland as binding, while the 'London Poles' were equally resolute in regarding its demonstration of the 'will of the people' as both fraudulent and illegal. They maintained tenaciously their right to the 1939 frontiers.[3]

The Polish Government had earlier laid plans for the underground army to stage a general rising in Poland, once it became clear that the German forces were fully in retreat. On 27 October 1943 instructions were sent to the Government Delegate in Poland and to the Commander of the Home Army (AK) regarding how to act once Soviet troops had entered the country. These instructions, though, were far from clear; they provided alternative courses of action to cater for a number of scenarios. In essence they ordered the Home Army to remain underground, limit activities to sabotage, and await further instructions. There was to be no fighting with Soviet units unless the Poles were attacked directly and had to defend themselves. Moreover, the instructions had been posited upon certain preconditions, one of which was the penetration of the continent by British and American forces to a point where they could support the Home Army's efforts by supply-drops and other means.[4] At the time the Red Army was crossing the Polish frontier in Volhynia and Podolia, D-Day was still six months away.

Modified instructions had therefore to be issued by the Home Army command itself on how – in the absence of any formal agreement between the two governments – local commanders were to conduct themselves in their encounters with approaching Red Army units. A particular concern of the AK leadership was the effect on morale of continuing passivity – but there was also a wider propaganda battle to be fought. In essentials, the orders of Home Army commander, General 'Bór'-Komorowski, issued at the end of November, for Operation Tempest, were that the underground forces were to take control of as much Polish territory as possible with a view to re-establishing sovereignty over it. They would strike at the rear of the German army and also attempt to save Poland from total destruction during the German withdrawal. At the same time, Home Army commanders and representatives of the civil administration would reveal themselves to incoming Red Army commanders. The political aims were clear. Poles were to greet the incoming Soviet troops as masters in their own house.[5] By implication therefore, fighting with Soviet units (partisan or regular Red Army forces) should be avoided. The mass flight of Polish citizens to the West – motivated not only by the approach of the Russians but, in the south-eastern districts of the prewar Republic, by the activities of armed bands of Ukrainian nationalists – should also be discouraged. It would lead to the weakening of the Polish presence in these areas. Furthermore, while Home Army commanders were to cooperate with their Red Army opposite numbers, all attempts to force Polish troops to join either the Soviet forces or Berling's army should be resisted.[6]

The first Polish Home Army formation that the Soviets encountered in Volhynia following the seizure of Łuck, was the 27th Infantry Division, commanded by Lt-Col. Jan Kiwerski ('Oliwa'). Kiwerski's forces were concentrated in an area south of Kowel and contact was initially established when a Soviet reconnaissance unit crossed the River Stochod in February. The Soviets were welcomed heartily, although it is not recorded what the Soviet commander said when informed that there was a whole Polish division in the area! In mid-March a joint Polish–Soviet operation was mounted against the town of Kowel, the Red Army attacking the town, while the Poles directed their attention to a nearby railway junction.[7]

Following the success of this initial cooperation, on 26 March Kiwerski attended a meeting with the Soviet commander, General Sergieyev, at which certain conditions for future cooperation were laid out. The conditions, which were put after consultation with central authorities, were reasonable. They included the request for the Polish force to become a regular formation, rather than remaining a partisan unit, and for submission to Soviet operational control for the remainder of the campaign. The Soviets in turn acknowledged that the division was Polish and owed allegiance to its own commanders in Warsaw and London. Furthermore, they agreed to equip it fully in order to bring it up to the standard of a regular army division.

Kiwerski communicated these conditions to the C-in-C of the Home Army and on the following day received orders from Warsaw to proceed; the division could be placed temporarily under Soviet operational command, but it could not be 'withdrawn to Soviet territory'. (According to Moscow's way of thinking it was already on Soviet territory, but the AK command presumably had in mind withdrawal to east of the prewar Polish–Soviet border.) Komorowski, in relaying this exchange to London, justified his decision by saying that it was worth seizing any opportunity to create Polish Army units subject to the London authorities and, if the Soviets were intent on deceiving them, then the deception would be of the most unambiguous kind and, as such, would provide ammunition for the Polish Government in its discussions with the Allies.[8]

The instructions for Kiwerski, which came with the approval of the Government Delegate, had to be returned to Kiwerski immediately, without awaiting confirmation from the authorities in London. However, when General Sosnkowski (C-in-C of the Polish Forces) replied, it was with some scepticism concerning Soviet intentions:

> I doubt whether the Soviet commander's promises will be kept, nor whether the additional conditions in your note will be observed. In any case I do not believe that the experiment will have a satisfactory outcome and the subordination of the division to you and me will most probably turn out to be completely illusory.[9]

Sosnkowski's doubts were understandable. The activities of Soviet partisans, who had been operating in the eastern Polish territories since the end of 1941, showed that they did not regard themselves as 'guests' in the region, but rather 'hosts'. An earlier note by the Polish government to Moscow had complained that diversionary and sabotage operations were being carried out by Soviet partisans without regard to the reprisals which the Germans exercised against the local population. Moreover, from the spring of 1943, reports began to filter through to Warsaw of incidents in which the Soviets had liquidated Polish self-defence units (created at this time to protect vulnerable Polish settlements against attacks from marauding Ukrainian nationalist bands). In April, for example, a Soviet partisan group under a Major Wasylewicz had descended on the small town of Nalibok in a night raid and murdered 120 men, later setting fire to buildings in the town.[10]

Proof of Soviet bad faith arrived when, following a clash with Soviet partisans in the province of Volhynia, a document found on the body of a dead *politruk* came into Polish hands. The document, dated 30 November 1943 and signed by the commander of the 'Stalin' partisan group, Colonel Gulewicz, referred to instructions issued by General Ponamarenko, Chief of Staff of the partisan movement attached to the Red Army High Command. The Soviet groups were, from 1 December 1943, to disarm all Polish partisan units they encountered, and direct the disarmed Poles, together with their arms and documents, to a 'Polish camp' at Nesterowicz (near Iwieniec). Those Poles who refused to give up their weapons or who resisted in any way were to be shot immediately.[11] A similar document, relayed to London and sent by prime minister Mikołajczyk to Anthony Eden on 17 January 1944, was signed by one 'Dubov' and ordered quite cold-bloodedly that 'All Polish underground organisations are to be exterminated and their leaders executed'.[12]

Unsurprisingly therefore, the cooperation between the 27th Volhynian Division and the Red Army came to a disastrous end in the course of April 1944. In a major battle with the German forces between Kowel and Włodzimierz, their backs against the River Turia, the Poles were abandoned by the accompanying Red Army cavalry division. Communiqués from the Soviet leader that help was on its way brought no tangible results. Ammunition trucks sent back across the river for supplies did not return. Facing the 'Viking' Panzer Division and a German mountain brigade, and bombed from the air by Stukas, the Poles suffered heavily during a five-day struggle for survival. In the process they lost their commander, Kiwerski. An attempt to break out of their encirclement led them north to the forested regions near Szack, where, concealed between the German and Soviet front lines, they attempted to draw breath and regroup. On the night of 20–21 April, after three weeks' fighting, Kiwerski's successor, Major Rychter, led one column west across the River Bug, where they made contact with detachments of the Lublin region underground. But the orders from Home Army command to move west did not reach the other column in time. Heading east in the direction of the Prypet region (Polesie), it was disarmed by the Soviets and transported to the Kiev region. From there the rank-and-file were directed to Berling's army, while the officers were taken deeper into Soviet territory.[13]

Similar disappointments were to accompany Polish efforts elsewhere to establish an effective cooperative relationship with Soviet formations. On the night of 6–7 July 1944, for example, Home Army units from the Vilnius and Nowogródek regions attempted to liberate the town of Vilnius from the Germans. The AK forces numbered some five-and-a-half thousand men and were under the command of Colonel Aleksander Krzyżanowski ('Wilk'). On the following day, forces of the Red Army's 3rd Byelorussian Front arriving at the city also began to take part in the battle. The town was freed on 13 July after six days of fierce fighting, and the Polish underground forces immediately set about re-establishing the town's administration.[14]

The exploits of the AK forces attracted the admiration of Soviet line commanders; one expressed his thanks in a personal letter to a Polish commander, while another reputedly even asked his superiors to reward soldiers of the 3rd battalion, 85th Infantry Regiment (commanded by Captain 'Jena') with Soviet military decorations.[15] As was the case in Volhynia, Krzyżanowski had come to an agreement with the Soviet commander, in this case General Cherniakovsky, that the Polish units would have their arms supplemented without any political conditions attached. They would form a regular infantry division and a cavalry brigade, which would go to the front as units of the Polish Army owing allegiance to the Polish Government and the Polish C-in-C. In the early days of the liberation of the city, Polish partisans walked freely in the streets of Vilnius, sporting armbands in the Polish national colours.[16] However, the atmosphere changed rapidly. Within days of Vilnius being secured, the Soviet authorities ordered the AK units to leave the city and gather on the edge of the Rudnicki Forest. On 16 July, Krzyżanowski, commander of the AK's north-east region, together with two senior colleagues, Lt-Col. Ludwik Krzeszowski, commander of the Vilnius region, and Lt-Col. Adam Szydłowski, commander of the Nowogródek region, went to a meeting with General Cherniakovsky. Not one of them returned from this meeting. AK officers who had gathered at Bogusze to continue talks with their Soviet counterparts were surrounded by Soviet troops and transported to the east. Also arrested were the Vilnius delegate of the Polish government, Zygmunt Federowicz and his deputy, together with their officials.[17]

At the news of their disappearance, the deputy commanders of the Vilnius and Nowogródek regions led their troops off deeper into the forests and ordered their men to form smaller groups and attempt to break out towards the towns of Grodno and Białystok. The Soviets initiated a round-up, as a result of which more than 5000 Poles were concentrated in a camp at Miedniki. The Home Army men, most of whom refused to be drafted into the Berling formations, were taken off to camps in the Soviet Union.[18] The epilogue to this sorry chapter was a battle between a Home Army unit under Lt-Col. Maciej Kalenkiewicz ('Kotwicz') and Red Army troops near Surkonty, during which the Polish commander and a large number of his troops were killed. According to reports reaching AK command, the Soviets, who had themselves suffered 132 men killed, finished off (*'dobijali'*) the wounded Poles.[19]

A pattern had started to develop which was to continue. Polish AK units revealed themselves to the incoming Red Army commanders, fought alongside the Soviet formations, often being supplied with armaments by the Soviets. They received both thanks and praise, were given assurances of further cooperation – and that they would be permitted to continue the fight for the liberation of Polish territory in regular formations alongside the Red Army. Even political conditions were waived. Then, in an almost casual way, Polish commanders would be invited for 'talks' only to be spirited away, their units to be broken up.

The strategy was played out once again in the south-eastern region, where soldiers of the 5th Infantry Division numbering some 3000 and commanded by Colonel Władysław Filipkowski, helped Red Army forces to take the city of Lwów in a battle which lasted some four days (23–27 July 1944). It should be pointed out that in the Lwów case, as with Vilnius and several other battles, the AK played a key role in the operation, since they were able to mobilise troops *within* the city. For as long as the battle lasted, relations were cordial and Soviet commanders even provided the Polish units with ammunition. With the fighting over, a special order was read out to some of the Polish units from Marshal Koniev, thanking them for their 'brotherly cooperation'.[20] Nevertheless, the Polish commanders were informed in no uncertain terms that Lwów now was Soviet and Ukrainian. The Poles were ordered to disband their units, the soldiers then being given the choice of joining Berling's forces or the Red Army. Filipkowski issued an order on 30 July for his men to disperse. Despite this, all the AK officers who assembled on the following day for a meeting with the Soviets were arrested.[21] At this point, events took a rather different turn than hitherto. Filipkowski and the commander of the Lwów district AK, Colonel Czerwiński, secured the permission of Soviet commanders to travel to Zhitomir to talk to Michał Rola-Żymierski, commander of the Polish Communist underground (Armia Ludowa – AL).[22] Their apparent willingness to agree to serve in the Berling units did not help them or their men. Filipkowski and his officers and men were arrested and imprisoned, to be eventually deported by the Soviet authorities.[23]

At more or less the same time, summary justice, Soviet-style, was also being meted out by the Red Army or NKVD against Polish underground units elsewhere. On 15 March 1944, Komorowski sent the following message to London:

Volhynia reports:–1) The Bolsheviks have disarmed our people in the town of Przebraże, 12 kms to the north-west of Kiwerce. Some of the people have been arrested, the senior officers shot. 2) On the 9 March in the town of Rożyszcze the AK commanding officer and three others were shot, around twenty people arrested and transported to Łuck, a few have been hanged. 3) They are forcing the young people into their ranks. In the light of the above, should similar actions against our units be repeated by the Soviets, I have ordered that our people in Volhynia should refrain from disclosing their identities as AK soldiers.[24]

The Polish leadership in London received detailed reports of how Operation Tempest was progressing in the eastern regions, and in particular – as we have seen above – of how the Soviets were abusing their role as Allies. They received reports about the arrests, executions and disappearances. Indeed, they received appeals for help. On 30 July 1944 the Commander of the Home Army and the Government Delegate sent a dispatch to the Polish prime minister and C-in-C emphasising the necessity of extending guarantees provided by international law to persons arrested by the Soviet authorities. They also requested formal recognition of the Home Army as one of the Allied armies.

> The Polish Government has the right to demand assurance of safety of people who are fighting to the end for the common cause, and who cannot be treated other than as Allies with full rights. . . .
>   We must do all we can to safeguard these people and not to let them be liquidated either by the NKVD or by their obedient Polish tools.[25]

Why should the Home Army commanders have been expected to continue the charade of collaborating? There are a number of answers. First, they felt they had little option. As suggested earlier, if they remained concealed and took no action against the Germans, the communists would have increased accusations levelled at the 'passivity' of the Home Army, and at the lack of support within Poland for the London leadership. Also to be considered was the morale of the Polish underground units, which had been preparing for such operations against the Germans for several years. It also forced the Soviets, by dealing with the 'Polish problem' in their time-honoured fashion, to demonstrate their bad faith as well as their underhand methods, to a wider audience. In this respect the Warsaw Rising, which broke out at the beginning of August, placed Soviet treatment of the Polish question in an even greater international spotlight.

There was yet another reason why Polish leaders felt that there was still some hope of retrieving something from the situation. Hitherto the encounters between AK units and Red Army formations had taken place in eastern Poland, on territory which was disputed between the Polish and Soviet governments. It was in effect a direct challenge to Soviet claims to the region. But there was, they felt, always a chance that the Soviet authorities would look more favourably upon the activities of the Polish underground, once the Red Army had crossed the 'Curzon Line'; that is, had crossed into what the Soviets recognised as 'ethnographic Poland'. In fact, as the Poles were to discover, the Soviets were determined not to leave any partisan units in the Red Army's rear. They regarded such forces as a security risk and a threat to supply and communication lines.

THE RED ARMY CROSSES THE RIVER BUG

On 18 July 1944 General Konstantin Rokossovsky's First Byelorussian Front renewed its summer offensive and, on the 20th, Soviet units crossed the River Bug, recognised by the Soviets as the eastern boundary of 'ethnographic Poland'. (The river had also formed part of the Nazi–Soviet demarcation line established in 1939.) Accompanying the Red Army troops were units of the First Polish Army, which by now consisted of four infantry divisions and ancillary units numbering altogether 78 000 officers and men. The 'Berling' forces had transferred from Zhitomir to join the front near Kiwerce (Volhynia) at the end of April.[26]

It was at this point – as the front moved into territory which was indisputably to remain within the frontiers of the postwar Polish state – that the problem of order and administration had to be addressed. On the day the offensive began, a conference took place in Moscow between communist delegates from Soviet territory (ZPP) and delegates from Poland itself (KRN), at which it was agreed that a KRN delegature for the Liberated Territories should be created. Members of the new body included Edward Osóbka-Morawski and General Michał Żymierski ('Rola') from the KRN, and Andrzej Witos, Bolesław Drobner, Stanisław Radkiewicz from the ZPP. On 19 July, representatives of the new Delegature, which had been created without consulting the Polish Government in London, met Stalin to discuss the possibility of an agreement on relations between the new Polish administration and the Red Army command west of the River Bug.[27]

As a result of these manoeuvres, on 21 July the Polish Committee of National Liberation (PKWN) came into being in Moscow, under the leadership of Edward Osóbka-Morawski. Deputies were Wanda Wasilewska and Andrzej Witos. The PKWN fused the two Polish communist camps – the Polish Workers' Party in Poland and the ZPP in the Soviet Union – and it became effectively a Polish Government-in-waiting. On 22 July the Committee's Manifesto – the 'July Manifesto'

– was made public. Although the PKWN was referred to as the 'Lublin Committee' (it was alleged to have crossed the Bug in the wake of the Red Army and issued its manifesto on Polish soil), in fact the Committee was still several hundred miles away in Moscow. While still there on 26–27 July, the PKWN leaders signed two important agreements with the Soviet leadership. The first involved acceptance of the 'Curzon Line' as the postwar Polish–Soviet frontier – and therefore acceptance of Polish territorial losses in the east.[28] The second agreement was on relations between the Polish administration and the Soviet military authorities west of the agreed new border.

As a result of this second agreement signed between the PKWN and the Soviet Government on 26 July 1944, the Soviet military authorities on Polish territory were accorded all power and responsibilities in matters concerning the conduct of the war. The PKWN agreed to supplement the Berling forces from available manpower, and to actively assist the Soviet Commander-in-Chief by providing administrative help and meeting the requirements of the Red Army during their operations on Polish territory. As soon as Polish territory ceased to be the site of military operations, the PKWN would take over direct administrative responsibility.[29] This agreement is of especial significance, in so far as Article 7 stipulated that crimes committed by the civilian population on Polish territory against the Soviet units in the zone of operations were subject to *Soviet* military justice. Not only was this a direct infringement of Polish sovereignty, but the terms of the agreement were not defined. What area did the 'zone of operations' cover? According to historian Maria Turlejska, it was only in February 1945 that the People's Commissar for Defence defined it as an area of between 60 and 100 km behind the front line but, she adds, this stipulation did not work in practice, in any case.[30] Furthermore, the length of time these provisions were to remain in force was also not specified. What 'crimes' were covered by the agreement? What of the 'crime' for example, of defending the civilian population against the repeated attacks which groups of Red Army troops made on weakly-defended settlements?

Significantly, the communist authorities kept the text of this agreement hidden. It had not been ratified by the KRN, and did not appear in the *Dziennik Ustaw* (Journal of Laws), as had the PKWN's July Manifesto. Indeed, it was not published in Poland until 1954.[31] Yet it was as a result of this agreement that many Home Army soldiers, political figures and civilians, such as landowners, judges and railway workers, were deported. Ironically, on the day this agreement was signed (26 July), a Soviet statement was broadcast over Moscow radio:

The Soviet armies have entered the territories of reborn Poland with one aim – to destroy the hostile German armies and help the Polish nation by freeing it from the yoke of the German invaders and building an independent strong and democratic Poland.

The Soviet Government declares that it considers the wartime activity of the Red Army on the territory of Poland as activity on the territory of a sovereign, friendly and allied state.[32]

On 28 July the members of the PKWN were flown to Chełm, the first Polish town of significance west of the Bug to be liberated by the Soviet advance. Consistent with the claims in its Manifesto, the PKWN described itself as the single source of legislative and administrative power on liberated Polish territory – a prerogative which, as we have seen, had already been partly signed away in Moscow. The PKWN assumed the powers of a government, and Bolesław Bierut, already chairman of the Homeland National Committee (KRN), took on most powers normally enjoyed by a head of state. Already on 21 July, the KRN had announced that it was assuming command of the Polish Army in the USSR and the underground People's Army (AL) in Poland itself. The two forces were to be combined on Polish soil under a joint command. Żymierski was designated Commander-in-Chief while his deputies were to be Berling (operations) and Zawadzki (political affairs).[33]

Within a short space of time, Nikolai Bulganin was appointed the Kremlin's plenipotentiary for the liberated Polish territories; the military authorities, the NKVD, frontier defences, and the PKWN become subject to him.[34] With Bulganin came Ivan Serov, who had been Khrushchev's NKVD chief in the Ukraine in 1939–41 and is widely held to have been responsible for ordering and supervising the earlier mass-deportations from Polish territory. Having in the meantime seen to similar deportations of nationalities from the Caucasus, he had now returned to exercise his talents in the 'liberated' lands on the western border.[35]

Under Soviet tutelage, the PKWN rapidly began to build up its own security apparatus. Stanisław Radkiewicz, holding responsibility for public security within the PKWN, began to establish Public Security Bureaus at county and district levels. However, in several important respects the establishment of 'people's authority' was hampered. In the first place, the Polish communists found it extremely difficult during the first weeks and months to find personnel suitable to fill administrative posts at local and regional levels. The ranks of the communist military underground (AL) were thin, and had to be drawn on for three purposes: the Berling Army, the civilian administration and the security forces. The UBP ('Bezpieka') depended at this stage on operatives trained by the NKVD – which was itself at this early stage operating in the Lublin region, in the Red Army's rear. The Bezpieka included among their ranks a number of young people trained at an NKVD centre in Kaluga. Some had reputedly been freed from labour camps on condition that they took up offers of such employment; others had, at an earlier stage, been forcibly drafted in from the Berling forces.[36] Alongside the 'Bezpieka', other security organs began to be formed. The People's Militia (Milicja Obywatelska, or MO) came into being, essentially as an policing unit, subject to the UBP. It drew recruits from the communist underground, but also from careerists and those demoralised by the war. Also formed at this time was the Interior Force (Wojsko Wewnętrzne).[37]

The crossing of the River Bug, into 'ethnographic Poland', did little to alter the policies of the Red Army and NKVD. On 26 July, Soviet troops surrounded and disarmed the 9th Infantry Division of the Home Army in the Lublin District. The Division's commander, General Ludwik Bittner ('Halka'), together with many of his men, was arrested and deported to the Soviet interior. On the following day, his deputy in the Lublin region, Colonel Kazimierz Tumidajski ('Marcin') was also seized.[38] On 19 August, further arrests of Home Army (AK) members took place in the Lublin region. More than 200 officers and 2500 men were rounded up and confined in the former German concentration camp at Majdanek. By 2 October, the number of those arrested in the Lublin area had reached 21 000. Many were held in Lublin Castle, where the Gestapo had earlier interrogated Polish underground soldiers under torture. Not content with this, the Soviets carried out further mass arrests on 19 October as a result of which 38 AK soldiers were shot without trial.[39]

Indeed, during August, arrests of AK soldiers by the Soviet authorities occurred frequently and widely. The outbreak of the Warsaw Rising on 1 August, and the decision by the Red Army commanders (or, perhaps, their political masters) to halt the summer offensive on the east bank of the Vistula, left communist security forces with more time to consolidate their hold on the territory so quickly seized – both the newly-incorporated territories east of the Bug and the 'Polish territory' between the Bug and the Vistula. On 24 August, wide-scale arrests of AK soldiers took place in the territories east of the Bug – in Baranowicze, Nieśwież and Słonim. These were to be augmented during late September by further mass arrests in the eastern *województwa* of the former Republic – in Lwów, Tarnopol, Stanisławów, Volhynia, Vilnius and

Białystok. To the west, many arrests took place in Radom (6 August) and Zamość (12 August); on 23 August, more than 150 Home Army soldiers were arrested in the Garwolin district. On 9 September, several hundred officers and men of the AK were placed in a Soviet concentration camp at Olcadowizna (near Minsk Mazowiecki).[40]

It is characteristic of Soviet policies at this time that, while the life-or-death struggle of the Warsaw insurgents raged, the Soviets intercepted and arrested Polish units from central Poland called to assist the Rising. Such a fate befell the remnants of the 27th Infantry Division (from Volhynia – see above) and also the 3rd, 9th and 30th Divisions of the Home Army.[41] From mid-August onwards, the NKVD began to carry out arrests of Home Army members and of those prominent members of the Polish community who, despite the influence and prestige they enjoyed, had not volunteered for work with the new authorities. This campaign was aided by units of the MO (Citizen's Militia) and the WW (Interior Forces) and given cover of respectability in an accompanying propaganda offensive as 'action against reactionary forces'. It is hard to escape the conclusion that the real aim was to pacify the population by a campaign of terror. Those arrested were incarcerated in centres which had already been made infamous by the Germans, and by the end of September an estimated 100 000 people were behind bars or barbed wire.[42]

The reports arriving at Polish HQ ('Centrala') in London from the regional commanders of the Home Army present a stark and desperate picture of what was happening in the wake of the Soviet advance:

1. From the commander of Vilnius region, 19 and 25 August 1944 (after reporting the arrest of Colonel Filipkowski and his staff):

> There are arrests taking place of political activists from the PPS, SP, KWP (political parties) . . . and further arrests of AK soldiers as the result of information from informers (in general some 180 people).
> There is a registration for call-up of age cohorts born 1894–1926 (i.e. those aged between 18 and 50 years) which has now been completed. . . . in the countryside a 'wild mobilization' is taking place . . . villages are surrounded and recruits taken forcibly. The medical examination is superficial. . . .[43]

2. From the commander of the Vilnius district to London, 22 August 1944:

> For a month now there have been no instructions from the Commander-in-Chief as to how to behave towards the Soviets who are carrying out a hostile policy of extermination.

AK units are disarmed and transported to Kaługa.

Several thousand (*kilkanaście tysięcy*) men have been deported for labour in Russia, and a further mobilization of those aged between 18 and 52 is in progress. We are threatened with a mass deportation of the population as happened in 1939–41.

It is essential that diplomatic steps be taken and instructions issued as soon as possible. . . .[44]

3. From the Lublin district to London, 23 August 1944:

The line of the River Bug, as well as Dubno, Łuck, Równe and a number of towns [NB east of the Bug – K.S.] have been hurriedly fortified. The Soviet border guard has taken up duties on the Curzon Line. Crossing has become very difficult . . . the state administration east of the Bug is Soviet. The złoty is not accepted as currency east of the Bug and so our people are in a very difficult situation. There are deportations of our people to Russia.

In our region there is chaos in the administration . . . mass arrests continue (carried out by the NKVD with the help of the PPR) . . . some of the arrested are being transported to Kiev. . . .[45]

4. From the Lwów district to London, 11 September 1944:

Recruitment has started again . . . recruits are being sent to Jarosław on foot, and then on to Lublin [NB in a westerly direction – K. S.].
In Stryj . . . from several places Poles have been chosen for the Red Army.

From Kołomyja many people have been taken to Soviet Russia.

In Złoczów the recruitment of women aged 18–25 for work in the Donetsk coalfield has begun. Poles are being deported to Russia. The Soviets are purposely removing the Polish element from this region.

Their attitude towards us is suspicious, hostile, arrogant – worse than in 1939. . . .[46]

5. From Commander of the Lublin region to London, 13 September 1944:

NKVD arrests are growing more numerous . . . the level of recruitment in Lublin is 70% and in outlying districts 20–25% . . . many officers are taken [it is not clear whether this is to the Red Army or to the Berling Army, or both – K.S.].

Many officers and candidates for retraining are taken to Russia. An oath has been devised for recruits to the army of General Berling which expresses loyalty to the PKWN and to the Red Army.

In Lwów many staff officers have been arrested and deported to Kiev, Zhitomir, Perm.

For the arrested officers and members of the temporary civilian administration. . . . new camps have been created in marshy, isolated areas. . . . Krasków Włodowski, Wierchy Radzyńskie.[47]

6. From Commander of Białystok region to the C-in-C, 8 October 1944:

Mobilization (to the Red Army) of fourteen age cohorts has been sabotaged . . . and ordered to be carried out again.

The struggle of the (Polish) population on the far side of the Curzon Line continues, such that recruits are being released from the Red Army and directed to Berling's army.

. . . arrests of AK soldiers continue . . . officers are tortured and then transported in unknown directions – probably to be shot. . . .[48]

7. From the Inspector of sub-district 'East' to the Minister of National Defence, 28 October 1944:

Mass arrests, mainly of AK and NSZ people are taking place. Nightly house searches and street round-ups are carried out by the NKVD assisted by the militia. An order has been issued for women up to 30 and men up to 50 to be registered.

The incidents of robbery and murder committed by Soviet soldiers are on the increase. The attitude of the Soviet authorities – hostile. In each 'obwód' there are several thousand people evading recruitment to Berling's army. Chased and hunted, they need help but our local funds are almost exhausted.[49]

8. From Commander of sub-district 'East' to Commander of Warsaw district, 29 October 1944:

In the town of Kreślin, Siedlce powiat, the NKVD have organized a punishment camp for members of the AK and the Government delegature. Those arrested sit in dug-out holes about 2 metres square with water up to their knees – in darkness. The camp is completely isolated. It contains an estimated 1500 people.

It is essential to arrange immediate intervention by international agencies to bring this Soviet brutality to an end.[50]

9. From Commandant of Warsaw District 'West' to London, 19 November 1944:

Białowieża reports that on 13 November some 2500 Poles, mainly from the AK, were taken by rail from prison and camps in the Siedlce region to the east. The next transports are being prepared.[51]

10. From acting commander of Lwów district to London, 20 February 1945:

From 3–15 January mass arrests took place: 60% were Poles, the rest Volksdeutsche. Among those arrested were 21 university professors, priests, members of the intelligentsia and people from other social and professional groups. Prisons are full to bursting . . . conditions are inhuman . . . there is ill-treatment, hunger. . . .

When people are arrested, as proof of their collaboration with the Germans it is sufficient to be found in possession of postage stamps with Hitler's face, German newspapers or books.[52]

11. General Okulicki to acting C-in-C, 9 March 1945:

Repressions and arrests of AK soldiers continue unceasingly. Intervention by the Anglo-Saxons is essential. So far more than 40 000 have been arrested. The fate of the arrested is unknown.[53]

The references to international agencies, and the Anglo-Saxon powers are particularly poignant, since it had been the British and US Governments which had acceded to Polish pressure and recognised soldiers of the Home Army as combatants under international law. This step occurred on 29 August, at the height of the Warsaw Rising and was taken in order to indicate to the Germans that the Warsaw insurgents were to be accorded POW status. Ironically, though, the remaining ally in this wartime alliance, the USSR, made no such recognition, and proceeded to treat Home Army soldiers as worse than common criminals.[54] Faced with the growing evidence of the disarming and arrest of underground fighters and the disappearance of their officers, AK commanders grew wary and began increasingly to simply disband their units. Nevertheless, former members of the AK still faced arrest or being drafted into Berling's army. They risked being informed upon, and hunted down if they fled to the forests.

Even for those who volunteered to serve in Berling's units, life was difficult. Friction between former AK and former AL elements grew. Hostility towards the AK recruits was to grow when the Polish communists received increasing evidence that they had miscalculated. In their haste to boost the numbers of their troops by 'press-ganging' Home Army troops, they had been infiltrated by large numbers of people who were hostile to the communist cause. They risked being sabotaged from within.[55] In one celebrated incident on 13 October 1944, virtually a whole infantry regiment (the 31st) of the Polish People's Army deserted, near Krasnystaw in the Lublin region. Altogether 667 men decamped, leaving behind 180 of their comrades. A factor contributing to their decision may have been disgust at the Soviet failure to aid the Warsaw Rising, which had collapsed only days earlier. Although the officers involved were sentenced to death for their 'negligence', this sentence was later commuted.[56]

At this point, realising that their military and security apparatus had been infiltrated by their political opponents, communist policies hardened even further. Władysław Gomułka stated at a Politbureau meeting on 29 October,

> Recently we decided to build the Polish Army with AK people. Now we discover that the majority of them are hostile to us. . . . The army which we built could become an instrument of the reactionaries. We are in control of the top levels but by no means do we control the whole machine. . . .[57]

Displeasure was also expressed by Stalin, to whom news of the desertions had been brought. Arrests and internment now began of those AK men who had earlier agreed to serve in the ranks of the Berling Army.[58]

FROM 'LIBERATION' TO 'CIVIL WAR'?

The most dramatic move, though, and the one which has been taken by some historians as initiating the 'civil war' in Poland during the 1940s, was the promulgation of the Decree for the Defence of the State on 30 October 1944. The issuing of this decree seems to have come about as a direct result of Stalin's demands that the struggle with Polish nationalist forces – in effect, with the majority of the population – should be stepped up.[59] The Decree anticipated the most severe measures – usually the death sentence – being used as punishment for relatively innocuous 'crimes'. For example, an individual could be sentenced to death for possessing a radio receiver, but so could someone who, knowing that his neighbour had such a receiver, had failed to inform the authorities of it (article 6). Peasant farmers could receive the death-sentence for failing to supply requisitioned quotas of foodstuffs (article 2). Articles 1 and 8 threatened all members of underground groups which had come into existence during the Nazi occupation with death if they did not reveal themselves; but, of course, they feared to reveal themselves, since they would be pressured into betraying their friends and in any case risked arrest and transportation. All such 'crimes' covered by the Decree came under the jurisdiction of military courts.[60]

Many of the AK soldiers afraid of revealing themselves and confused by the lack of clear instructions emanating from London, returned to underground concealment. There was a growing feeling that they should refrain from offensive military activity against the communists. With some 2.5 million soldiers of the Red Army pouring into the area of central Poland controlled by the Lublin Committee (PKWN) – an area which covered some 78 000 sq. km and contained only some 6.5 million inhabitants – there was little sense in attacking the Soviet units. This is not to say that battles did not break out between the AK and Polish security units. They did, and with increasing frequency, initially as a self-defence measure against the repressive policies of the PKWN, but some partisan attacks also took place on outposts of the UB and MO; attempts were made to liberate AK prisoners and to assassinate recruiting officers from the 'People's Army'.[61] From 1945 onwards this struggle grew in scale and took on all the aspects of a fully-blown civil war.

On December 1944 the KRN, 'in accordance with the demands of the people', approved a resolution to call into being a Polish Interim Government. This step was taken despite warnings from President Roosevelt only days earlier that such a step would lead to a split in the policies of the Big Three, since the Western allies would continue to recognise the Polish Government in London. The Soviet Government nevertheless exchanged ambassadors with the new 'government', having accorded it diplomatic recognition on 4 January. The new government was recognised by Czechoslovakia on 31 January and by Yugoslavia on 30 March. However, for the next six months, Moscow's puppet regime in Poland remained unrecognised by the Western allies, or indeed by any states independent of Moscow.[62]

On 12 January 1945, the Red Army renewed its westward offensive. In the north the 3rd Byelorussian Front crossed the East Prussian border near Königsberg (Królewiec); in the central region, the 1st Byelorussian Front moved forward to take possession of the ruins of Warsaw, and then onwards towards Poznań; while in the south, the 1st Ukrainian Front advanced towards Breslau (Wrocław), taking Kraków on the 18th and reaching the River Oder a week later. As this new offensive took place, the final act of Operation Tempest was being played out. Home Army units attacked the retreating Germans in the

Warsaw and Kielce regions and helped the Red Army take Kraków. In the latter operation, AK units within the city attempted to ensure that buildings of especial historical importance were not destroyed. Similarly, at Częstochowa, a special AK unit was delegated to protect the monastery-shrine from despoliation by the retreating Germans. But everywhere the NKVD and UB, following in the wake of the Red Army, continued their earlier policy of arresting AK members, imprisoning them and eventually deporting them to the east.

The situation from the viewpoint of the Polish underground authorities was hopeless. They had attempted to carry out orders from the London political leadership in the hope of advancing the Polish cause in Allied councils, but there was little to gain from further sacrifice. On 19 January, therefore, the C-in-C of the Home Army, General Okulicki, gave the order for the Home Army to disband.[63] This order was confirmed by President Raczkiewicz some three weeks later (8 February) in a radio broadcast to the homeland. Arriving at almost the same time as news of the Yalta Conference decisions, the double blow struck at the morale of the Polish community and sapped their will to continue the struggle – an exhausting struggle, already in its sixth year.

Attempts were made by leaders of the Polish political parties to come to an understanding with the Interim Government. But all calls for compromise and negotiation ended in March 1945 when 16 Polish underground leaders, called to talks with Soviet representatives, were arrested and flown to Moscow. The arrest of the 16, who included the last C-in-C of the Home Army, General Leopold Okulicki, and Jan Jankowski, Polish Government Delegate for the Homeland, was probably the single most arrogant act of bad faith carried out by the Soviets during this period. The 16 were put on public trial in Moscow, showing complete contempt for the opinions of the Western allies. Two of the convicted, including Okulicki, did not survive the year and died in Soviet prison cells.[64]

The round-up of politicians continued. Wincenty Witos was arrested, since he was one of the few leaders with international standing and prestige in the community at large, whom the new powers would willingly have incorporated into their structure. Witos, however, refused to give the usurping regime his seal of approval, and the communist authorities, faced with an international scandal, were forced to let him go.[65] His health subsequently deteriorated and he died shortly afterwards. The NKVD arrested Mieczysław Jakubowski (Nationalist Party), Jan Hoppe (Labour Party), Stefan Rzeznik (Socialist Party), Tadeusz

Seweryn ('Roch' faction of the Peasant Party), and others. The security agencies arrested many whom the Germans had not thought to touch, such as Adam and Maria Tarnowski of the Polish Red Cross, Janusz Machnicki from the Main Welfare Committee (Rada Główna Opiekuńcza) and numbers of aristocrats (Janusz and Karol Radziwiłł, Jan and Maurycy Potocki) and many more.[66]

In the spring of 1945 the representatives of 'people's power' themselves began a widescale campaign aimed at terrorising the population into submission and compliance. Brutal pacification, along with pillage and summary shootings, spread over the whole of eastern Poland, from Białystok to Rzeszów. On 8 May (the day of the formal German capitulation) a Soviet detachment, numbering 200 people, carried out a pacification operation in Kurylówek. Sixty buildings were burned down and 25 people were either shot or else thrown into the flames of the burning buildings. The reason for the outrage was the disarming of a militia outpost in Leżajsek and the quartering in the district of partisans from the NOW group.[67]

On 25 May 1945 the commander of the AK's Białystok region, Colonel Władysław Liniarski ('Mścisław') reported:

> The NKVD and militia from the Lublin Government have carried out a systematic pacification of the Wysoko–Mazowiecki district. Each of the villages is surrounded in the night by NKVD forces and robbed of clothing and food. Those arrested are beaten most cruelly and taken away on suspicion of belonging to the AK. Along with the NKVD troops there is usually a column of armoured vehicles to be used in the event of resistance from the population.
>
> On 18 May the village of Bodaczki in the Bielsk powiat was surrounded, pillaged and then burned. Thirty-two people were killed on the spot.
>
> On 23 May the villages of Skarzyn Nowy, Stok, Miodusy, Stasiowięta, Zochy, Trzcianka and Krajewo in the Wysoki Mazowiecki powiat were surrounded and pillaged. Fifty-eight people were arrested.[68]

This kind of report can be duplicated scores of times for the period from the autumn of 1944 to the summer of the following year. In most cases the reports specify that the NKVD carried out the atrocities, rather than the MO or the UB. Indeed, there are cases recorded of the NKVD incarcerating MO platoons, which were suspected of not being either sufficiently zealous or enthusiastic about their work. In those cases, the MO operatives not infrequently found themselves occupying cells with Poles they had arrested earlier.[69]

As a result of such activities, the prisons and internment camps – of which there were many – rapidly filled with prisoners. The internment camps used during this period included those of Krzeslin, Skrobów, Krzesimów, Glusk, Kraczewice, Mątwy, Lęgnowo, Zimne Wody, Polulice, Mielęcin, Starogard, Lipno, Poznań, Ciechanów, Czynów, Sosnowiec-Radocha, Strzemięszyce, Świętochłowice, Katowice airport, Janów Podlaski and Rembertów. From these camps and prisons, many of which had previously been used by the Gestapo but were now under Soviet administration, regular transports of prisoners were taken into the Soviet Union.[70]

THE DEPORTATIONS

In attempting to analyse the renewed process of deportation from the Polish lands between 1944 and 1948, the task becomes possibly even more complex than it was in 1939–41. The process of arrest, internment and incarceration of Poles – whether civilians or Home Army personnel – took place both on territory to the east of the River Bug and on that lying to the west. But there was a difference. Although the Polish authorities in London continued to regard the prewar frontiers as sacrosanct, and authorised underground activity, both military and civilian (i.e. political), east of the Bug, we must bear in mind that the Soviet authorities, by contrast, considered all those east of the new frontier as *Soviet* citizens. The Soviet claim was based on the formal annexation of the region in November 1939, which followed on from the 'plebiscite' of the previous month. All residents of the region were deemed at that time to have acquired Soviet citizenship. Indeed, they had been issued with Soviet identity documents which many still held.[71] Here the Polish communist authorities (PKWN) had no jurisdiction. The military could recruit to Berling's forces, but the arrests and deportations which took place were carried out exclusively by Soviet agencies.

Logically, therefore, when the Red Army returned to the region, the Soviet legal code once again came into force. One Pole deported from Lwów in January 1945 states that only much later did the deportees discover that all Soviet citizens who lived for any length of time under German occupation, underwent the rigours of *'gosudarstwiennoj pierewierki'* – or, in other words, a review of their attitude towards the occupying powers. During the three years of the occupation, 1941 to 1943, the NKVD supposedly investigated all aspects of collaboration with the Germans. But honest citizens too were investigated on charges of 'collaboration' – a term which the Soviets extended to include anyone who had continued their profession under the Germans.[72] It is not surprising, therefore, that Poles in towns such as Lwów should be regarded by the Soviet legal authorities as having infringed paragraph 58 of the Soviet penal code.

It is clear, though that the communists adopted a casual approach to legal niceties. Polish citizens west of the Bug were just as liable to arrest, incarceration and deportation – whether under Polish military law, Soviet military law, or by the NKVD, who, if they were constrained by any considerations of legal propriety at all, presumably still operated according to the Soviet penal code.

Several Polish studies (most written outside Poland during the years of communist rule) refer to a figure of 50 000 Poles deported by the Soviets during the period 1944–48. It is not clear though whether this estimate refers only to serving Home Army members (i.e. those who had sworn the oath of allegiance, borne arms, taken part in operations, etc.) who revealed themselves to the communist authorities, or whether it includes the many 'civilian' Poles who were also rounded up and deported at this time.[73] Other reports and eye-witness accounts make it clear that hundreds and thousands of people were deported 'on suspicion' of belonging to the AK. Maria Kulczyńska estimates that during the mass round-up that took place in Lwów alone between 3 and 8 January 1945, some 17 300 people – mostly civilians – were taken.[74] If this is a correct figure then it seems that the overall number taken must be greater than 50 000. One Polish historian has estimated that 50 000 AK soldiers were deported from Polish territories within their 1939 frontiers, but claims that as many again were taken in the winter and spring of 1945 – mainly from Pomorze, Upper Silesia and Wielkopolska – for work in the USSR.[75] This would mean some 100 000 people altogether but, again, it would not include the non-combatants taken from the many towns and villages east and west of the new border.

What was the fate of these people, once they were apprehended? Their fate depended in large measure on what kind of category they belonged to – how and why they were seized by the Soviet authorities. In very broad terms, four main categories of people can be identified among those who were taken to the Soviet Union during the period 1944–48.

First were the 'internees'. These were people who emerged from the underground – both military and political – and revealed themselves to the Soviet military authorities, mostly in the course of the Operation Tempest. In many cases, as we have seen, the AK members had cooperated with the Red Army in driving out the Germans. Although the group would have included soldiers of the Home Army, the right-wing NSZ and the Peasants' Battalions who had refused to serve in the Berling units, it would also have numbered those who served with the People's Army and yet were arrested in the period after October 1944. The overall number of internees taken during the period 1944–45 has been estimated at between 15 000 and 17 000 people.[76]

In general they were not subjected to court process and thus were held as 'internees' rather than 'prisoners' – although this distinction did not mean a great deal in practice, since their treatment did not seem to differ greatly from that of captured Axis soldiers. Not all were deported. Many rank-and-file members of the AK who were detained on Polish soil (i.e. west of the Bug), and later held in camps, were eventually released. In most cases, though, the officers were deported. Those seized east of the River Bug, on what was now Soviet soil, were virtually all deported. Those who were taken to Soviet territory were released within a matter of months or at least within a few years. Few were held beyond 1948.

One of the first transports of internees was that of AK soldiers from Vilnius (the circumstances surrounding their apprehension have been outlined earlier). The transport numbered some 4000 people and left the detention camp at Miedniki around 28 July 1944, arriving at its destination – the Kaluga transit camp – on 4 August.[77] The only officers on this train were those who – perhaps mindful of the fate of their predecessors at Katyn – had not revealed their rank to the Soviet authorities. When they reached Kaluga, however, and their true status was discovered, the officers were removed from the camp – all except the doctors, in whose hands lay the running of the camp's medical service.[78]

The experience of this first group of internees is unique in that the Soviet authorities attempted to induct them *en masse* into the Red Army. A few days after their arrival at Kaluga they were transformed into the 361st infantry regiment of the Red Army, consisting of four battalions. All important command positions were held by Soviet officers. Once the regiment had been formed, it embarked on a six-week recruitment training programme. When training ended they were given arms and new uniforms, and were invited to swear an oath of allegiance to the Red Army. The Poles refused to swear this oath, however, and were disarmed, stripped of their uniforms and directed to work in forestry clearance. The battalions were divided up and one was eventually disbanded as a result of losses due to desertion.

That the prisoners wanted to desert is hardly surprising. Accommodation

was primitive – the men had to live in dug-out shelters they themselves had made. Their work norms, at first manageable, were doubled
and then increased further. And their food ration, although consistent
with what they might have expected as soldiers, was insufficient, given
the heavy work they were engaged in. What is surprising is that camp
security was so lax as to allow them to escape. It is not recorded how
many made their way back to Polish territory. The remainder continued to work at Kaługa until the end of 1945. In the third week of
December they received new uniforms and were moved to a collecting
point at Sieredniakow, from where they travelled via Moscow to
Smolensk. After a delay of a further month they were taken to Brześć.
This transport reached Polish soil (Biała Podlaska) on 16 January 1946.[79]

In his short, exploratory study of the internees' journeys and their
camp conditions, historian Ireneusz Caban has identified 47 camps in
which AK internees were held on Soviet soil. All of these camps were
in the European part of the Soviet Union, although the two most northerly
and easterly groups of camps, close to the northern Urals, were not far
short of Siberia. Some of these were only transit camps. In many, the
Poles formed only a minority of the camp population; other groups of
internees or prisoners encountered in the camps included Austrians,
Hungarians, Romanians, Spaniards from Franco's 'Blue Division', Czechs
and Slovaks, Finns, Greeks, Italians, Albanians, Bulgarians, French-
men, Norwegians, Dutchmen and Yugoslavs. The Griazoviets camp
system, north of Vologda, was one of the largest camps for German
prisoners-of-war and for the captured prisoners of the Nazi satellite
nations. Most of the above-listed nationalities were found there in the
period 1945–47.[80]

German prisoners-of-war were encountered in many camps, and it
was an unpleasant surprise for the Poles to find on occasion not only
that they were occupying a camp vacated by German prisoners, but
that, frequently, the German administrative staff was left behind to
run the camp for and exercise supervision over, the Poles! In the
Griazoviets camp, for example, the administration was run by German
officers. In the Jegolsk camp (Borowicze), at which Poles arrived in
the last weeks of 1944 from the Lublin region, not only were the administrative functions in German hands, but the camp's internal commandant was a German. Only determined protests by the Poles and a
number of clashes between German and Polish inmates, persuaded the
authorities to remove the Germans from the camp.[81] In a number of
camps, the Poles were marked out for especial restrictions – the most
common of which was the ban on correspondence with their families

– a ban not extended to other nationalities (even to the Germans). This reducing of Home Army soldiers to the level of the defeated enemy, against whom they had been fighting until only a few months before, was a particularly provocative move by the Soviets.

The conditions the internees faced varied widely, although in general it seems that officers were treated reasonably well and were not ex- pected to carry out physical work. The men, however, were engaged in mining, forestry work and work in camp workshops or else in neigh- bouring collectives and state farms. In the Diaghilev camp no. 178 (near Riazan) more than 2000 Home Army soldiers from the Lublin and Białystok region were concentrated during 1945. In the course of 1946 the camp inmates included five AK generals, together with 500 other AK officers. In an effort to uplift spirits and build morale, the Poles embarked on a number of cultural initiatives: a choir was formed, and a theatre group – 'Nasza Buda'; courses began in languages (Eng- lish, French, Russian), as well as in farming, forestry, teaching and music; there were talks on literary and historical themes; groups be- came involved in repairing radio receivers and cameras; finally, with four priests in the camp it was possible to organise religious life on a regular basis – although camouflaged from the camp authorities.[82]

Despite these relatively relaxed conditions, many escape attempts were made from the camp. While most ended in failure, as many as a dozen men are estimated to have reached Poland again. The camp also became well-known for a famous hunger-strike which took place in June–July 1947 – as a protest of the inmates against the continued refusal to allow them to return to Poland after some three years of captivity, or even to give them any idea of how long they would be held. The strike lasted for ten days and was only halted when a special commission arrived from Moscow and stated that the internees would gradually be freed and allowed home.[83]

A certain number were allowed to return to Poland, but the camp as a whole was divided up into five groups and despatched in different directions, the aim clearly being to block any future concerted action of this kind. A small group of some 340 people were taken to the Ustishora camp in the Marysk Republic. There they worked on dig- ging potatoes and building embankments to regulate the river-flow. There, too, in a camp which had been vacated only a few days earlier by German prisoners, they found evidence (medals, crosses, carved objects in wood and metal) of the internment of Polish prisoners during an earlier period (1940–41).[84]

Among the Poles transported to the Ustishora camp was one Jerzy

Dzierżyński, nephew of Feliks, the founder of the Czeka and thus ultimately, of the NKVD. Jerzy had been one of the AK brigade commanders in Vilnius (where, incidentally, his famous uncle had attended
high school) and had been 'interned' together with other Home Army
personnel. The NKVD commandant of the Ustishora camp (named
Cyganow) could scarcely believe whom he had under his care and
how he had got there. He frequently came to sit, look at and talk to
Dzierżyński. But within a few weeks, on 10 September, an NKVD
officer came from Moscow and took Dzierżyński from the camp. On
18 September he arrived in Warsaw and was reunited with his family,
who had intervened on his behalf with the Soviet authorities.[85]

The second group to be deported were Home Army prisoners sentenced by Soviet courts. These were people in the eastern territories
who did not reveal themselves to the Soviet authorities but were subsequently arrested as a result of NKVD round-ups, and investigations.
In a number of cases they were encouraged to come out of hiding by
colleagues or superiors. For the most part, therefore, they were apprehended in towns such as Lwów and Vilnius many months after the
front had passed to the west – indeed in some cases after the war in
Europe was formally over. Their fate was similar to that of many Poles
arrested during the 1939–41 period: long periods in prison, interrogations, and then a sentence which took them by stages to labour camps
often in the extreme north. Many of these AK people – both men and
women – spent their period of corrective labour in the Vorkuta camp
complex – mining. Most spent at least ten years in the camps and did
not return until the late 1950s.

This later wave of deportations, perhaps not as well recorded as the
mass-movements of 1940–41, nevertheless has produced some detailed,
if harrowing, documents. Adolf Popławski, for example, was working
with the Government Delegate in Vilnius in the early part of 1945. It
was a period during which the NKVD was announcing an amnesty for
AK personnel, and representatives of Berling's forces appeared, trying
to induce the partisans to come out of hiding. Popławski himself was
tricked by the deviousness of the NKVD, which, having arrested members
of his units, persuaded them that if they could encourage colleagues to
reveal themselves, all would go free. Popławski was in fact promised
during an early meeting with an NKVD official that he would be allowed to remain in Vilnius, or to travel to Poland. In any event he
would not be subject to arrest.

Of course, these undertakings proved worthless. Arrested on 15 June
1945, during his initial period of imprisonment he was interrogated

and beaten repeatedly. Eventually he was sentenced by a Soviet Military Tribunal (together with the very colleagues who had induced him to reveal himself) under Paragraph 58 of the Soviet penal code, for 'treason'. It was of little use arguing that since they regarded themselves to be Polish citizens, they could hardly be guilty of treason against the Soviet state. Pop ławski was sentenced to 15 years in corrective labour camps – *katorga*. He had a varied experience of the Soviet labour camp system, having 'visited', in the course of his sentence, camps in Vorkuta, the Ural region, Taishet and Magadan. After serving eleven-and-a-half years, he returned to Poland on 30 November 1956.[86]

A further, unpublished account is that of Maria Wierzbicka, a wartime courier for the Home Army in Lwów. She, together with her husband, who had also been active in conspiratorial work during the German occupation, fell victim to the wave of NKVD arrests which followed the 'liberation' of the city and began in July 1944. She was arrested on 10 August, but it was only after several months of life in prison cells and a holding camp (Pe łtewna, on the outskirts of Lwów) that she was brought before a Military Tribunal on 13 January 1945. She was one of only two women in a group of 20 being sentenced for their involvement in underground activities coordinated by the London Polish Government, 'which was hostile to the Soviet Union'. 'This organisation, active during the period of the German occupation, had as its goal the rebuilding of the Polish State in its pre-1939 frontiers.' In other words, the prisoners aimed to 'tear away' the Lwów, Tarnopol and Stanis ławów administrative districts from the Soviet Ukraine. Their cause was weakened by the apparent collaboration of the arrested Government Delegate, Adam Ostrowski, with the NKVD. He had been released together with a few close friends, and was later to enjoy a prominent career in communist Poland.[87]

The group were sentenced under article 54 of the Ukrainian Legal Code (equivalent to art. 58 of the Soviet Code), paragraph 11 – which referred to membership of illegal, underground organisations. Seventeen of the group, who were proved by their German identity documents (*Kennkarten*) to be permanent residents of the region annexed in 1939 by the Soviets, were further accused of treason. Wierzbicka and two other defendants were acknowledged to be Polish citizens, since they possessed identity documents issued west of the new Yalta frontier. She received the lowest sentence – ten years in corrective labour camps – although, like the other members of the group, received a further five years' sentence 'deprived of legal and civic rights'. On 15 November 1945 she was transported to the Ural region (Po łowinka camp, near Perm). Later she also worked in a camp in the Komi Republic. She did not return to Poland until December 1955.[88]

A further account by a convicted AK activist is that by Edward Buca who, at the age of 19, had been sentenced to death by a Soviet Military Court for an assassination attempt on a Polish communist official. Like Wierzbicka, he had been active in the Lwów area and was held in the Zamarstynów prison for three months before his sentence was commuted to 20 years' hard labour and he was moved to the Pełtewna transit camp. Buca subsequently worked in labour camps in the Vorkuta complex and in Siberia (Taishet) for more than a decade, returning to Poland only in May 1958.[89] On his return to Poland, Buca was regarded as such a dangerous individual that he was again put on trial by the Polish communist authorities; 'I was in fact being tried by a Polish court for my activities in 1945, which were no longer political in character and for which I had already been tried and sentenced in the Soviet Union.'[90] The court found him guilty, but because of various amnesties proclaimed during the intervening period, was able to release him. (The period spent in the Soviet Union was regarded by the Polish authorities as only 'temporary isolation'!) For a further twelve years, it remained possible for the court to reimpose the sentences. Indeed, Buca recalls that he was rearrested with monotonous regularity each time a high-ranking Party official, whether Polish or foreign, visited his home town of Katowice. In 1971 he escaped to the West via Sweden.

The third category of people detained and deported in the 1944–45 period by the Soviet security organs were Polish civilians. In some cases these were suspected and accused of involvement in underground activities, but more frequently other, on occasion dazzlingly trivial, motives were found. Romana Gruber-Zych was arrested in Lwów on 3 January 1945 and transported some 1500 km to a labour camp in the Donbas region (Krasny Don). The reason? As she took her dog out for a walk at the beginning of the new year, it was noticed that her Scottish terrier was wearing a red ribbon around its neck. In the charge papers she was described as having attempted to debase the state flag and the symbol of the Revolution by tying a red ribbon around the neck of a dog. She was charged with 'anti-Soviet agitation'.

Some days earlier, just before Christmas 1944, Stanisław Krzaklewski had been arrested, also in Lwów, in the strangest manner. Walking along the street, he observed on the other side two men in fur caps coming towards him and between them a colleague with whom he had studied veterinary science. He bowed his head slightly in greeting to his colleague, whereupon, the men in Russian hats produced pistols and ordered him to go with them. He was taken to Lwów's Łącki jail where he was held for six weeks.

On the night of 5/6 February 1945, the prisoners were taken to the railway station and loaded into wagons. As they waited in the trucks, men and women desperately scribbled notes for relatives, which they then slipped between the planks of the railway wagon and allowed to drop on to the track – hoping that they would be picked up by a kindhearted soul and delivered. An observer noted that the next day, after the train had departed, the Russians collected seven sackfuls of paper from along the track. Few of the messages reached their destination. The transport was taken to NKVD camp no. 0310 in the Donbas and the prisoners – both men and women – were employed in mining. Their daily routine involved a march of two km through the steppe, then they were forced to wait in the frost for a small lift, before going down the mine shaft – and then a further two km underground to the coal-face. They worked hacking at the coal in a kneeling position, or sometimes lying down. Two points in the account of their experiences are worthy of mention. The first is that American UNRRA supplies arrived at the camp, including powdered egg, tinned meats, etc. However, none of this reached the prisoners, who saw only empty tins, which had to serve as cups and plates, or sometimes scraps of cardboard from the packaging. The prisoners were hungry for most of the time and, indeed, died of hunger in large numbers. Krzaklewski, who was 24 years old at the time, was employed in disposing of the corpses outside the perimeter wire of the camp compound. Only half of the three thousand people who had been deported in this January transport ever returned to their homes.[91]

Maria Kulczyńska, who was arrested in Lwów on the night of 8–9 January 1945 and transported to the Donbas in the same transport that took Krzaklewski and Gruber-Zych, estimates that around 17 300 people were arrested in Lwów between 3 and 8 January. She states that those arrested came from the most varied social strata and, so, those Poles arrested for their 'political' activities found themselves in company with thieves, murderers, prostitutes, informers, Volksdeutsche, and Ukrainian nationalists. Large numbers of academics from the Lwów Polytechnic and University were taken, as well as many doctors, engineers and artists grouped in unions or associations – categories which had previously been protected, if not privileged, under Soviet rule.[92] For unexplained reasons, she was released and sent to Poland after only two years – in 1947. This period of mass-arrests of civilians seems to have coincided with a similar wave in Vilnius and other towns.[93]

The fourth category of deportees were those conscripted into the Red Army. We have seen that some of the AK personnel were given the option of serving in the Red Army or in Berling's formations. To judge from the reports of AK commanders, though, male civilians of military age were not always given the choice and, as in 1940–41, were taken forcibly. Not much is known about this category, however, either about the numbers involved, the length of service or their experiences.

CONCLUSION

If the 1939 Ribbentrop–Molotov Pact and the Soviet seizure of Polish territory following the German invasion was an act of opportunism and bad faith by the Soviet leadership, what happened in the Polish lands between 1944–45 was a disgraceful episode in Moscow's relations with its neighbours. The NKVD's activities on Polish soil conceded little in brutality and savagery to those of Hitler's Einsatzgruppen five years earlier. The above account has done little more than hint at the full horror of the conditions under which Poles were held by the NKVD and their frequent summary fate. In time the virtual civil war which erupted in Poland after 1944 merged into the campaign of terror that preceded the 1947 elections.

The period marked a further chapter in the series of violent uprootings practised by Moscow on the Polish people. The large-scale movement of the Polish population was the third time within a decade (if one includes the liquidation of the Polish autonomous regions in Ukraine and Byelorussia that took place during the years 1936–38). It was admittedly the smallest of the three movements. This may have been due to the difficulties of large-scale rail-movements on the devastated territory in the Red Army's rear, or due perhaps to the Polish communists' apprehensions about an even more violent rejection of their cause by the Polish population. The fact, though, that so many of the deportees were combatants – people who had fought a brave five-year struggle against the Nazi occupation of their homeland – was also a shameful one for the Western partners in the wartime anti-Nazi alliance.

It is a great and unexplained mystery, why so many Home Army soldiers – including senior commanders – who fell into Soviet hands in 1944, were released relatively quickly, often within months, while others of lesser rank and significance were sentenced as criminals and passed periods both in prison cells and in hard labour. One could perhaps surmise that the earlier seizures had included many people who had both fought alongside the Red Army and had declared their presence before the front passed. Those apprehended later had not, as far as was known by the NKVD, distinguished themselves through 'brotherhood of arms' with their Soviet 'liberators'. Moreover, they had not revealed themselves willingly to the new authorities, which may have led to the suspicion that they were planning to resume activity in the rear of the Red Army.

Once again, however, attempts to analyse and fathom Soviet methods and intentions founder in the face of the apparent caprice of the NKVD. Many of the arrestees-deportees were taken straight from the street for the most trivial reasons. The inescapable conclusion is, therefore, that this was a preventive measure only in so far as it was intended to terrorise the population into passivity and acceptance of the inevitability of Soviet rule.

7 Repatriation from the Soviet Union, 1944–48

EARLY MOVES TOWARDS REPATRIATION

In 1944, as the Red Army's divisions pushed inexorably west, whole tracts of Polish territory were liberated from German control. Yet the eastern provinces (*województwa*) of Poland, which Stalin had annexed in 1939 as a result of the Nazi–Soviet Pact and subsequent territorial agreements, were once again – this time with the Allies' compliance – incorporated into the respective Soviet rep..blics. The new Polish–Soviet border ran along the River Bug leaving towns and cities such as Lwów, Vilnius, Tarnopol, Pińsk, Brześć, Baranowicze and Grodno on the Soviet side. (But the town of Białystok, which had been the capital of Western Byelorussia between 1939 and 1941, was restored to Poland.) A further inescapable consequence was that the Soviet Union reacquired several million Polish citizens within its borders.

The Polish communists, who had agreed to the concession of territory, began moves to transfer Poles from the Soviet Union. The migration that occurred in 1944–48 brought hundreds of thousands of people, some of whom had been forcibly removed during the earlier years of the war, 'back' to their homeland. The movement was one of considerable size – and for the most part was organised and controlled. It was only one of several migratory processes which were taking place at this time to bring Polish citizens, cast by wartime activity to the various corners of the world, back to their homeland. However, it was one of the largest return movements from a single country. Indeed one historian of postwar Polish repatriation movements has observed that it was only surpassed in size by the return of Polish prisoners of war, forced labourers and Wehrmacht draftees from Germany.[1] The comparison is a telling one.

Just as the Poles' journeys to the USSR had been due a variety of causes, so the return journeys too fell into different categories. The first returnees to Polish soil were, of course, the men and women of Berling's Army – although their wartime march was to take them on into German and Czech territory, before they eventually returned finally to their homeland at the cessation of hostilities.[2] A further Polish migration of considerable size moved west during 1943–44 – and therefore in some cases before the Red Army's arrival. These were the Polish refugees who fled west to escape the 'ethnic cleansing' policies of Ukrainian nationalist gangs in Volhynia and Eastern Galicia. The number 'cleansed' in this way has been estimated to be as high as 200 000.[3]

In addition to these two categories, a third embraced a number of individuals who, according to historian Krystyna Kersten, 'returned on the strength of visas given by the Soviet authorities in individual cases from July 1944–July 1945'.[4] This special category seems somewhat mysterious; one can only speculate as to who came under this arrangement. Kersten does not elaborate. It seems likely, however, that she is referring to a token group of Poles amnestied and released from Soviet labour camps during the period in question. During the Moscow talks which led to the formation of the Polish Committee for National Liberation (PKWN) in July 1944, some of the Polish communists intervened for the release of compatriots held in prisons and camps. They were doubtless motivated by political considerations – concern for their domestic popularity – rather than pure philanthropy, but the appeal had some effect. On 10 August, by a decree of the Supreme Soviet, an amnesty was declared for Polish citizens sentenced by Soviet courts 'for crimes committed on the territory of the USSR'.[5]

One of the prisoners released under this amnesty was Jerzy Drewnowski, who had been arrested in 1940 for illegally crossing the border from the General Government. Significantly, he had not been released under the earlier amnesty of 1941, and even when recruitment began to the Kościuszko Division, he was detained by the NKVD. Languishing in the Vietlosian labour camp, near Uchta (Komi ASSR), the first he heard of impending release was on 21 October 1944, when orders for his release were transmitted from Moscow to the Uchta region NKVD. Drewnowski himself attributes his mysterious liberation to the intervention of the KRN/PKWN leaders, but adds that otherwise their intervention had in general only limited results.[6]

By far the largest group, however, were Poles who moved west under the formal 'repatriation' agreements concluded by the PKWN or the Provisional Government with the Soviet authorities. These agreements and their implementation will be discussed in more detail below.

We encounter a methodological difficulty, however, with the use of the term 'repatriation'. 'Repatriation' is generally taken to mean the return to their homeland by persons who have earlier left its frontiers – whether voluntarily or otherwise. But many of the people who moved west under the Polish–Soviet 'repatriation' agreements were not, strictly speaking, being repatriated. They had never left their homeland. Many indeed had never left their homes. Nevertheless with the shifting of the Polish–Soviet frontier, millions of Poles found themselves outside the borders of their homeland – just as indeed, almost a quarter of a century earlier the establishment of the 'Riga Line' (the interwar Polish–Soviet frontier established at the Treaty of Riga in 1921) had left so many of their fellow-countrymen on the wrong side of the frontier and at the mercy of the infant Soviet regime. In a sense then, in the case of these people, one could say that they had not left Poland – Poland had left them.

On the other hand, some hundreds of thousands of Poles who left, or were removed from, Polish territory in 1939–41, still languished in the Soviet interior. Of their return, one can indeed use the term 'repatriation', even though they were returning to a 'homeland' that was completely unfamiliar to them (most originated from the eastern provinces but were being returned to central and western Poland). It seems sensible, therefore, to restrict the use of the term 'repatriation' to those deportees and others who had moved, voluntarily or involuntarily, east of the Riga Line during the period of 1939–44. The terms 'resettlement', or 'transfer' might better be applied to those from the former Polish *kresy wschodnie* (eastern borderlands) who decided to leave homes and moved to Poland within its new borders. In practice, though, this distinction in terms is not easy to maintain and scholars have tended to use the word 'repatriation' for both categories of migrant. It is true, as Kersten has stated, that the two problems – that of repatriating those refugees displaced by wartime activity and transferring those residents of former Polish territories in the east – were closely linked to one another.[7] Indeed, the same 'repatriation' agency dealt with both return movements to the homeland.

The first major agreements relating to 'repatriation' from the Soviet Union had already been concluded during September 1944, at a time when the territory east of the Curzon Line had been liberated by the Red Army and the Soviet offensive had crossed the River Bug to 'ethnographic Poland'. As a result of a Soviet constitutional amendment of February 1944, granting Soviet republics the power to establish their own foreign commissariats, separate agreements were signed with each of the three neighbouring republics. On 9 September, therefore, the PKWN, in the person of Edward Osóbka-Morawski, signed agreements with the Byelorussian and Ukrainian governments (represented by A. Shavrov and N. Khrushchev respectively). On 22 September a similar agreement was signed with the Lithuanian government.[8]

There must be some doubt over the legality of these agreements since the PKWN, which had been established less than two months earlier, had no mandate to act as a government and conclude pacts of this kind with foreign powers. Furthermore, as Tadeusz Romer, Foreign Minister of the Polish Government and former Polish ambassador in Moscow, pointed out in a letter to the British Government of 7 October 1944, the agreements concluded with the 'so-called' Polish Committee of National Liberation (PKWN),

> are attempting by means of accomplished facts and unilateral decision to change the traditional ethnographic face of these territories by arbitrarily moving . . . millions of people. It would be impossible to exaggerate the calamity inflicted on this population by the expulsion from their ancestral homes of a large mass of people who have already endured the afflictions of the last five years and their settlement in new places of domicile while the war is still going on.[9]

Romer drew attention also to the fact that the relevant agreements did not cover the case of Polish citizens deported to the interior of the USSR in 1939–41, which seemed to indicate, he suggested, that the Soviet Government had a purely political effect in view (i.e. that outlined in the quotation above). In fact, an agreement concerning the repatriation of Poles from the remaining areas of the USSR was signed the following summer.[10]

On the day that Romer sent his protest to the British Government, the PKWN took a further step towards securing the repatriation of the millions of Poles dispersed outside the frontiers of the homeland – a task regarded as among the most important facing the PKWN and, later, the Polish Government of National Unity.[11] The Polish Repatriation Bureau (Polski Urząd Repatriacyjny, PUR) was called into existence on 7 October by a decree of the PKWN. Its first director was W. Wolski, and its tasks included organising the repatriation of Poles from the territory of all other states. Of course, at the time PUR was founded, only days after the collapse of the Warsaw Rising, the Soviet Union was the only state from which it was possible to consider repatriating Poles. In the event, its role eventually became limited to supervising the transport of migrants and their welfare within Polish borders. Most other repatriation activities were taken over by the Office of the General Government Plenipotentiary for Repatriation, created in the spring of 1945. The Government Plenipotentiary's Office was divided into two sections – that concerned with repatriation from the east (i.e. the USSR) and that concerned with repatriation from the west. Wolski, first head of PUR, was appointed to the position of Government Plenipotentiary in April 1945. (PUR was subordinated to the Plenipotentiary's Office.)[12]

REPATRIATION FROM THE NEIGHBOURING REPUBLICS

What were the provisions of these agreements and how were they put into operation? Essentially, they seem to have much in common with the Nazi–Soviet agreements for exchange of populations dating from the early months of the war. They provided for the exchange of populations on a voluntary basis between the signatory parties. Specifically, all those of Polish and Jewish ethnic background who were Polish citizens before 17 September 1939 – before, that is, the Red Army invaded Poland – and lived within the newly-extended western borders of the Lithuanian, Byelorussian or Ukrainian Soviet Republics, could apply for transfer (or 'repatriation') to Poland. Similarly, those Lithuanians, Ukrainians or Byelorussians residing on the territory of the new Polish state could likewise apply for transfer to their home republics within the Soviet Union.

Although outlined in this way, the issue sounds straightforward, in fact there were considerable obstacles to be overcome. Behind the choice of whether or not to transfer lay the thorny question of citizenship. The Soviet authorities had, on more than one occasion, stated their view that residents of Western Ukraine and Western Byelorussia had become Soviet citizens by choice, following the 'plebiscite' of October 1939. Therefore conversations on the subject between the Polish communists and Moscow during 1944 ran into difficulties. They were only resolved on 22 June 1944, when the Supreme Soviet, conceding ground to the Poles, agreed to make certain exceptions to the November 1939 citizenship decree. Soviet citizens of Polish ethnic background, from all republics and districts, if they had served in the Berling Army or had otherwise actively contributed to the liberation of Poland, had the right to change their Soviet citizenship for Polish. The same rights were extended to their families.[13]

This agreement was only regarded as a first step by the Polish communist authorities, and negotiations on the subject continued. Nevertheless, this June 1944 decree did introduce an interesting anomaly. Whereas the Soviet authorities had at no time been prepared to allow Lithuanians, Byelorussians or Ukrainians who had formerly been Polish citizens to opt for transfer to Polish territory, the decree nevertheless allowed for certain categories of Poles who had been Soviet citizens before the war (e.g. those Red Army personnel that had been drafted into service with Berling's forces) to 'return' to Poland.[14]

Further anomalies surfaced. Discussions regarding Poles in the remaining areas of the Soviet Union (those not covered by the September agreements) continued from the autumn of 1944 into 1945. The right of option had not yet been extended to them, and the PKWN–ZPP negotiators pointed out that those Poles who had retained their original identity documents and had steadfastly refused to accept Soviet passports during 1943–44, despite the urgings of the ZPP, were often readily recognised by the Soviet authorities as Polish, whereas the 'loyal ones' (those who had accepted Soviet citizenship!) were deprived of all rights to amnesty and repatriation.[15] It is not recorded whether the ZPP representatives appreciated the irony of this situation.

Another sensitive area was that of Polish Jews. Former Polish citizens of Jewish origin were not initially mentioned as candidates for repatriation from the Soviet republics. Yet Jews had constituted a large proportion of the inhabitants of the eastern territories deported in 1940–41. Indeed, an estimate by the Repatriation Bureau (PUR) in mid-1945 was that, of 750 000 Polish citizens still on the territory of the USSR (other than territory formerly belonging to the Polish Republic), Jews accounted for 40–50 per cent.[16] The exclusion of Jews from this early repatriation scheme aroused strong feelings and was in the end unsustainable. The Polish Communist Party had always had a disproportionately large number of Jews among its members and the situation of the Polish communists in the USSR was little different. The already small cadre from which communist ideologists, educational advisers and administrators were being selected would have shrunk to even smaller – and probably unmanageable – proportions, had Jews been excluded. In October 1944 the Union of Polish Patriots intervened with the Soviet authorities in order to have the terms of the 22 June decree extended to include those of Jewish origins.[17]

Under the provisions of the agreements, several categories of kin could accompany individual repatriates. The agreements list marriage partners, children, parents, grandchildren, and even extend to non-kin who had worked together within the same economic unit. It seems fair to assume, therefore, that, despite the general restriction of the provisions to ethnic Poles and Jews, that a number of non-Poles who were related by marriage made their way west. Indeed the statistical material available shows that some 15 103 people who were not classified as 'Poles' or 'Jews' but as 'Others' were transported to Poland in the period 1944–48.[18]

Certain incentives were also applied to encourage waverers to make the decision. Those moving would be released from all outstanding taxes, insurance premiums and production quotas on their farms. Furthermore, they would remain exempt from state taxes and insurance premiums for two years after resettlement. Tranferees could take with them livestock, poultry and household or farming equipment up to a limit of two tons per family. Those in the professions could take with them their tools or equipment. However, resettlers were eligible for a loan of 5000 złoties (5000 roubles) to replace farm equipment and other necessary items. Furthermore, the export of gold, silver, platinum, precious stones, and objects of artistic and archaeological value was forbidden.[19]

The work of registering potential repatriates and organising travel arrangements was carried out by the Office of the Government Plenipotentiary for Repatriation. Office representatives established their bases in Vilnius (Lithuanian SSR), Baranowicze (Byelorussian SSR) and Łuck (Ukrainian SSR). The officials were endowed with wide powers and could employ not only the organisational network of the local Polish community but also the republic's information media (press, radio, etc.) to reach potential repatriates. Local repatriation commissions were established in each of the neighbouring republics. By March 1945 there were 45 of them. For the western Ukraine this meant offices in Kowel, Włodzimierz, Rawa Ruska, Lwów, Sambor, Drohobycz, Stryj, Chodorów, Stanisławów, Tarnopol, Czortków and Kamionka Strumiłowa; in Byelorussia – Brześć, Bereza Kartuska, Grodno, Kobryń, Lida, Pińsk, Prużany, Słonim and Wołkowysk. The personnel of each regional office varied between 15 and 30 people, depending upon the needs of the area.[20]

In the case of the 'repatriation' agreements with the neighbouring republics of September 1944, candidates were expected to register between 15 October and 1 December 1944. It was anticipated that the transfers would take place between 1 December 1944 and April 1945.[21] This timetable indicates a quite surprising degree of haste, bearing in mind that transport of repatriates was being planned for the most severe winter months. It also displays great confidence about the Red Army's ability to clear the Germans from Polish soil. After all, when the original agreements were being signed and plans laid, the Warsaw Rising was still raging. The Red Army was stalled on the east bank of the Vistula and, in fact, as we now know, was not to resume its offensive until January 1945. Indeed, TASS reported that the first trainloads of Poles from the Byelorussian republic left the towns of Baranowicze, Stołpce,

Grodno and Wolkowysk on 12 December 1944 – before the winter offensive began.[22]

We can speculate as to whether the desire for haste was more motivated by a wish by Moscow to see Poles leaving Soviet territory or, as seems more likely, an attempt to promote the speedy – and, it would be hoped, irreversible – colonisation of the German territories handed to Poland.[23] Whatever the reason, the transports had to be stopped, not only because of the resumption of military activity, but also because there were difficulties in settling the transferees. Some 200 000 refugees had already flooded into central Poland, and were being temporarily accommodated in villages and on estates in the Lublin and Rzeszów administrative districts. But until the western districts were cleared of German troops and their inhabitants expelled, and farms and apartments abandoned, there was insufficient space to locate newcomers.

On a personal level, the decisions to be taken by potential repatriates were agonising. In some areas, the question of identity and national affiliation was particularly complex. In the Byelorussian regions, for example, a considerable number of people in the Polesie marsh region regarded themselves as '*tutejsi*' (local, from hereabouts) and did not feel a particularly strong pull to either Polish or Byelorussian communities. They were more attached to their homes and their land. By contrast, for those of Polish stock from the former '*kresy wschodnie*' to leave during 1944, while the war was still continuing, was tantamount to betrayal of the Polish cause; by leaving apartments, farms, houses and villages to the new 'hosts' – national groups such as the Lithuanians, Byelorussians and Ukrainians – they were serving the immediate and long-term aims of the Soviet regime. Once these territories were denuded of ethnic Polish stock, it would be difficult for Polish statesmen and diplomats to argue for their restoration to Poland. The Polish Government in London, aware of this problem, had advised the Home Army to do its utmost to prevent a mass exodus of the Polish population at the time it issued orders for the 'Burza' operation at the end of 1943.[24] Remaining behind signalled a determination to fight for one's home and community; leaving was equivalent to resignation, giving up. As one report summarised the situation: 'There began on the part of each Pole a struggle with his conscience. . . . He loved his true homeland, but also loved the village of his ancestors. . . .'[25]

In the period to the end of 1944, therefore, only 117 212 repatriates – all from the Ukrainian SSR – entered Poland. The fact that most of these repatriates originated from the southern regions indicates the change

that conflict with Ukrainian nationalists had brought about. The
maraudings of the *Banderowcy* had convinced many people, especially
those most exposed to danger in the countryside, that they had to move
to regions where the authorities could do a better job of protecting
them. But the violence of war and ethnic strife had also, for many,
brought about a change in attitudes – a heightened sense of their ties
to Poland and the need for the homeland.[26]

In the Lithuanian and Byelorussian republics, an interesting problem was posed by the existence of small Karaite and Tartar communities.
A 'long correspondence' evidently took place between the Poles and
the Lithuanian authorities regarding some 1500 Karaite families in the
Vilnius region. (The source of this information gives no indication as
to how the matter was resolved.) The Byelorussian authorities reportedly refused to allow Tartar and Karaite communities within their republic to leave for Poland, although statistics show that some 1437
Tartars apparently did so.[27]

The repatriation movement really gathered momentum during the
following year (1945). This was due to a number of factors. One was
no doubt the news of the Yalta conference, when there could no longer
be any doubt that the former eastern *kresy* had been handed to Moscow and the need for a decision become more evident. Also, the advance of the Soviet–German front, when the offensive resumed in January,
meant that the territories granted to Poland as compensation for its
losses in the east were soon conquered and the expulsion of the German population could begin.

ZPP officials who visited Lwów during March 1945 reported that
the number of Poles registering for transfer was rising in direct relation to the liberation of Polish territory. In Lwów, despite the underground authorities' campaign to prevent the Polish element of the
population leaving, which had been long and intense, a turnaround in
attitudes had occurred. There was a widely-voiced concern as to whether
the official repatriation agreement would cease to be effective once
the official termination date of 1 April had been passed. In other words,
the prospect that the decision-making period was coming to an end
was helping to concentrate people's minds.[28]

On 16 March 1945 the Polish Council of Ministers (of a Polish
Provisional Government which was as yet unrecognised by the western powers) authorised the State Repatriation Bureau (PUR) to set up
branches in the 'recovered territories'.[29] All repatriates – and most of
those refugees who had arrived in Poland before the formal repatriation process began – were henceforth directed to these western re-

gions. Now mass repatriation by the trainload was theoretically possible – but it remained hampered by transport difficulties. The Chief Plenipotentiary in March 1945 described the situation as 'desperate' (*rozpaczliwa*).[30] This was not surprising, given the extent of the military activity there had been on Polish soil and destruction of rolling stock, track, signalling equipment, etc.

In the course of 1945, 720 573 Poles (including Polish Jews) were repatriated from the three neighbouring republics. This included 73 042 from Lithuania, 135 654 from Byelorussia and 511 877 from Ukraine. The average monthly figure for movements was just over 60 000, but this average disguises a particularly strong movement during the second and third quarters of the year, which indicates no doubt a preference to travel during the summer months, when weather conditions were much milder.

Table 7.1   Repatriation from the neighbouring Soviet republics (i.e. from former Polish territory) 1944–48[31]

	Lithuanian SSR	*Byelorussian SSR*	*Ukrainian SSR*
1944	—	—	117 212
1945	73 042	135 654	511 877
1946	123 443	136 419	158 435
1947	671	2 090	76
1948	—	—	74
Total	197 156	274 163	787 674

Many of the repatriates were directed to the 'recovered territories'. A large number (31 596) of those transferring from Lithuania, for example, moved to the Olsztyn region of what had been East Prussia. Other large groups moved to the Gdansk region (31 842), Szczecin (13 946) and Wrocław (18 050). An overwhelming majority (247 936) of those from Byelorussia settled in the four provinces of Gdańsk, Szczecin, Poznań and Wrocław (but none, interestingly, moved to Olsztyn or Silesia). The movement from the Ukraine followed a slightly different pattern. Again, the vast majority (612 405) settled in the 'recovered' territories – Wrocław again proving popular (216 483) and Silesia providing a new home for almost a quarter of a million (232 111). The earlier, 'wild' migration – or flight – of Poles from the Ukrainian republic during 1944 resulted in early settlement in the central provinces (especially Lublin, Kielce and Rzeszów regions), but thereafter this diminished.[32]

REPATRIATION FROM THE INTERIOR OF THE USSR

On 6 July 1945, a further agreement was signed in Moscow between
Zygmunt Modzelewski, the representative of the Polish Provisional
Government of National Unity (its Polish acronym TRJN) and Andrei
Vyshinsky on behalf of the Soviet authorities.[33] This further repatriation agreement, signed by a Polish government which had now been
accorded full diplomatic recognition by the Western powers, contained
similar provisions to the earlier agreements, but extended their geographical scope. The Soviet Government agreed to grant to 'Poles and
Polish Jews who were citizens *living in the USSR* the right to renounce
their Soviet citizenship in favour of Polish and the choice of returning
to Poland if they so wished'.

As before, the agreement related to those who could prove that they
were citizens of the Polish Republic before 17 September 1939. As a
matter of form, both to maintain balance and to keep to the pattern set
by the earlier treaties, the Polish side agreed to extend to 'Russians,
Ukrainians, Byelorussians, Ruthenians and Lithuanians' the right to
change their Polish citizenship should they wish, and move to Soviet
territory.[34] Once again, too, the agreement listed the categories of people
entitled to accompany the individual repatriate, stating that 'other relatives,
irrespective of nationality, [might be included] if they were part of a
single economic unit and expressed a wish to move'.[35] This gave the
opportunity, therefore, to Poles who had married local inhabitants, to
go back to Poland with them. However, the right of option had to be
exercised by all adults within the family as individuals; the household
head could not automatically register all his family members for return.[36]

Those leaving for Poland were entitled to take with them all personal belongings, except certain items which it was forbidden to export from the USSR. The weight of these goods was not to exceed
two tons for farming families, one ton for urban families. It seems
unlikely that many Poles returning from exile in the furthest reaches
of the USSR had this weight of worldly goods to bring with them.
Nor that many 'artists, engineers, researchers and other professionals'
would have had professional equipment and tools with them. However, we must remember that the Moscow agreement was modelled on
the earlier agreements of September 1944 providing for exchange of
populations across the new Polish–Soviet frontier. People leaving their
homes in Lwów, Vilnius, Grodno or Łuck would certainly have wanted
to carry as much as possible with them. Repatriates were also able to
take with them cash to the value of 1000 roubles, much less than the

5000 allowed to transferees from the former Polish *kresy wschodnie*.[37]

Under the further terms of the agreement, a Polish–Soviet Commission to supervise the repatriation movement was called into being. It had six representatives – three from each side – and the Polish members (H. Wolpe, A. Juszkiewicz, J. Kuczyński) were all members of the ZPP. TASS news agency reported that the Commission began its work on 25 July – some two-and-a-half weeks after the signing of the agreement. The Commission had the task of broadcasting news of the repatriation to Poles. It also had the right to appoint its representatives to areas of Polish concentration, with the aim of settling matters relating to their registration and evacuation. Over one hundred were selected for work at local level and at the border crossing-points. In fact, this work was entrusted to the ZPP, which was also called on to finance the repatriation operation on Soviet territory.[38]

Those wishing to take advantage of the option were enjoined to register by 1 November 1945. This was a tall order, given the size of the country and the remoteness of some centres of Polish settlement.[39] Even more unlikely was the stated aim of carrying out the transfer, not later than 1 December 1945. The deadlines were subsequently extended to 1 January 1945 and 15 June 1945 respectively – but return movements took place well after this. Statistics from official sources show that return from the 'interior' of the USSR only began in late 1945 and gathered momentum during 1946 when the overwhelming majority were transferred. 'Stragglers' continued to be moved, at an average of some 2000 every three months, until the end of 1948.[40]

Priority in repatriating Poles was to be given to military families (i.e. families of those serving in the 1st Polish Army), but farmers and highly-skilled workers – people who would be of most help in rebuilding the economy and infrastructure of their war-shattered country – were also given preference.[41] A geographical order of priority was also established: first, those from the eastern and northern regions of the USSR where the climate was most severe; second, those from the European part of the country; third, those from other regions, including the southern, Asiatic republics.[42]

The ZPP leadership attempted to make political capital out of the agreement, pointing out with some satisfaction that the displaced Poles in the USSR were the first overseas contingent to be returning home *en masse*. This illustrated the political wisdom of the 'democratic camp' (the ZPP) and was a blow to the traitorous reactionary forces which were attempting 'with all their might to oppose the return of millions of their compatriots from Germany, France, England and other countries'.

The repatriation agreement gives the lie to the suggestions of the reactionaries, who feeding on the patriotic feelings of Poles in the USSR, on their longing for their homeland, murmured that not all would return to Poland, attempting to cause divisions among the refugee group. The repatriation agreement is based on the principle of universality and opens the way to Poland for all those former Polish citizens wishing to return to their homeland. This is taking place because the agreement which has been concluded is an expression of the most accommodating response of the Soviet Union to the requests of Polish refugees in the USSR, it is the fruit of Polish–Soviet friendship.[43]

The first point to be made is, of course, that not all 'former Polish citizens' were able to return to their homeland. Those of Ukrainian, Byelorussian or Lithuanian extraction were certainly not. It is known also that many thousands of NKVD captives in prisons and labour camps were not included in the spirit of this agreement. But a further difficulty relates to the phrase 'return to their homeland'. Kersten points out that most of those Poles who were east of the prewar frontier came from the *kresy wschodnie* – the former eastern Polish provinces annexed by Moscow. She writes that their choice was therefore 'of moving to Poland or moving back to their former homes, or resigning themselves to Soviet citizenship. . . .'[44] There is no indication in the official agreement that the right of 'option' exercised by these refugees extended to being taken back to their former homes in Western Ukraine and Western Byelorussia – a region from which, as we know, Poles were being resettled. Another Polish author cites letters reaching the ZPP representatives from Poles asking to be returned to their former homes in the *kresy*. The desire to be reunited with their families and return to family homes and property was mentioned as justification.[45] However, he gives no indication as to whether these requests were successful. If true, it would mean that the Soviet authorities agreed to a relocation, or internal migration. Leading on from this, it is not clear why such a move, were it approved, should have been carried out within the framework of a 'repatriation' operation.

How many people were expected to register for transfer to Poland? By contrast with the situation in the former *kresy wschodnie*, where Polish residents in many areas were undecided about the wisdom of moving, those Poles who had been displaced to the Soviet interior had no such qualms. There was an eagerness to register which amounted to desperation in some cases. How desperate this urge was can be judged from the firsthand account by Maria Łęczycka, appointed ZPP delegate for the Semipalatynsk region of Kazakhstan:

> On the first day at four o'clock in the morning a crowd of some four and a half thousand people gathered in front of the main NKVD building. Even though the documents concerning change of citizenship had to be dealt with in alphabetical order, everybody came on this first day. Even the Zalewskis, Zakolickis and Zyzwaks. There was no force on earth that could chase away this weeping, impoverished, feverish vortex. They stood until late in the evening, only to begin their vigil at dawn the next day. Thus it continued for thirty hot, work-filled days of the 'option', until the last Zyzwak had added his signature. . . .[46]

The Mixed Commission established that some 273 321 people on Soviet territory had the right to opt for Polish citizenship and return to Poland. This estimate was based on ZPP reports, yet A. Juszkiewicz, the Secretary-General of the ZPP, estimated the number of Poles in the further Soviet republics as 400 000, a figure repeated by W. Wolski, the deputy Minister for Repatriation.[47] On 8 June 1945, the Repatriation Bureau (PUR) estimated that the number of Polish 'emigrants' in the USSR was 750 000.[48] The ZPP figure is considerably lower than London Polish circles would have accepted, on the basis of those deported, taken into captivity as POWs and mobilised to the Red Army during the period 1939–41. It seems certain that the ZPP had not penetrated to all groups of Poles, many of whom were living in extremely isolated regions. The ZPP figure was subsequently revised downwards – to 248 000 – as a result of the first slow movement of repatriation which took place over the second half of 1945. A breakdown of the figure according to republics shows that the majority were in the Russian Federative Republic, with large colonies in Kazakhstan, Uzbekistan and eastern Ukraine:

RSFSR	107 249
Kazachstan	63 933
Ukraine	30 862
Uzbekistan	29 574
Kirghiz	11 387
Tadzikistan	4 000
Turkmenistan	940
Georgia	200[49]

Łęczycka's memoir gives a rare view of the role of the ZPP delegates. Although not a communist herself, like many others she became drawn into the work of the ZPP, partly through the need to find work to support not only herself, but her parents and children. Naturally, the registration process threw up some anomalies and some cases which caused doubt and anguish. The rule that Poles could take their local spouses with them was carried out, but not always smoothly. Łęczycka describes how a Polish agronomist, his Russian doctor-wife and their four-year-old son were booked to leave on the first transport, but did not arrive in time for the nine o'clock departure. Had the wife, she wondered, changed her mind about travelling to Poland? If so, then the husband was faced with the difficult decision of whether to leave for Poland alone, or to remain in Kazakhstan as a Soviet citizen. The train's departure was delayed, however, and the couple arrived at the station some time after the scheduled departure, to explain breathlessly that the wife's parents, concerned for her future happiness, had locked them into a room of their house, in order to prevent them leaving. Only after ten o'clock, when they were convinced the train had left, did they release the couple.[50]

Not all Poles wished partners to accompany them. One Lothario from Lwów, who had enjoyed great success among the female population of Semipalatynsk, had married a local girl during his stay. When the time came to leave, he informed the delegate that his wife would be following him on a later transport. Subsequently, it became clear that he had not signed the necessary authorisation papers and, as both Polish and Soviet representatives concluded, had decided to abandon her. The young wife, five months pregnant and inconsolable, was convinced that it was a mistake and took to camping outside the delegate's office.[51]

In another case, described by Łęczycka, the Polish widow of a former *osadnik wojskowy* (military settler in the former eastern provinces of the Polish Republic) had married a Soviet citizen, a resident of the Zan-Semia township, Łęczycka writes that the choice before her was either to stay with her new husband, or return to Poland without him. (The obvious conclusion is that while Polish men could take their new partners with them, Polish women did not enjoy the same right – although the Repatriation Agreement had not discriminated in this way.) The woman had a 12-year-old daughter, who was desperately eager to return to Poland but, as a minor, could not travel without her mother. On the evening that the last transport left Semipalatynsk, the girl arrived at the station, to inform the delegate that her mother had been taken to a mental hospital. Her last chance of returning to Poland had vanished. Since she was not yet 14 years old, she could not exercise the right of option herself. Yet as her mother had not died, she could not be repatriated as an orphan either. She was thus compelled to remain in the Soviet Union, dependent upon a father-in-law who was good to her mother but with whom she herself did not get on.[52]

The repatriation of Polish children in orphanages, in schools, and those who had been 'adopted' by Polish or Soviet families required special attention. The repatriation Agreement had specified that the repatriation of Polish children and their guardians should be carried out in an organised manner. There were estimated to be some 5000 children in orphanages and homes, with a further 700 children in schools.[53] The first transports of children left at the end of February 1946 and during early March. On 20 March a train left the Byelorussian Station in Moscow with 103 Polish children on board. They were aged between 2 and 16 and had come from a home at Zagorsk. At the station to bid farewell were Soviet and Polish representatives, including Wanda Wasilewska, representing the ZPP, who made a speech of farewell.[54]

Transports of children returning from the USSR were directed to institutions in Poland which had been prepared to receive them. Thus children from the Zagorsk home were directed to a home near Bielany; children from an orphanage at Chkalovsk went to Szklarska Poręba in Lower Silesia.[55] On 16 June 1946 the last transport of Polish children left Kozielsk in Siberia and six weeks later crossed the Polish border. By then all the children registered – 5079 – had been brought back to Poland. But this was only a fraction of the estimated 50 000 children whom the Polish Government had wanted to evacuate from Soviet territory in 1942.[56]

A Polish journalist, meeting some of the returning children at a dispersal point near Gostynin, marvelled at the fact that after so many years of exile they had not forgotten how to speak Polish, and that they had passed the whole of the tiring journey in tolerably good conditions.[57] The overall picture was neither so straightforward nor so positive as far as retention of Polish identity and language were concerned. Many of the younger children, especially those who were orphaned early and taken into care by Russian foster parents, rapidly forgot their native language. Maria Łęczycka reports touring Soviet orphanages and kolkhozes to find and gather Polish children, some of whom had been adopted by Kazakh or Russian families. They were covered in fleas, half-wild and worked as shepherds. Most had forgotten their parents and their Polish. Some were even resentful when repatriation officials appeared with a view to tearing them away from their adopted families:

At the last moment, when the doors of the wagons had been slammed shut, I received the information that two children who had not been included in the list – Franek and Marysia Sobiepański – remained in one of the suburbs of Semipalatynsk. I held up the train's departure, to the great irritation of the station master. Accompanied by the secretary of the ZPP and the head of the Polish orphanage I travelled to the address indicated. In a small, free-standing wooden house, I found the door open. In the first room next to a cobbler's last sat a boy of perhaps thirteen, dressed in an apron. With precision and with assured blows he was hammering at a large, man's leather sole. Next to him stood a small girl with a snub nose, who was at the most six years old. She was eating a piece of bread that had been thickly smeared with crackling. She watched me with wide, black eyes.

– Are you called Franciszek and Maria Sobiepański? I asked.

– The boy nodded from the height of the cobbler's bench.

– *Da. A kakoye vam dieło?*

So he understood Polish well, but spoke Russian like a native of Semipalatynsk.

– We have come for you, we are going to take you to Poland.

– *Nie znayu* – he replied with indifference – *papasza* will soon be here and then you can talk with him. Please wait.

He continued hammering at the sole. Marysia looked at me enquiringly. Her chubby face moved ceaselessly. I tried to engage her in conversation. She did not understand me. Then I turned to the boy, standing silently.

– Have you lived in this house for long?

– *Nie znayu.*

– Do you remember your mother?

– *Niczego nie znayu.*

– Would you like to travel to Poland?

– *Czort s vami i s vaszej Polszej!* When *papasza* comes you can talk to him.

– *Da! Pridiot papka. Siejczas pridiot* – the little one warbled – *i mamasza toze pridiot.*

I began to feel uncomfortable. I sensed that the matter would not be settled without a scene. The children had forgotten completely that they were Poles. And they felt at home here, as they would have with their real parents. I was curious to know how their guardians would react. At the sight of us *papasza* and *mamasza* widened their eyes. When I showed them the document from our consulate,

stamped by the Soviet authorities, empowering me to collect Polish orphans wherever I might find them, they burst out laughing so heartily that I felt, in my honoured post as local repatriation delegate, irritated.
– There's no reason to laugh – I stated coldly – the children must return to Poland! I am responsible for that!

Papasza looked at me with a jovial expression and replied merrily:
– *Idi k czortu! Moya dorogaya!* I will not give you the children, *moya dorogaya! Ja ich polubił, moya dorogaya! Ja ich kormil, moya dorogaya! Wot i Wsio, moya dorogaya!*

He sat down on a stool, took a little tobacco out of a pouch and looked around for the local newspaper with which to roll a cigarette. He was laughing the whole time. I tried to convince him, arguing that their mother's family were waiting for them in Poland, that they would be well looked after in Poland, that as a Polish consular representative I had no right to leave them, since they were Polish and not Russian orphans!

He lit his cigarette. Looking at me through a thick cloud of smoke he again burst out laughing, as though he had heard something unusually funny:
– Orphans! What orphans? . . . They are not orphans! They have a mother and a father! Tell your consulate that Vasyl Antonowicz Grigorenko will not give up his children and *wsio! Poniatno? . . . Doczenka! –* he turned to the little girl – do you want to go to Poland without *papka?*

The girl knitted her brows in a severe expression:
– *Nie choczu.*
Franek standing near *mamasza* in an aggressive posture, added:
– *Ja toze nie choczu nikakoy Polszy!*
I knew that without the help of a militiaman I was going to get nowhere. I returned with one after an hour. By now the old man had stopped laughing. he scowled. He and his wife stood in front of us, shielding the frightened children.
– What right do you have to them, why do you dare to oppose the authorities in this way? I asked in irritation.
His beard shook.
– What right? – he shouted – a human being's right. I gave four sons to the Red Army. Four sons have met their death in this war. Two are lying somewhere on the other side of Warsaw. This gives me the right to these children! Don't take them away from me, *moya dorogaya!* Their mother died five years ago. She asked me to look after the children. She shared my house. She was good, kind. We

became attached to them as though they were our own. We are old and alone. My wife is too old to bear any more children. And she cares for Maria as though she were her own.[58]

Despite this appeal the children were returned to Poland, but not before – the train having been delayed yet longer in Semipalatynsk – they had once more escaped and returned to their adoptive Russian parents.

Although the Polish and Soviet authorities began early on to make arrangements for the repatriation, the movements themselves hardly gathered momentum at all during the second half of 1945. This was caused by a number of factors; the difficulties of obtaining rolling stock, the widespread dispersal of the Polish population (some lived 200–300 km from the nearest railway station), and also weather conditions, as delays lasted until the end of the year. For people who had heard rumours as early as March 1945 that repatriation might be on the cards, then that it would take place in the autumn, then (in October) that it would not take place until the following spring, the waiting bred impatience, cynicism and doubts over whether the movement would ever take place at all. Rumours circulated that only the *Kościuszkowcy* families (i.e. relatives of soldiers serving in the Kościuszko Division) and those who declared themselves to be communists would be permitted to return.[59]

The ZPP itself received letters from the regions protesting about the delay, and bemoaning the poor conditions Poles were living under. Many feared that they could not survive another winter. The ZPP group in Pavlodar wrote:

We have been waiting six years for this moment. 1945 is drawing to a close and still we hear nothing of the evacuation. . . . Autumn has come and with it mud, cold; people are working in the vineyards barefoot and in rags. The work is hard. . . .

The Polish population, both children and adults, are emaciated by malaria, which in these regions is chronic, there are no medicines. People fall ill and walk about like shadows. On 7 October they gave us three days off work, but over the same period refused to give us any food. After the signing of the repatriation agreement, the attitude of the local authorities towards us has changed for the worse.[60]

Because of the continued postponement of the transport movement, the desperation to be included in the first transport exceeded all rational bounds. Although the categories of people to be sent home first had been set out in the Repatriation Agreement, nevertheless people fought for the chance to join it. In Semipalatynsk windows of the ZPP delegate's office were smashed and the door broken in. Attempts were made both to bribe and threaten the delegate, who had to return to her quarters in the evening under guard.[61]

A further factor delaying the return movements – although it may have been an incidental consideration – was the poor physical and psychological state of many of the refugees. Considerable efforts were made to ensure that the Poles' lack of clothing, footwear and food was made good. Distributions by the ZPP of UNRRA and Red Cross welfare goods, was supplemented, according to reports, by gifts from local Soviet administrations in some cases. In addition to improving their physical condition, the ZPP also made efforts to cultivate a positive attitude towards the Soviet Union by means of rallies, meetings and lectures. There was a clear campaign both to avoid a public relations disaster by sending the refugees back to Poland in a half-starved state, and also to wean the Poles away from the hostility and loathing that most felt for the Soviet regime.

The departure of the first transports took place in a festival atmosphere, with flowers, speeches, bands, songs, votes of thanks, etc. These carnivals were not spontaneous local affairs but were orchestrated by the ZPP hierarchy and were part of its political campaign. In instructions to local delegates the ZPP administration recommended,

> Immediately before the departure a farewell rally should be organised for those leaving, in the course of which the Polish emigrants' achievements in the USSR generally, and in the locality particularly, and the problems of the task facing us in Poland in the future, should be set out. At these rallies too resolutions should be passed concerning the repatriates' readiness to undertake the rebuilding of our homeland, and also to thank the Soviet Union for its hospitality.[62]

As the transports prepared to leave, papers were checked and gifts were handed out for the journey. For the first transport to leave Semipalatynsk, linen and money were distributed. The first to leave Kiev was a transport of some 63 wagons (1160 people) on 1 February 1946. (It had been due to leave some three weeks earlier, but had been held back through lack of warm clothing and footwear; this was then supplied by the Soviet authorities.) Since it was still winter the trucks had been prepared with small stoves, sleeping bunks, fuel and lighting. A doctor and two nurses accompanied the transport and the repatriates received food for twelve days. Their documents included authorisations signed by both Polish and Soviet delegates, enabling them to cross the frontier. The repatriates were sent on their way with a ceremony in which ZPP took part. A Polish engineer thanked the ZPP representatives on behalf of those departing, and also acknowledged the goodwill and help of the Soviet authorities.[63]

From Semipalatynsk, four main transports, or *eszelons*, left, at intervals of approximately three weeks. The first, as we have already heard, carried the military families, farmers, specialists and skilled workers and, as Łęczycka describes, expectant mothers. It left in March 1946 and was preceded here, as elsewhere, only by transports of children duly clothed, fed and supplied for the journey. The third carried mainly Jews who had been deported in June 1940. The fourth and final transport had to stop to pick up latecomers – some fifty or so Poles who had been hospitalised (typhus) and unable to register earlier.[64]

Between 3 and 14 February some ten transports left the Ukraine for Poland, taking repatriates from centres such as Poltava, Czernikov, Zhitomir, Sumy, and Zaporoza. In keeping with the planning of the Mixed Commission, transports from the whole of the Russian Federative Republic were to be moved during March–May 1946; in the period April–May, refugees from Central Asia were to be moved, and in the summer months those from the southern republics. On 17 February a transport carrying 3000 people left the Voronez *obwod*. On 11 March a transport leaving the Byelorussia Station in Moscow carried all those who, until then, had been resident in the Moscow area, the majority being workers from industrial plants just outside the city. On 13 March there were 1000 people in the first transport to leave Novosibirsk – 70 per cent of them military families. On 20 March the first transport to leave Chkalov carried with it 1307 people. Altogether, in the seven weeks between 1 February and 20 March, some 56 000 Poles returned to their homeland as a result of the repatriation scheme. They passed through border check-posts, such as those at Brześć, Medyka and Jagodzin, where their documents were checked by representatives of the Mixed Commission. Within Poland, as the transports moved west, staging-posts had been set up at which the repatriates could receive hot food.[65]

There were some Poles who 'returned' by an unimaginably complicated route. Among them were the Poles whose homes lay beyond the new Polish–Soviet border, but had been drafted as forced labour to the Reich. When liberated by the Allies they often lacked the documentary proof of their Polish nationality. In the course of 1945 a number of these Poles found themselves at Włodzimierz, which was the main centre of concentration for Polish citizens returning from Germany. One young Pole from Złoczów (Tarnopol province) was liberated by the Americans at the beginning of May 1945 but thereafter, in company with Russian repatriates, travelled via Hungary and Austria to Moscow. There he was able to write a letter to the ZPP, appealing for help in repatriating him.[66]

The total number of Poles repatriated at this time from the interior of the USSR (i.e. beyond the 'Riga Line') was as follows:

1945	22 058
1946	221 717
1947	7 964
1948	7 251
Total	258 990[67]

When added to the number who arrived in Poland from the newly-acquired western regions of the USSR, the total of Poles 'repatriated' during the period was 1 517 983. The repatriates were once again directed in the main to the former German territories in the north and west. A mere 6029 settled in the central region of Poland and these were latecomers, most of whom did not return until 1948.

Help for the repatriation movement sometimes came from unexpected quarters. In June 1946, when the date for the transfer of Poles from the Vilnius region (and from Polesie, Nowogródek) was fast running out, 400 000 Poles, who had opted to leave, put off their departure, refusing to leave. Jakub Berman, Polish Politbureau member with responsibility for ideological and security questions, asked Labour Party politician Karol Popiel to act as an intermediary by asking the Roman Catholic Church for help in speeding the repatriation process. After Popiel had held talks with the Episcopate, the Church did indeed make an appeal to Poles in the former eastern provinces to travel to Poland.[68]

Among the 217 144 Poles who returned during the first half of 1946, more than half – 136 500 – were Jews.[69] But the majority of Jews did not intend to settle in Poland, and many of those who did were quickly dissuaded – by the prevailing atmosphere, particularly hostile towards those who attempted to reclaim property. Most migrated onwards – to North America, Western Europe, or Israel.

There seems to be a fixed pattern to the wanderings of these Jews. They return to their country; they look around and do not find any of their families, relatives and friends; they bid farewell to the ashes of their dearest ones and to the ruins of their homes and their communities; then they proceed directly to the West, towards the strategic passageways, towards the 'gates' that lead to Palestine and to other lands overseas.[70]

The final meeting of the Polish–Soviet Commission for Repatriation took place on 30 April 1949, and the conclusion of the repatriation scheme was discussed. Despite the air of satisfaction and mutual congratulation which abounded, it is clear that a considerable number of Poles – Polish citizens in September 1939 – remained on Soviet territory.[71] Certainly numbers of Poles did choose to remain behind on Soviet territory. But written requests and appeals for help from Poles who wished to be repatriated continued to arrive at the Polish Embassy in Moscow. How many there were is uncertain, but it is known that in February 1947 the Chief Polish Plenipotentiary for Repatriation made a strong case for extending the validity of the repatriation scheme for three categories of people:

(a) Poles who had been pressed into Wehrmacht service and were being held by the Soviets as prisoners-of-war.
(b) Poles deported to the USSR during 1939–40 who had not been able to register and join the repatriation movement in time.
(c) Those civilians and members of the Polish Home Army who had been interned by the Soviet authorities during 1944–45 (and had not subsequently been released).[72]

FURTHER REPATRIATION IN THE 1950s

Pressures to reactivate talks with Moscow on repatriation came from Polish communities abroad, as well as from domestic opinion. But moves to bring yet more Poles home had to wait until the 'thaw' which followed the death of Stalin. In November 1956 Polish leaders Gomułka and Cyrankiewicz, visiting Moscow for talks, signed a declaration with their Soviet counterparts concerning the possibility of further repatriation. (Soviet signatories were Bulganin and Khrushchev, both of whom had had dealings with the Poles during the 1940s.) A further repatriation agreement was signed in Moscow on 25 March 1957, providing for the return of all those who, for whatever reason, had been unable to take advantage of the earlier scheme.[73]

In most respects the 1957 agreement mirrors those of 1944–45. An initial deadline for registration of 1 October 1958 was eventually extended by a further twelve months. However, a significant departure from the wording of the 1940s agreements was Article 3. This allowed for Poles in Red Army service to be demobilised and repatriated. Even more surprisingly, though, it provided for Poles in places of confinement to be released, whether or not their sentences had run their course, and be either repatriated or handed over to the Polish authorities.

In one sense, then, this was a precedent – although it should be remembered that the earlier agreements had been accompanied by a separate 'amnesty' for Poles (however loosely observed by the NKVD). Moreover, there is some evidence that Poles returning from Soviet camps and handed over to the Polish authorities soon found themselves again incarcerated. A number of such 'criminals' were placed in camps near Warsaw before angry protests from the local population forced the authorities to release them after a matter of weeks. Still others were retained by the Soviet security forces. These included Poles sentenced on the basis of paragraphs 58/6 (spying) and 58/8 (terrorism) of the Soviet penal code. Home Army soldiers held by SMERSH were brought together in transit camps before being despatched to camps in distant Siberia.[74]

Expectations were that some 400 000–500 000 Poles would benefit from this new repatriation agreement, but such hopes were disappointed. The figures for repatriation were as follows:

1955	6 429
1956	30 786
1957	93 872
1958	85 865
1959	28 400
Total	245 000[75]

It can be seen from this table that the beginnings of the renewed movement started in 1955. This was not only before the formal agreement had been signed, but before the Moscow declaration signed by Gomułka and Khrushchev. It is not clear why or how the repatriation flow started so early.[76] Indeed, information on this later wave of repatriates is scarce. There is little knowledge of their origins. One author has stated that only 50 000 came from the Soviet interior (the rest presumably coming from the former Polish territories) but he does not justify such a figure.[77] There is no knowledge either of where the newcomers were settled; whether they were 'directed' to the west, as previous repatriates had been. Certainly, those who had been deported from the re-

gions east of the River Bug were not permitted to return to homes in
Lwów, Tarnopol or Vilnius. Most made their way to the 'recovered
territories' to where kin and friends had been resettled.

POSTSCRIPT

In the first postwar Soviet Census in 1959, the number of ethnic Poles
throughout the Union was stated as 1 380 622. The most significant
concentrations were in Byelorussia (538 881), Ukraine (363 297), Lithuania (230 107), the Russian republic (118 422), Latvia (59 774) and
Kazakhstan (53 102). In percentage terms, the Polish element in the
Soviet population, and in the individual republics, was insignificant.
Only in Lithuania, where it constituted between 7 and 8 per cent of
the overall population and was very much concentrated in the south-
east of the country around Vilnius and Soleczniki, has the Polish element been of any political importance.

However, these figures, and subsequent Census returns, are believed
to understate the Polish element, since great pressure was brought to
bear on Poles not to declare themselves as such – often at the cost of
release from labour camps or conditions of exile. On the other hand,
the nationality declaration in a Soviet passport does not tell us a great
deal about the closeness of the individual's ties with Poland, or with
Polish language and culture. A Soviet ethnographic atlas published in
the 1960s shows pockets of Poles in rural areas of the Ukraine around
Zhitomir and Berdichev – that is, in areas which have not been part of
Poland since the late eighteenth century. But most of the Poles in
these communities speak little Polish and their links with their ethnic
homeland and its culture are tenuous. Another factor to be taken into
account is that the Polish element has been eroded by intermarriage
and gradual assimilatory pressures – difficult to resist for the deported
and dispersed Poles, cast, like their nineteenth-century forebears, far
from their family homes.

The Soviet Census shows a gradual decline in overall numbers of
Poles over subsequent decades:

1970	1 167 525
1979	1 151 000
1989	1 126 334

Although these figures cover a significant decrease in two of the largest
(and adjacent) communities – in Ukraine and Byelorussia – there have

been healthy increases in Lithuania and, surprisingly, in Kazakhstan. It remains to be seen what figures for the Polish element will be provided by the first post-Soviet censuses conducted in the individual republics. By the time these statistics are collected, the next large-scale repatriation movement of Poles may have begun.

Notes

PREFACE

1. K. Sword with N. Davies and J. Ciechanowski, *The Formation of the Polish Community in Great Britain, 1939–1950.* London, 1989.
2. N. Davies, *God's Playground. A History of Poland.* Vol. II. *1795 to the Present.* New York, 1984, p. 286.
3. E. Szemplińska, 'Krótka relacja z bogatego życia'. (Conversation with Jan Plater-Gajewski.) *Ład*, no. 35 (1988), pp. 3 and 14.
4. Throughout the communist period the academic historian who wanted to research the wartime experiences of Poles in the Soviet Union was compelled to consult materials held in Western archives such as the archive of the Sikorski Institute in London, or the holdings of the Hoover Institution in California.
5. There are three main collections of documents from the Moscow archives cited in this book. The first group, relating to the Katyn massacre and dealing with the administrative measures taken by the NKVD at the time, were handed over by President Gorbachev to General Jaruzelski during the spring of 1991. Many of these documents were published in the Warsaw paper *Rzeczpospolita* in the second half of 1991.

   The second group were made available to the Polish authorities in the late autumn of 1992 (some were handed to President Lech Wałęsa by a representative of the Russian President, Boris Yeltsin). These also concerned the Katyn massacre, and provide proof of Politburo approval for the extermination of the Polish officers, since a key document is signed by Stalin and other leaders. Some of these were published under the title *Katyn. Dokumenty Ludobóstwa.* Warsaw, 1992.

   Finally, a large collection of documents concerning the deportation of Soviet nationalities during the period 1920–57 has also emerged. These were obtained by Dr Martin McCauley of the School of Slavonic and East European Studies via contacts in Moscow in the course of 1992. They are to be published as a collection in the near future.
6. *Informator* of the Archiwum Wschodnie. Warsaw, undated.
7. W. Zygulski, 'Take us home'. *Warsaw Voice*, no. 11 (229). 14 March 1993. A great problem, both in Kazakhstan and in other republics, is knowing what the size of the operation is going to be. According to the 1989 Soviet Census, there were some 60 000 Poles in Kazakhstan. Polish community representatives put the number at nearer 200 000.

1 THE MASS MOVEMENT OF POLES TO THE USSR, 1939–41

1. According to V. Molotov, Soviet Commissar for Foreign Affairs, the Soviet Union annexed 196 000 sq. km. (52 per cent) of the prewar Polish Republic and increased its population by 13 million (40 per cent of the

prewar Polish population). *Documents on Polish Soviet Relations (DPSR)*. Vol. 1. London, 1961, p. 68.

2. See J. Gross, 'The First Soviet-Sponsored Election in Eastern Europe'. *East European Politics and Society*. Vol. 1, no. 1 (Winter 1987), pp. 4–29. Also (in Polish) Gross, 'Wybory'. *Aneks* (London), no. 45 (1987), pp. 129–60 and 'Wybory II'. *Aneks*, no. 46–7 (1987).

3. See, for example, the German–Soviet Boundary and Friendship Treaty of 28 September 1939, in which it is stated (Article III) that, 'The necessary reorganisation of public administration will be effected west of the (agreed demarcation line) by the Government of the German Reich, in the areas east of this line by the Government of the USSR.' *DPSR*, p. 52.

4. J. Gross, 'Wywózki'. *Aneks* (London) no. 51–2 (1988), pp. 46–7.

5. Ibid., p. 52. The term 'passport' is sometimes used in referring to these identity papers, and the process of issuing them is referred to as *paszportizatsiya*, from the Russian. This might be misleading to a Western reader, however, since the documents did not authorise ordinary Soviet citizens to travel abroad.

6. *Krasnaya Zviezda* (Red Star), No. 218/4667, 17 September 1940.

7. Quoted in Z. S. Siemaszko, 'Jeńcy wojenni'. *Zeszyty Historyczne* (Paris), no. 82 (1987), p. 101. Siemaszko suggests that the true number of Polish troops taken prisoner was 230 000. This matches the estimate made by Bogdan Podoski, *Polska–Wschodnia 1939–1941*. (Rome, 1946), p. 10. However, Podoski does not include the 12 000 Polish troops interned in Lithuania and Latvia who fell into Soviet hands when the Red Army occupied the Baltic States in the summer of 1940. *W sowieckim osaczeniu*. London, 1991, p. 54.

8. General Olszyna-Wilczyński, commander of the Grodno garrison, which had offered brave but ultimately futile resistance to the Red Army's advance, was dragged from his car by Red Army troops near the town of Sopóckinie and shot, together with his adjutant. The shooting was witnessed by his chauffeur and by his wife, who was accompanying him. K. Liszewski, *Wojna polsko–sowiecka 1939r*. London, 1986, p. 87.

9. Z. S. Siemaszko, 'O Polakach w ZSSR'. *Zeszyty Historyczne*. no. 31 (1975), pp. 174–5.

10. Colonel K. Rudnicki and General M. Karaszewicz-Tokarzewski were seized at the beginning of 1940 (though not together) while attempting to cross the demarcation line to Soviet-occupied eastern Poland. Rudnicki travelled as 'Józef Rumiński', while Tokarzewski travelled as 'Dr Mirony'. Their mission was to take command of the resistance movement in Lwów (ZWZ). Siemaszko (1991), p. 137. Rudnicki wrote about his experiences in his book *The Last of the Warhorses*. London, 1974, pp. 109–14.

11. However, some of those released at this time were subsequently caught up with their families in the mass waves of deportation in early 1940 – notably where the household head had in the meantime been arrested.

See the case of 'Witek', who fought in the battle for Lwów and was captured by the Soviets and allowed to return home some four months later. In the meantime his father, a power-station official, had been arrested and was held in a Soviet prison from November. 'Witek' and his family were taken during the April deportation. M. Januszkiewicz, *Kazachstan*. Paris, 1981, p. 20.

12. Following agreement with the Germans at diplomatic level and a decree
    from the Supreme Soviet, prisoners were exchanged at prearranged points
    on the Nazi–Soviet demarcation line. Although it is not known how many
    prisoners were handed over to Soviet charge, NKVD documents indicate
    that 42 492 prisoners were handed over to the Germans at two transfer-
    points in the four-week period between 24 October and 23 November.
    Rzeczpospolita (Warsaw), 21–2 July 1990.

13. Ibid.

14. J. Stypułkowski, *Droga do wojska*. London, 1967, pp. 57–63. Quoted in
    Siemaszko (1991), p. 39.

15. The Katyn tragedy has been widely discussed in the West since the war.
    See J. K. Zawodny, *Death in the Forest. The Story of the Katyn Forest
    Massacre*. London, 1962; C. Fitzgibbon, *Katyn Massacre*. London, 1977.
    Also, the memoirs of a survivor, S. Swianiewicz, *W cieniu Katynia*. Paris,
    1976. (Published in English under the title *In the Shadow of Katyn*.)
    J. Czapski, who in 1941 was ordered by General Anders to look for the
    missing Polish officers, wrote of his frustrating search in his *The Inhu-
    man Land*. London, 1987.

16. In the course of 1990 and 1991 Soviet archival documents concerning
    the fate of Polish prisoners interned at the three camps began to appear
    in published form. At the same time the Soviet authorities gave permis-
    sion for the exhumation of bodies from two mass graves at Kharkov and
    near Kalinin. The former was found to contain bodies of Polish officers
    from the Starobielsk camp, while the Kalinin site contained the bodies of
    prisoners from the Ostashkov camp. L. Bójko, 'Czarna droga Starobielska'.
    Gazeta Wyborcza, 29 May 1990; B. Węglarczyk, 'Pogrzeb ofiar
    Starobielska'. *Gazeta Wyborcza*, 12 August 1991.

17. For more on Berling's career and general biographical details, see J. Nowak,
    'Sprawa generała Berlinga' *Zeszyty Historyczne*, no. 37 (1976) and the
    same author's 'Jeszcze w sprawie Berlinga', *Zeszyty Historyczne* no. 41
    (1977). Berling wrote of his own period of service in the Polish Army in
    the USSR. See his 'Wspomnienia' in *Kultura* (Warsaw), 16, 23, 30 April
    and 21 May 1967; 5, 12 and 19 March 1977.
    A further small group led by reserve Captain Mikołaj Arciszewski went
    over to the Soviet side. When the Germans attacked the Soviet Union in
    1941, they were given training by the Soviets before being parachuted
    back into Poland (behind German lines) in August 1941. Arciszewski's
    intelligence work for the Soviets lasted almost a year, before the Ger-
    mans discovered him with his radio-set. He was shot by the Gestapo
    after interrogation. M. Turlejska, *Prawdy i fikcje*. Warsaw, 1968, pp. 643–4.

18. J. Gross, 'The Polish POW camps in the Soviet-occupied Western Ukraine'.
    In K. Sword (ed.), *The Soviet Takeover of the Polish Eastern Provinces,
    1939–41*. London, 1991, pp. 44–56.

19. An account of this journey based on the experiences of Sergeant W.
    Pasternak and A. Bierzyński was included in a report sent by General
    Karasiewicz-Tokarzewski to the Polish ambassador in the USSR, S. Kot,
    on 17 October 1941. Polish Institute and General Sikorski Museum, London.
    (PIGSM) A.9.III.2a/58.
    Z. S. Siemaszko has suggested – on the basis of the timing of the

prisoners' move – that it may have been linked to the murder of Polish officers in Katyn. Alternatively, that it was linked to strikes which broke out in Polish POW camps in Ukraine during the winter of 1939–40. Siemaszko (1991), pp. 44–5 and 56.

20. The categories of people to be deported included, apart from the more obvious 'enemies of Soviet rule' such as members of political parties and military or police personnel, the following: those travelling abroad, involved in overseas correspondence, or coming into contact with representatives of foreign states; esperantists; philatelists; those working with the Red Cross; refugees; smugglers; those dismissed from the Communist Party; priests and active members of religious congregations; and the nobility, landowners, wealthy merchants, bankers, industrialists, hotel and restaurant owners.

Source: Order no. 0054 issued by the People's Commissar for Internal Affairs of the Lithuanian SSR, Guzevicius. It was dated 28 November 1940. K. Pelekis, *Genocide: Lithuania's Threefold Tragedy*. Germany, 1949, pp. 30, 273–8.

21. Public Record Office, Kew. (PRO) Foreign Office General Correspondence Files. FO371/23159, C19080. Subsequently, as a result of Stańczyk's efforts, a TUC delegation headed by Sir Walter Citrine made representations on behalf of their fellow socialists at the Foreign Office.

22. G. Herling, *A World Apart*. Oxford, 1987. (Originally published by G. Herling-Grudziński under the title, *Inny Świat. Zapiski sowieckie*. Paris, 1985.)

The Soviets were very interested in Polish military potential and gathered detailed intelligence on their defensive capabilities. This much is proven by the author's conversations in a Soviet jail with Colonel Lavrenti Ivanovich, whose role in Soviet Army Intelligence had been to gather information about the Polish units on the eastern frontier. Ivanovich, writes Herling, 'knew the region like the back of his hand';

He could remember the dispositions of garrisons, regiments and divisions of the Polish frontier guard, as well as the names and the personal idiosyncracies of their commanding officers. . . . He asked me excitedly what part each had taken in the September campaign, as a ruined horse-owner might enquire about the performances of his horses on foreign race-tracks. (op. cit., p. 14)

23. Julian Stryjkowski has pointed out that monitoring of residents' movements by NKVD-trained janitors was more effective when the former did not have their own key, but had to ring on every occasion to be admitted. J. Stryjkowski, *Wielki Strach*. London, 1980, p. 130.

24. See, for example, the account by Beata Obertyńska (Marta Rudzka) in her *W domu niewoli*. Chicago, 1968 p. 21.

25. See similar account in Gross (1988) p. 147.

26. PIGSM Kol. 138/289 (1732).

27. PIGSM Kol. 138/289 (6584).

28. M. Begin, *White Nights*. London, 1977, p. 24.

29. Siemaszko (1975), p. 177.

30. According to a recently-released NKVD document, the number of people

in prisons in eastern Poland who were under sentence of 'the ultimate sanction' in March 1940 was some 11 000. *Katyn. Dokumenty ludobójstwa.* (Dokumenty i materiały archiwalne przekazane Polsce 14 października 1992r.) Warsaw, 1992, p. 39.

31. K. Zamorski, 'Arrest and Imprisonment in the Light of Soviet Law', in K. Sword (ed.), *The Soviet Takeover of the Polish Eastern Provinces.* London, 1991, p. 213.

32. Obertyńska (op. cit.), p. 236.

33. PIGSM Kol. 138/292 (12966).

34. For more details of the NKVD killings of prisoners and the forced evacuation marches, see J. Gross, *Revolution from Abroad. The Soviet Conquest of Poland's Western Ukraine and Western Byelorussia.* Princeton, NJ, 1988, pp. 178–86. Also N. Tolstoy, *Stalin's Secret War.* London, 1981, pp. 243–50.

   By the beginning of July 1941 word had already reached London of the murder of Polish prisoners in Lwów, before the Russians withdrew. The Germans were making a great deal of propaganda from the story. Foreign Office enquiries via Moscow elicited the following reply from ambassador Cripps:

   > Molotov has informed me in writing that amongst prisoners left at Lwów in Brigidki prison when Soviet forces withdrew, were not more than 150 Poles. Evacuation of these prisoners in existing conditions would have endangered their lives. 'A special investigation' has established that they were not ill-treated in any way. Molotov suggests that the Germans themselves may have butchered prisoners and accused the Soviet authorities to cover up their traces. . . .

   In the Foreign Office, F. K. Roberts wrote:

   > We cannot hope to know what really happened, but it is clearly politic to accept this statement at full value and to give it full publicity.

   PRO FO371 26755 C7693 and C7890. Cripps's telegram is dated 14 July 1941.
   This exchange – both the Soviet response to the massacre enquiry and the British resignation in the face of it – have uncomfortable similarities to the aftermath of the Katyn graves discovery almost two years later.

35. PIGSM A.9.III.2c/61, p. 28.

36. Studium Polski Podziemnej (SPP – Polish Underground Study Trust, London) 3.19.1 'Okupant Sowiecki, 1939–41' (Raporty). Dok.1 Raport z Lwówa (2.XII.1940).

   It may have been rumours of this kind – deliberately spread by the Soviet authorities – which eventually reached the Polish Government in the West and led to Sikorski's controversial aide-mémoire to the British Government of June 1940. Without consulting his ministerial colleagues, Sikorski raised the possibility of forming a 300 000-man Polish army in the Soviet Union. This was a reckless step at a time when Stalin was regarded by most Poles as an aggressor second only to Hitler. Sikorski was very nearly forced to resign over it. *DPSR*, p. 95.

37. Ibid.

38. PIGSM A.9.III.2c/61, p. 28.
39. The figure of 200 000 was arrived at by Polish Army historians and statistitians in the following way. Three age-cohorts were called up: those born in 1917, 1918 and 1919. A certain number born in 1920 and in the following two years were also taken (i.e. young men between the ages of 17 and 22 were taken). The total number of each cohort for the whole of Poland (based on Census figures) was approximately:

1917	175 000
1918	150 000
1919	205 000
1920	250 000

Since there were only some 13 million of Poland's prewar population of 35 million in these territories, one age-cohort from eastern Poland would have averaged some 70 000 young men. However, with war losses (killed, wounded, POWs), refugee flight to neighbouring states, evasion, and natural wastage, a figure of 55 000 taken for each of the main three cohorts may be more realistic. This would yield over 160 000. To this must be added the unknown number recruited from the younger three cohorts (1920–22) and it cannot be ruled out that members of the refugee population from Western Poland were also caught in the net. PIGSM Kol. 138/281 'Obywatele polscy w Armii Czerwonej', Paper prepared by the Historical Department of the Polish Army.
40. Ibid. See also L. A. Sułek, 'Wojenne losy Polaków żołnierzy Armii Czerwonej (1940–1945)'. *Zeszyty Historyczne*, no. 99 (1992), pp. 30–9.
41. PIGSM Kol. 138/281. 'Obywatele polscy w Czerwonej Armii'.
Many doctors were also taken at this time; notably around 200 from Lwów and some 20 from Równe.
Rudolph Fałkowski was one of a small group of Poles released from Red Army service in 1941–42 who left the Soviet Union for Great Britain in June 1942, where they were to join the Polish air force. To their surprise, nobody had any idea that thousands of Poles had been *forcibly* conscripted into the Red Army. It was widely assumed that they must have volunteered, and he writes that their arrival was greeted with wariness and suspicion. R. S. Fałkowski, 'Polacy w czerwonej armii (1940–1945)' *Zeszyty Historyczne*, no. 101 (1992), pp. 115–42.
42. PIGSM Kol. 138/281.
43. Edward Ochab, for example, who occupied various positions within the party/government hierarchy in postwar Poland (until 1968) had joined the Polish Communist Party in 1929 and been imprisoned five times in the period to the outbreak of the Second World War for his political activities. In prison when the war broke out, he moved to the Soviet Union and volunteered for Red Army service following the German attack in 1941. He was directed to a *stroybat*, however, and employed on digging defensive ramparts. T. Torańska, *Oni*. London, 1985, p. 25.
44. Y. Litvak, 'Polish-Jewish Refugees in the USSR, 1939–1946.' (PhD thesis) University of Jerusalem, 1988, pp. 178–9.
45. These included the musical review group, 'Ref-Ren', the Henryk Wars orchestra, Stanisław Laudan's jazz group and Ryszard Frank's dance

orchestra. Z. S. Siemaszko, in listing these and other entertainment artistes, points out that following the 1941 'amnesty' for Poles some of these people had difficulty in being acknowledged as Polish citizens and coming under Polish Government care and protection. They had not gone to the USSR as prisoners and in some cases had willingly accepted Soviet citizenship, so technically were not covered by the amnesty. Z. S. Siemaszko, (1991), pp. 106–7.

See also R. Turkow Kaminska, *Mink Coats and Barbed Wire*. London, 1979; an account of the period spent in Soviet Russia by a Polish jazz trumpeter and his actress wife.

46. R. Buczek, 'Działalność opiekuńcza Ambasady RP w latach 1941–43' *Zeszyty Historyczne*, no. 29 (1974).

This figure has been challenged by Siemaszko as too high. Siemaszko argues that if 30 000 people were recruited for work in the Donbas and Ural regions, it would mean that almost all the industrial workers of eastern Galicia travelled east. But there is no reason why industrial workers alone should have travelled to Soviet territory, unless their factories were being moved *en bloc*. Indeed there was good reason for them to stay; they already had jobs, homes and a degree of security. It was the large numbers of refugees in the region which proved the most fertile recruiting ground and there is no reason for supposing that they were predominantly industrial workers. Irrespective of their former occupations, they could always be employed. Z. S. Siemaszko (1991), p. 106.

47. J. T. Gross, *Revolution from Abroad*, p. 191. Gross draws attention to a report in *Czerwony Sztandar* of 4 March 1940, which indicated that 16 000 volunteers were working in the Donbas and other industrial centres in the Soviet Union. If this was correct, then either there had been a marked slowdown in the numbers recruited since December, or else significant numbers had been returning.

48. Some 9000 soldiers who had fought during the struggles on Polish soil between 1914 and 1920 had been rewarded by the state with the gift of small parcels of land in the eastern borderlands. This settlement programme took on something of the characteristics of an ethnic plantation, but never developed on a great scale. See H. Łappo *et al.* (eds), *Z kresów wschodnich R. P. Wspomnienia z osad wojskowych, 1921–1940*. London, 1992. Also, T. Böhm, 'Osadnictwo Wojskowe na kresach wschodnich w II Rzeczypospolitej', *Dzieje najnowsze*, Vol. XXIV (1992), no. 1–2, pp. 3–12.

49. USSR Sovnarkom decree no. 2122–617, 29 December 1939. Instructions of the USSR People's Commissariat of Internal Affairs (signed by Beria). This order is one of a number of documents from Moscow archives concerning the deportation of national groups during the Soviet period, which has recently appeared in the West. A collection of these documents will shortly be published: Martin McCauley (ed.), *The Deportation of Soviet Nationalities, 1920–1957* (forthcoming).

50. K. Pelekis (op. cit.), pp. 30, 273–8.

51. M. Fainsod writes of the 1936–38 Stalinist purges in the Soviet Union:

The purge swept out in ever-widening circles. . . . The endless chain of involvements and associations threatened to encompass entire strata of Soviet society. Whole categories of Soviet citizens found themselves singled out for arrest because of their 'objective characteristics'. Old Bolsheviks, Red Partisans, Communists of German, Austrian or Polish extraction, Soviet citizens who had been abroad or had relations with foreign countries or foreigners.... were automatically caught up in the NKVD web....

> M. Fainsod, *How Russia is Ruled.* Cambridge, Mass., 1964 (revised edition), p. 440.

52. K. Zamorski (op. cit.), pp. 213–15.
53. N. Tolstoy (op. cit.), p. 122.
54. Ivan Serov was later in charge of the deportations of the Muslim peoples of the Crimea and the Caucasus (e.g. Tatars), during which thousands of people died. Serov was awarded the Order of Suvorov in 1944 and became head of the KGB in 1954. R. Conquest, *The Nation Killers.* London, 1970, pp. 192–3.
55. M. McCauley *Deportation*, op. cit.
56. PIGSM Kol. 138/166. P.9690.
57. PIGSM Kol. 138/289 (1859).
58. Maria Łęczycka records that while waiting in the wagon for the transport to pull out, a pregnant woman with four children was put on board – but without any luggage. Having heard that people from the village were being deported she had fled with her children into the forest. Unfortunately she was seen and a cart was sent to pick her up. The family was taken just as it was found, without food or spare clothing for the children. M. Łęczycka, *Zsyłka.* Wrocław, 1989, p. 11.
   Further eye-witness material quoted by Gross suggests that elsewhere too, despite the instruction contained in the NKVD order, the February deportees were seized without being permitted to bring any warm clothing; children were already dying during the journey by cart or sledge to the railway station. Gross, 'Wywózki', p. 76.
59. Pelekis (op. cit.), pp. 72–82.
60. Gross, 'Wywózki', p. 74.
61. Ibid., p. 69.
62. Gross quotes the account by Leopold Bakalarczyk, despatch clerk from Baranowicze, of the preparations made in the course of January 1940 for the mass deportation that was to take place the following month; the boarding-over of windows, construction of bunks, provision of stoves, etc. in the freight trucks. Ibid., p. 60.
63. The difference between the narrow European gauge and the wider Soviet-gauge tracks meant that many of the passengers had to be transferred at established points on the old Polish–Soviet border. (In some areas work had begun on extending the Soviet-gauge track west of the former frontier.) This provided the first opportunity for most of them to stretch their legs outside the confinement of the wagon.
64. In the NKVD December order providing for the deportation of the 'osadniks', there was no indication of how long should be allowed for packing. M. McCauley, *Deportation*, op. cit.

65. Under the Nazi–Soviet agreements of late 1939, there was an undertaking that certain groups who wished to move to the other side of the demarcation line would be transferred. This concerned, in the main, ethnic Germans from east of the Nazi–Soviet partition line and Ukrainians and Byelorussians from west of the line. *DPSR*, Vol. 1, p. 53.

When German repatriation missions began their work in the Soviet zone, large numbers of Jews turned up at the offices seeking to register for transfer to the German zone. It was to a large extent upon the basis of these applications that the lists for the June 1940 deportation were compiled.

One of those who was astonished to see so many Jews queueing to be taken to Germany was the NKVD chief for the Ukraine, Ivan Serov. S. Talbot (ed.), *Krushchev Remembers*. London, 1971.

66. Siemaszko suggests a figure of 200 000–300 000 people deported from Lithuania in the course of the June 1941 deportation. This seems unreasonably high, if one recalls that the deportations were taking place from all three of the Baltic states simultaneously. Furthermore, it is not clear from his listing how many of these 'Lithuanians' were Polish citizens prior to 1939 (i.e. residents of the Vilnius region), nor how many were ethnic Poles. Siemaszko (1991), p. 95.

67. Łęczycka, op. cit., pp. 12–13.

68. Ibid., p. 16.

69. D. Tęczarowska, *Deportation into the Unknown*. Braunton, Devon, 1985, pp. 31–4.

70. Łęczycka, op. cit., pp. 24–5.

71. 'Krystyna' (Z. K. Kawecka), *Journey without a Ticket*. Nottingham, 1989, p. 42.

72. Łęczycka, op. cit., p. 12.

73. Conversation with Mr W. Bednarek. Glasgow, 18 November 1985.

74. Łęczycka, op. cit., p. 16.

75. J. Głowala, *Purga. Wśród więzniów i zesłanców w ZSRR 1941–1955*. Warsaw, 1990, p. 39.

76. Just as the food provisions for deportees in the NKVD instruction document seem in practice to have been largely absent, so the existence of nurses or medical facilities on the transports too are rarely mentioned. Janina G. deported from Białystok during the April 1940 deportation wave remembers that there were a doctor and nurses in the *eszelon* with which she travelled east, but maintains that the 'nurses' were simple girls without any medical training and that, in any case, they had no medicines to speak of. J. T. and I. Gross, *W czterdziestym nas matko na Sybir zesłali. . . . Polska a Rosja 1939–42*. London, 1983, pp. 470–1, no. 165.

Overall, however, the mortality rate during the Polish deportations of 1940 – even the more severe February operation – was less than some of the subsequent wartime movements. Robert Conquest reports the estimate that 46 per cent of the Crimean Tatars deported during 1943–44 died *en route*; entire trains were reported as abandoning the journey after the death of all the deportees aboard. Conquest, op. cit., pp. 12 and 162.

77. Interview with Mr and Mrs Szwajkowski, Slough, 17 March 1980.

78. I have stressed three categories rather than the two mentioned by Z. S.

Siemaszko (*W sowieckim osaczeniu*, London, 1991, p. 97). It may be that the second and third categories both belonged to the 'special settler' group as he suggests. However, the important point is that there was a difference in the treatment of the two groups of 'settlers'. This is implicitly acknowledged by Siemaszko. Perhaps, though, a more important reason for insisting on three categories is Vyshinsky's division. This was his categorisation and given his qualifications (see below), I see no need to argue with it.

79. Andrei Vyshinsky (1883–1954) was born in Odessa and had been a member of the Menshevik Party from 1903. He graduated from the law department of Kiev University in 1913, and was thereafter engaged in writing and teaching. Despite his earlier Menshevik affiliations, his career blossomed following the Bolshevik revolution. He became Rector of Moscow State University from 1925 to 1928 and a member of the collegium of the People's Commisariat for Education, 1928–31. During the period 1935–39 – the period of the notorious show trials in Moscow – he was chief procurator of the USSR.

Vyshinsky became deputy minister of foreign affairs between 1940 and 1949 and from 1949 to 1953 he was minister of foreign affairs. During the last year of his life he was the USSR's permanent representative at the UN. He was recognised as an authority on Soviet law and wrote a number of books on the subject. However, history was not too kind to him. A Soviet reference work states:

> His theoretical works contain serious errors, which resulted in an incorrect characterization of the Soviet state and law. Vyshinsky overemphasized the role of compulsion and underestimated the role of education and prevention. He also exaggerated the importance of the confession of the accused as evidence in cases of counterrevolutionary conspiracies, and he made other errors as well. In practice his mistakes led to major violations of the socialist legal order.

Great Soviet Encyclopedia, Vol. 5, Moscow, 1970. (This quotation is from the English translation of the Third Edition. London and New York, 1974.)

80. S. Kot, *Conversations with the Kremlin and Despatches from Moscow.* London, 1963, p. 30.

81. From chance remarks made by Stalin and other Soviet leaders, it is clear that certain prisoners were considered as not coming under the 1941 amnesty.

Stalin assured Sikorski during their meeting at the Kremlin on 3 December 1941 that the Soviet Government had not the slightest reason to retain even one Pole. But then Molotov added that the Soviet authorities had detained people who, 'after the war' (i.e. after the German attack) had 'committed felony, stimulated diversion, set up radio stations (?) and the like'. See *DPSR*, Vol. I, p. 233.

An NKVD document from the period mentions two categories of Polish POW which were not released under the 1941 'amnesty' for Polish prisoners:

(i) 'Those held in Aktiubinsk camp and withheld from the call-up on the basis of materials held by the Special Units (457)'.

(ii) 'Those persons of Polish origin held in Spasozawodski camp and not called up to the Polish army (197)'

(M. McCauley, *Deportation*, op. cit.).

If special categories such as this existed for prisoners of war, then there is every reason to believe that similar categories existed for convicted civilians who were regarded as particularly dangerous.

82. Y. Litvak, 'Polish-Jewish Refugees in the USSR 1939–1946', op. cit.
83. B. Podoski (P.B.), *Polska Wschodnia 1939–1941*. Rome, 1945.
84. Siemaszko (1991), p. 95.
85. W. Wielhorski, *Los Polaków w niewoli sowieckiej*, London, 1956; also the same author's *Trzy pytania i trzy odpowiedzi*. London, 1964.
86. Gross suggests that the estimate of 1.25 million put forward by the wartime Polish Foreign Office is a 'cautious estimate'. Gross (1988), p. 193.
87. *DPSR*, Vol. I, p. 180. This figure was quoted by deputy commissar for foreign affairs, Andrei Vyshinsky, during a conversation with Polish ambassador, S. Kot, on 14 October 1941.
88. Gross (1988), p. 193.

2 THE SIKORSKI–MAISKY PACT OF 1941 AND THE 'AMNESTY' FOR POLES CONFINED ON SOVIET TERRITORY

1. On 21 June 1941, on the eve of the German attack, Stalin had once again rejected British warnings about Germany's hostile intentions. Indeed, Stalin not only ignored British and American warnings, but disregarded intelligence reports from one of the Soviet regime's best spies, Richard Sorge. L. Rotundo, 'Stalin and the Outbreak of War in 1941'. *Journal of Contemporary History*. Vol. 24, no. 2. April 1989, p. 289; J. Erickson, *The Road to Stalingrad*. London, 1975, pp. 73–98; N. Tolstoy, *Stalin's Secret War*. London, 1981, p. 215.
2. Churchill's radio speech of 22 June 1941. Quoted in J. Garliński, *Poland in the Second World War*, London, 1985, p. 104.
3. Polish Institute and General Sikorski Museum (PIGSM), London. Dziennik Czynności Naczelnego Wodza, June 1941, Zał. 1. Zaleski had pressed Foreign Secretary Eden for the British Government not to use words such as 'ally' in relation to the USSR, for the time being, until a formal agreement on Polish questions had been reached. See also W. Pobóg-Malinowski, *Najnowsza Historia Polityczna Polski*. Vol. 3, pp. 172–3.
4. *Documents on Polish–Soviet Relations, 1939–45* (henceforth DPSR), Vol. 1 (1939–43), London, 1961, pp. 108–12. Less than a week earlier, in talks with Sir Stafford Cripps, Sikorski had brought up the question of whether anything could be done to assist the Poles in Russia:

> The British Ambassador to Moscow had stated that he was unable to do anything for the Poles, and that the Bolsheviks had not only refused all conversations with British representatives on that matter, but had also seen to it that any interventions of that kind should have very unpleasant consequences for the Poles concerned who became a target for Russian persecution.

DPSR, p. 107. The conversation took place on 18 June 1941.
5. Stalin's broadcast was referred to by Sikorski in his letter to Eden of 4 July. Ibid., p. 113.
6. Ibid., p. 116.
7. Ibid.
8. Critics of Sikorski have pointed to the anomalies inherent in this situation. Firstly, they claim, the prime minister was usurping the functions and role of his foreign minister, and 'honouring' a diplomatic representative of a technically hostile, foreign power by entering into direct talks with him. Although well-meant and an attempt to cut through red tape, this may perhaps have been construed as a sign of weakness and desperation in Moscow. Secondly, there was the irregularity of conducting these talks with a diplomat who was accredited to a foreign power (I. Maisky was the Soviet ambassador to the United Kingdom).
W. Pobóg-Malinowski, op. cit., pp. 177 ff.
9. *DPSR*, p. 118.
10. Ibid., p. 142.
11. The word 'amnesty' comes from the Greek *amnestia* meaning 'forgetfulness'. Chambers' Dictionary defines the term as meaning 'a general pardon' or 'an act of oblivion'.
The declaration of an amnesty followed a pattern established in the eighteenth and nineteenth centuries by the Russian Imperial court, by which successive generations of Polish exiles – prisoners-of-war or later insurgents against Tsarist rule – were pardoned.
An amnesty clause was also written into the Treaty of Riga, which marked an end to Polish–Bolshevik hostilities in March 1921.
12. *DPSR*, p. 145. The clause stipulating the 'amnesty' for Polish citizens was apparently settled in Moscow between the British Ambassador in Moscow, Stafford Cripps, and Stalin:

> I pointed out (to Vyshinsky) that was not so and explained to him exactly how the clause as to the amnesty came to be agreed between myself and M. Stalin. . . .

Note from Cripps to Foreign Office following his interview with Dep. Commissar Vyshinsky on the demand of the Polish Government concerning the fulfilment of the Polish–Soviet Agreement of 30 July 1941. Ibid., p. 191. See also p. 193.
However, another source states that Polish chargé, Józef Retinger, was responsible for the use of the word 'amnesty'. S. Stroński in *Wiadomości* (London), no. 34, 1950.
13. *The Times*, 1 August 1941.
14. Ibid., 31 July 1941.
15. President Raczkiewicz considered resigning over the issue of the Polish–Soviet Agreement. He was also opposed to the appointment of Stanisław Kot as ambassador to the USSR. W. Pobóg-Malinowski, op. cit., pp. 192–3.
16. Bartel had been prime minister of Poland for three short periods following Piłsudski's coup in May 1926. He was one of several professors from Lwów University who had been invited to Moscow by the Soviet authorities

in the late summer of 1940. The reasons for these visits are somewhat
obscure, but on the basis of these contacts, the Germans decided that
Bartel was a collaborator and executed him together with 21 other academics
in July 1941 after they had occupied Lwów. See M. Bartlowa,
Wspomnienia'. *Zeszyty Historyczne*, no. 102 (1987), pp. 34–65.

  Bartel was suggested as a possible ambassador in talks between Sikorski
and Maisky, *DPSR*, p. 118.
17. K. Sosnkowski, 'Układ polsko-rosyjski z 30 lipca 1941', *Kultura* no. 42
    (1951), pp. 122–3.
18. Z. S. Siemaszko, *W sowieckim osaczeniu*. London, 1991, p. 169; Pobóg-
    Malinowski, op. cit., p. 194.
19. *DPSR*, p. 145. Vyshinsky said that he considered the Agreement 'an epoch-
    making event of historical importance'.

    However only weeks later, an irritated Vyshinsky stressed to Polish
    Ambassador, S. Kot, that 'the Polish–Soviet Treaty was signed by us
    more from motives of sentiment than of reason. It is also difficult to say
    that it has advantages for us, rather the contrary.' (Ibid., p. 181)

    While it is quixotic to think of someone as hard-headed and ruthless
    as Stalin pursing foreign policy on a basis of 'sentiment', Vyshinsky's
    words may indicate that even at this early stage the Soviet leadership
    was having doubts about the wisdom of concluding the Agreement with
    the Poles – or at least, about having granted so many concessions.
20. K. Pruszyński, *Russian Year*. New York, 1944, pp. 12 and 31.
21. S. Kot, *Conversations with the Kremlin and Despatches from Russia*.
    London, 1963, p. 70. British ambassador Stafford Cripps confirmed that
    the journey took five days rather than the usual 20 hours and added that
    the Soviet Government had not provided food for the diplomatic evacuees.
    Consequently 'there was a brisk trade in eggs and milk by peasants on
    the way'. Quoted in G. Gorodetsky, *Stafford Cripps' Mission to Moscow,
    1940–1942*. Cambridge, 1984, p. 253.
22. S. Kot referred to Zhukov as being 'completely in Stalin's confidence',
    op. cit., p. 58.
23. *DPSR*, pp. 145–7.
24. L. Mitkiewicz, *Z generałem Sikorskim na obczyźnie*. Paris, 1968,
    p. 169.
25. W. Anders, *Bez ostatniego rozdziału*. London, 1959, pp. 53–4; also *PSZ*,
    p. 225. Why Anders did not meet the same fate as the victims of Katyn
    in April 1940 will probably never be known. Certainly the Soviets cap-
    tured him early enough (in September 1939) and they were aware of his
    identity (by contrast with some other officers, who were arrested and
    deported under assumed names). Furthermore, it seems, according to Anders
    himself, that his interrogators never even attempted to persuade him to
    work on their behalf. His prison conditions improved within days of German
    aircraft appearing over Moscow.
26. Reports of the first two meetings (in English) are contained in *DPSR*, pp.
    149–53.
27. Sikorski wrote to Churchill, on 17 December, following his visit to the
    USSR:

Full freedom is finally granted for the exercise of religious practice within the Polish Army for Roman Catholics, Orthodox and Jews. In my conversations with Vyshinsky he promised me that para. 123 of the Russian Constitution granting religious freedom would not be a dead letter in the future and he himself attended a Catholic service in one of our camps.

PRO FO371/31077 (The letter was sent from Teheran via J. Retinger.)
In the spring of 1942 Father J. Gawlina, Bishop of the Polish Forces, travelled into the Soviet Union to visit Polish troops and civilian refugees and coordinate their religious welfare. He spent five months there, travelling across the vast expanses of the Soviet interior by car, aircraft and railway wagon before leaving for Persia with the last evacuation convoy in September. Z. Kotkowski, *Biskup Polowy Ks. Józef Gawlina.* London–Baghdad, 1964.

28. Józef Czapski was the officer delegated by General Anders to locate the missing officers. His account of this fruitless search can be found in his memoir of the period; J. Czapski, *The Inhuman Land.* London, 1987.
    The fate of the officers became clearer when the mass grave of some thousands of Polish officers was discovered in the Katyn forest by the Germans in the spring of 1943. The most authoritative study on the subject of Katyn is J. K. Zawodny, *Death in the Forest: The story of the Katyn Forest massacre.* London, 1971. See also L. Fitzgibbon, *Katyn: Crime without parallel.* London, 1971; and J. Mackiewicz, *The Katyn Wood Murders.* London, 1950.
29. *Polskie Siły Zbrojne w Drugiej Wojnie Światowej* (hereafter *PSZ*). Edited by the General Sikorski Institute. Vol II, part 2. London, 1975, p. 235.
30. K. Zarod, *Inside Stalin's Gulag. A true story of survival.* Sussex, 1990, p. 158.
31. J. Głowala, *Purga. Wśród wieznióe i zesłańców w ZSSR. 1941–1955.* Warsaw, 1990. p. 49.
32. Kot, op. cit., p. 17.
33. B. Obertyńska, *W domu niewoli.* Chicago, 1968, p. 212.
34. S. Skrzypek, *Rosja jaką widziałem.* Newtown, Wales, 1949, p. 140.
35. Ibid.
36. Kot, op. cit., p. 93. Also *PSZ*, p. 245.
37. A. Kowalska, *Moje Uniwersytety.* London, 1971, p. 24.
38. Skrzypek, op. cit., p. 140.
39. Siemaszko, (1975), p. 100.
40. Conversation with Mrs Z. Żaba, Manchester, 26 March 1993.
41. The information about the daily allowance was contained in a pro-memoria from the Narkomindiel (Soviet Foriegn Ministry) dated 28 August 1941 and sent in reply to a note from the Polish chargé, J. Retinger. *DPSR*, p. 157.
    It may be assumed, however, that the Soviet estimates of travelling times were drawn from peacetime experience, and did not allow for the disrupted journeys which the Poles actually faced.
42. Interestingly, one account mentions the release of *Czechs* under the amnesty. These apparently fell into two categories; (i) members of the Czech division under Colonel Svoboda which had crossed into Poland at the

time of the German annexation of Czechoslovakia and subsequently fought in the September 1939 campaign in Poland; and (ii) Czech colonists deported from Volhynia in 1939–40. B. Dańko (ed.), *Nie zdążyli do Andersa (Berlingowcy)*. London, 1992, p. 93.

43. Quoted in W. Sukiennicki, 'Z ziemi nieludzkiej – relacje obcych i swoich'. *Kultura* (Paris), no. 36 (1950), pp. 121–57.

44. Quoted from W. Moskoff, *The Bread of Affliction. The Food Supply in the USSR during World War II*. Cambridge, 1990, pp. 30–1.

45. Anders to S. Kot, 20 October 1941. Quoted in *PSZ*, p. 237.

46. W. Hort (H. Ordonówna), *Tułacze dzieci*. Beirut, 1948, pp. 47–8.

47. Archiwum Akt Nowych (Modern Records Archive), Warsaw. File no. 1575. (Paper on the Mortality Rate of Polish Nationals in the USSR, compiled for the Polish Embassy.)

48. Ibid.

49. S. Skrzypek (op. cit.), p. 200.

50. From the very beginning the Embassy adopted the attitude that where free settlers have a roof over their heads and the possibility of at least minimal earnings, they should not move. S. Kot to Raczyński (Polish Minister of Foreign Affairs), 8 November 1941. Kot (op. cit.), p. 96; also *PSZ*, p. 247.

51. Stanisław Kot writes in his memoirs:

    it was not possible to eradicate Stalin's suspicions concerning the illegal (*sic*!) irruption of Poles, against the Government's agreement into Uzbekistan; and from 25 November onward a forced, violent evacuation of 45,000 Poles began from there. The Ambassador's sharp protest secured a partial hold-up of the evacuation, an improvement in its technical and sanitary conditions, and the withdrawal of the transfer to Semipalatynsk.

    Op. cit., p. 163.

52. J. Litvak (op. cit.), p. 353. Note that the date of commencement of the transfer given by this informant is four days earlier than that mentioned by Kot.

53. Nor was he released in 1943 to join Berling's forces! J. Drewnowski, *Cynga. Wspomnienia z łagrów połnocy1940–1944*. Warsaw, 1989, p. 134.

54. J. Głowala (op. cit.), p. 58.

55. From J. Margolin, *La Condition Humaine*. Paris, 1949. Quoted in W. Sukiennicki (op. cit.), p. 129.

    Kot writes that hunger-strikes were caused by despair on the part of those who had not been released, yet did not know why. Not all hunger-strikes were successful. Some merely led to the transfer of prisoners to other camps. S. Kot, op. cit., p. 97. Also *PSZ*, p. 248.

56. Kot claimed that a large number of death-sentences had been passed in Soviet prisons with the intention of terrifying Poles into signing their agreement to cooperate. *PSZ*, p. 246.

57. Account given by Stanisław S. cited in J. T. Gross and I. Grudzinska-Gross, *W czterdziestym nas matko na Sybir zesłali. . . . Polska a Rosja, 1939–42*. London, 1983, p. 166 (doc. 83). See in the same volume the

account by Kajetan K. in which Poles were refused carts or horses to help transport their possessions to the nearest rail-point and had to make their way on foot through the tundra with what they could carry (p. 143, doc. 63).

58. S. Mora and P. Zwierniak, *Sprawiedliwość Sowiecka*. Italy, 1945, p. 230.
59. Ibid., p. 253.
60. Ambassador Kot confirmed that cases had come to light of Polish prisoners being despatched to more remote areas of the USSR. This was presumably done in order to avoid having to release them. He also pointed out the ways in which the release from camps of healthier Polish elements was delayed in various ways. The Poles were often forced to sign contracts to engage in free labour. These contracts, in the Soviets' view, made it impossible for the signatory to leave for the army. Others had their payments for work performed held back or else their personal effects were not handed over. Kot to MSZ, 8 November 1941. S. Kot, op. cit., p. 94; also *PSZ*, p. 245.
61. General Anders, in referring to the delay in the release of Poles, brought proof from Poles who had been released that other healthy Poles were being detained by camp commanders because without them it would be very difficult to fulfil the quotas imposed upon them. According to the record of this conversation Molotov nodded his head in agreement and Stalin said (no doubt jokingly) that these commanders should be brought before the courts. Minutes of conversation held in the Kremlin on 3 December 1941 between General Sikorski and M. Stalin. Also present: Kot, Molotov, Anders. *DPSR*, p. 232.
62. Notes from conversation between Kot and Vyshinsky, 14 October 1941. Ibid., p. 180.
63. PIGSM A7/682/10.
64. W. Sukiennicki, 'Akcja Interwencyjna Ambasady R.P. w ZSSR', *Zeszyty Historyczne*, no. 59 (1982), p. 170.
65. Kot, op. cit., pp. 85–6.
66. Sukiennicki, op. cit. (1982), pp. 171–2; and *DPSR*, doc. 153, pp. 220–1 and doc. 158, pp. 228–31.
67. PIGSM A7/682/10.
68. Ibid.
69. A. Nove, *An Economic History of the USSR*. Harmondsworth, 1986, pp. 261–4.
70. PIGSM, Kol. 210/3, p. 116. A curious aspect of this problem is that in mid-June 1942 some 157 volunteers from the Caucasus region, evidently sent on by the local *wojenkomat*, came through Krasnovodsk to join the Polish Forces. (The Polish account does not make clear in which direction they were travelling – out of Krasnovodsk to join the Polish units evacuated to Persia, or in through Krasnovodsk, possibly from Baku, to join the remaining Polish units in the southern Soviet republics. I have assumed the latter.) However, in the light of the ethnic composition of the group – particularly the fact that there were Soviet citizens who were not even of Polish extraction in the transport – it was assumed that they had been sent on by mistake. PIGSM Kol. 210/4, p. 70.

71. At Yangi-Yul, after the transfer of Polish Staff headquarters, at one of the conference held to discuss recruitment (in mid-January 1942), Soviet liaison officers were informed of the recruitment plan worked out in Buzułuk. At the following conference they presented their own plan, which excluded members of the ethnic minorities – wherever in the prewar Polish Republic they had resided – and also excluded Poles serving in the Red Army and labour battalions. Although this was not consistent with the terms of the Polish–Soviet Military Agreement, Anders was compelled to comply so as not to risk the recruitment programme. PIGSM Kol. 210/3. (Lis Papers). 'Polskie Siły Zbrojne w ZSSR'. Cz.II, p. 111.
72. *PSZ*, p. 314. Originally 25 000 had been the anticipated ceiling.
73. PIGSM Kol. 210/3, p. 111.
74. Ibid.
75. J. Lis, 'Geneza tworzenia Polskich Sił Zbrojnych w ZSRR i umowy polsko–sowieckiej'. *Niepodległość* (London), Vol. I (1948), p. 147.
76. *DPSR*, p. 246. Declaration of Friendship and Mutual Assistance signed in Moscow by Sikorski and Stalin, 4 December 1941.
77. General Anders wrote that on occasion people froze to death in the tents, which lacked even the most basic equipment for keeping them warm. W. Anders, op. cit., p. 108.
78. *PSZ*, p. 259.
79. PIGSM Kol. 210/3 pp. 152–3. Figures were 37 510 at 15 December, 47 367 at 15 February and 63 825 at 15 March 1942. These figures include officers, NCOs and other ranks, but also a small number of civilian workers, Red Cross nurses and members of the Women's Voluntary Service (PSK). Recruitment was effectively halted by the Soviet authorities at the beginning of April, following the first evacuation of Polish troops from Soviet territory. *PSZ*, p. 279.
80. Ibid., p. 260.
81. Ibid.
82. Lis, op. cit., p. 147.
83. *DPSR*, doc. 157, pp. 227–8.
84. Lis, op. cit., p. 152.

3   THE EVACUATION OF POLES FROM THE USSR DURING 1942

1. Scalene was the British codename for the first evacuation of Polish troops from Russia to Persia and ultimately to the Middle East, while Scrivener was the codename for the evacuation of 25 000 Polish troops (including air and naval personnel) who were to be transferred directly from Russia to the United Kingdom. The second evacuation of Polish troops from the Soviet Union to Persia in August–September 1942 was codenamed Brimfield. *The Second World War. A Guide to Documents in the Public Record Office.* (PRO Handbooks No. 15), London, 1972.
2. See, for example, W. T. Kowalski, *Walka dyplomatyczna o miejsce Polski w Europie, 1939–1945.* Warsaw, 1970, pp. 275–6.
3. Polish Institute and General Sikorski Museum, London (hereafter PIGSM) A.11.49/Sow/6. This document is quoted in *Documents on Polish–Sovie*

Relations, 1939–1945 (hereafter DPSR), Vol. 1 (1939–1943). London, 1961, p. 159.

4. PIGSM, 'Dziennik Czynności Naczelnego Wodza' (Commander-in-Chief's Diary of Events), June 1941, Zał. 1.

5. 'General Sikorski's instructions to Lt-General Anders concerning the political conditions under which the Polish Forces in the USSR should be used', *DPSR*, Vol. 1, doc. 120, pp. 162–5.

6. Public Record Office, Kew (hereafter PRO). PREM 3. 351/9. Telegram no. 1357 of 24 September 1941.

7. P. Zaron, *Kierunek wschodni w strategii wojskowo-politycznej gen. Władysława Sikorskiego, 1940–1943.* Warsaw, 1988, p. 77.

8. Ibid.

9. As early as September 1941 Stalin was calling on the British Government to transfer 25 to 30 divisions to the eastern front. See Llewellyn Woodward, *British Policy in the Second World War,* Vol. II. London, 1971, pp. 28ff and pp. 40ff.

10. *DPSR*, Vol. 1, doc. 132, p. 182.

11. 'Minute of the conversation held in the Kremlin between General Sikorski and M. Stalin on the outstanding problems of Polish–Soviet relations', 3 December 1941. *DPSR*, Vol. 1, doc. 159, pp. 231–43.

12. Ibid.

13. W. Anders, *Bez Ostatniego Rozdziału.* London, 1959, p. 108.

14. Sikorski's report to the Council of Ministers on his visit to Russia and the Middle East, 12 January 1942; cited in *DPSR*, Vol. 1, no. 171, p. 266.

15. PRO FO371/31077 1024, Mason-Macfarlane's talks with Panfilov (January 1942).

16. Both Britain and the USSR had become concerned about the degree of German influence in Iran in the early years of the war, but Britain lacked the troops available and the Soviets were restrained by their 1939 Pact with Nazi Germany. Once the Germans attacked the Soviet Union, however, and especially as the Wehrmacht moved closer to the Caucasian oilfields, there was more interest on both sides in dealing with this pro-German thorn in the Allies' side. (In strategic terms, a pro-German regime was felt to threaten the new railway line from Teheran to the Persian Gulf, along which Western supplies for the Soviet war effort were being carried.)

    On 25 August 1941 British and Soviet forces crossed the southern and northern borders of Iran. Following their entry into Teheran on 17 September, the Shah abdicated. Iranian troops were requested to withdraw from the British occupation zone in the south-west and the Soviet zone in the north. An Anglo–Soviet–Iranian Treaty was ratified on 29 January, which provided for the removal of foreign troops within six months of the ending of hostilities. Llewellyn Woodward, op. cit., pp. 23–7 and 54–7; also B. Rubin, *The Great Powers in the Middle East, 1941–1947. The Road to the Cold War.* London, 1980, pp. 73–5.

17. Sikorski complained that the Poles were not present at these Anglo-Soviet talks. See *DPSR*, Vol. 1, p. 595, note 198.

18. PRO FO371/31077 C425.

19. *DPSR*, Vol. 1, doc. 175, p. 268; 'Note from Ambassador Bogomolov to

the Polish Government concerning Minister Raczyński's interview in *The Sunday Times* of 11 January 1942'. See also Sikorski's reply to Bogomolov on this matter. Ibid., doc. 178, pp. 272–3.

20. *DPSR*, Vol. 1, p. 279. See Panfilov's insistence on this to Wolikowski (DPSR, bottom of p. 283).

21. *DPSR*, Vol. 1, doc. 188, p. 286. ('Report made by Counsellor Weese on the subject of Soviet broadcasts to Poland.')

22. PRO FO371/31077 C1220. General A. Nye wrote to Cadogan at the Foreign Office on 30 January 1942, that the evacuation of at least 25 000 Poles from Russia was of urgent military importance in order (a) to expand the Polish forces in the Middle East to a full infantry division (15 000 required) and (b) to expand Polish armoured forces in this country to a full armoured division (10 000 required).

23. PRO FO371/31078 C1960. Telegram no. 3828; 30 Military Mission (Gen. Macfarlane) to War Office, 18 February 1942.

24. PRO FO371/31079 C2643. Telegram no. 3473; 30 Military Mission to W. O., 8 March 1942.

25. 'Telegram from Lt-General Anders to General Sikorski transmitting the text of Stalin's telegram announcing the reduction of food rations for the Polish Army in the USSR', 9 March 1942. *DPSR*, Vol. 1, doc. 190, pp. 294–5. See also *PSZ*, Vol. II, part 2, pp. 269–70.

26. 'Record of a conversation between Lt-General Anders and M. Stalin on reduction of the Polish Army to 44 000 and evacuation of the surpluses to Iran', 18 March 1942. *DPSR*, Vol. 1, doc. 193, pp. 301–10. Also *PSZ*, pp. 270–7; Anders, op. cit., pp. 113–22.

27. General Z. Bohusz-Szyszko, who was Anders' chief of staff at this period, wrote in his memoir of these events:

> The commander of the base at Krasnovodsk was Lt-Col. Berling. It was necessary to transfer him there, since he could no longer remain in the areas of larger military concentration. The history of the 'Villa of Delights' was too well known. The soldiers did not harbour any respect or sympathy for him and there arose the danger that hostility towards him might be openly demonstrated.

Czerwony sfinks. Rome, 1946, p. 244.
        See also Anders, op. cit., p. 111. Berling had earlier been appointed Chief of Staff of the Polish 5th Division, despite the widespread knowledge of his collaboration with the Soviets. Anders believed that to have ostracised Berling might have provoked a reaction from the Soviets.

28. PRO PREM 3. 354/1. Telegram 3715, British Military Mission (Moscow) to WO, 19 March 1942.

29. Ibid.

30. Bohusz-Szyszko, op. cit., pp. 241 and 243.

31. PRO FO371 32630. 'Report on Evacuation of Poles from Pahlevi, 25 March–25 April 1942' by Lt-Col. A. Ross. (hereafter 'Ross report'), p. 2. The report is dated 3 June 1942 and is one of three reports on the 1942 evacuations that Ross compiled. Ross, who was a Russian speaker (his mother was Russian) and also spoke some Polish, served in the Highland Light Infantry and was, at this time, Officer in Charge of the

British Base Evacuation Staff at Pahlevi. When he returned to Pahlevi in August to supervise the second evacuation of Poles, he arrived as an official of the Middle East Relief and Refugee Administration (MERRA) which shortly before had taken over responsibility for the reception and onward movement of all Polish civilian refugees.

32. Ibid.
33. PRO PREM 3. 354/1. This minute by Churchill was attached to telegram no. 407, dated 31 March 1942, from Sir Reader Bullard (Ambassador in Teheran) to the Foreign Office, in which the large exodus of Polish civilians was reported.
34. Reference as above.
35. Letter from W. W. Kulski, Counsellor at the Polish Embassy in London, to Sir A. Cadogan, Permanent Under-Secretary of State at the Foreign Office. 31 March 1942. PRO FO371/32627 W5163.
36. PRO FO371/32627 W5648. Sir A. Clark Kerr (Kuibyshev) to Foreign Office. Telegram no. 478, 12 April 1942.

    Anders confirms that on 26 March he received, 'totally unexpectedly', a telegram from Ambassador Kot with the information that the news of the evacuation of civilians together with the army had spread and had caused uncontrollable movements of Polish civilian personnel from the north and in the southern regions. Kot asked Anders to take steps to ensure that the evacuation was carried out more 'discreetly'. Anders, op. cit., p. 124.
37. Bohusz-Szyszko, op. cit., p. 243.
38. PRO FO371 32630. Ross report, p. 3. Polish sources report that nearly 200 people died in the transports during the crossings and furthermore, that the total number of deaths to June 1942 was 150 soldiers and 434 civilians, including 200 children. *PSZ*, p. 278.

    The physical state of the evacuees who arrived at the Polish General Civilian Hospital in Teheran is discussed in an article by M. Kruszyński, 'The State of Health of Poles Evacuated from Russia to Persia in 1942', *Antemurale* (Rome), Vol. XX (1976), pp. 133–205.
39. Ross report, p. 9.
40. Ibid., p. 5.
41. *PSZ*, p. 305.
42. Ross report, p. 4.
43. *PSZ*, p. 278.
44. Ross report, p. 11.
45. Ibid., p. 13.
46. *PSZ*, p. 305.
47. PRO FO371/32627 W5303. Telegram no. 444 (Teheran to Foreign Office), 7 April 1942.
48. *The Times*, 20 June 1942. Note that the term 'evacuation' used in this extract is a euphemism. What is referred to in the article is in fact the original mass round-up by which the Poles were deported to the Soviet interior in 1940.
49. *PSZ*, p. 279.
50. Bohusz-Szyszko, op. cit., p. 249.
51. *DPSR*, Vol. 1, doc. 219, pp. 351–2 (Molotov's note to Ambassador Kot

220 *Notes*

on the discontinuance of the 'enrolment into the Polish Army in the USSR',
14 May 1942.)

52. Anders expressed this scepticism not only to Sikorski but also to staff
at British military headquarters during his stay in London. *Polski Czyn
Zbrojny*, p. 321.
53. Anders, op. cit., pp. 150–2; *PSZ*, p. 280.
54. *PSZ*, p. 280.
55. Ibid., p. 281.
56. *PSZ*, p. 66.
57. Ibid. Also *DPSR*, pp. 372–3.
58. *DPSR*, p. 374. This information is contained in a letter from Sikorski to
General Anders of 23 June.
59. This direct contact between Stalin and the British may have been a deliberate rebuff to the Poles, or at least for ambassador Kot, for whom
Stalin expressed contempt. Although Kot was still in the Soviet Union
at this time – he did not relinquish his position until 13 July 1942 – he
had been recalled by the Polish Government as early as 22 May. See
Kot, op. cit., p. xxvii.
60. PRO PREM3 354/7. Moscow Embassy to Foreign Office. Telegram no. 51,
30 June 1942.
61. Ibid.
62. Sikorski had told Anders, when giving his assent to the second evacuation of Polish troops on 2 July, that the Polish Government's agreement to a further evacuation of troops from the Soviet Union was linked
to that of 'a further call-up, the setting-up of a reserve centre there and
the evacuation of children and the civilian population in the area where
the troops are quartered'.

Furthermore, he attached 'the greatest importance to leaving a strong
and well organised reserve centre under the command of General Bohusz.
It should be able to organise further recruitment and evacuation. You
must insist on this very strongly.' *DPSR.* doc. 233, p. 375.

The Soviet Government rejected such conditions for the evacuation
of Polish troops, indicating that its proposal had been purely a military
matter designed to ease the situation in the Middle East.
63. *PSZ*, p. 284.
64. Lt-Colonel Klemens Rudnicki recalled that secret plans were laid in case
the Soviets attempted to take charge of the Polish units by force – perhaps to drive them into kolkhoz work. Escape routes to the Iranian and
Afghan borders were secretly reconnoitred by the Polish military in preparation for a mass break-out. The disposition of the nearest Soviet garrisons, where stores and equipment could be obtained, were also checked.
K. Rudnicki, *The Last of the Warhorses*, p. 242.
65. PRO PREM3 354/7. Prime Minister's personal minute, dated 5 July 1942.
66. PRO PREM3 354/7.
67. P. Zaron, *Ludność polska w Związku Radzieckim w czasie II wojnie
światowej.* Warsaw, 1990, p. 222.
68. *PSZ*, p. 291.
69. PIGSM Kol.25/25a. Report by H. Jacyna to the Polish Interior Ministry
on the evacuation from the Polish Army's organisational centre in Guzar.

70. J. Kowalska, *Moje uniwersytety*. London, 1971, pp. 84–5. The author (true name Hanna Swiderska) began this memoir immediately after leaving the Soviet Union (see p. 61). A further, though brief, child's account of Hanna Swiderska's period in the Soviet Union is quoted in J. Gross and I. Grudzińska-Gross, *W czterdziestym nas matko na Sybir zesłali. . . . Polska a Rosja 1939–1942*. London, 1983, pp. 77–9.
71. PIGSM Kol. 210/4. pp. 45–6. The evacuation base at Krasnovodsk was wound up by an order of 29 September and the remaining personnel transported to Iran in the last transport. However, the base commander, Lt-Colonel Zygmunt Berling, opted to remain behind. With him stayed Colonel T. Wicherkiewicz, Lt J. Juszkiewicz and Maria Mika (Mikka?), a member of the Polish Women's Volunteer Service (PSK), who later became Berling's wife.
72. Quotations from Berling's memoirs in *Polskie Czyn Zbrojny*, p. 328.
73. PRO War Office files. WO 204/8711. 'Evacuation of Polish citizens from Krasnovodsk – report on the refugee camps', p. 3.
74. Ibid., p. 4.
75. PSZ, p. 295. Further statistics show that 2430 officers, 36 701 NCOs and other ranks were evacuated, together with 112 military officials, 1765 members of the Women's Voluntary Service (PSK), and 2738 cadets. Of the civilian evacuees, 9633 were children.
76. Ibid. The same figure for the number of deaths (568) is quoted in *PSZ*, p. 295.
77. PRO FO371/42781 W8364. Lt-Colonel Ross's report on Polish refugees in Persia, April 1942 to December 1943 (MERRA report), p. 7.
78. PRO WO 204/8711.
79. The Aschabad orphanage was eventually evacuated from the Soviet Union in July 1943, according to Sir P. Heydon, op. cit., p. 203. News of the impending evacuation of the 311 orphans and 26 staff was sent to London on 13 July. Telegram no. 791 from Teheran (Bullard) to FO. PRO FO371/34584 C8076.
80. The Polish authorities began to make soundings of the British regarding a large evacuation of children following the first (March/April) exodus. See PRO FO371/32630 W9241. See also Kot, op. cit., p. 324; *DPSR*, Vol. 1, pp. 356, 361–3, 558.

    A telegram from the Minister of State (Cairo) to the Foreign Office raised the spectre of independent action by the Poles to evacuate these children (there were 10 000 Polish civilian refugees already in Persia) as 'a serious potential embarrassment'. The consensus of opinion in London was that such an exodus would not help the war effort and everything should be done to prevent it, or at least delay it until preparations could be made to receive them. In the event permission for such an evacuation was never given by the Soviet authorities.
81. *DPSR*, Vol. 1, doc. 319, p. 538.
82. *DPSR*, Vol. 2, p. 9.
83. MERRA report, p. 22.
84. Ibid., p. 8. The Nyasaland resettlement project never came to fruition.
85. MERRA report, p. 9.
86. Ibid., p. 12. On the fate of Polish refugees in British East Africa, see

R. Królikowski, 'Operation Polejump', *Zeszyty Historyczne* (Paris), no. XIV (1968), pp. 150–88.
87. K. Skwarko, *The Invited: The story of 733 Polish children*. Wellington, 1974. A follow-up study of this group was carried out in the early 1980s by a social anthropologist. See T. Sawicka-Brockie, 'Forsaken Journies: the Polish Experience and Identity of the Pahiatua Children in New Zealand'. (PhD thesis) University of Auckland, 1987.
88. R. C. Lukas, 'Polish Refugees in Mexico', *Polish Review*, Vol. 22 (1977), no. 2.
89. PRO FO371/42781 W6392 Tel. no. 125, from Bullard (Teheran) to FO, London, 23 April 1944.
90. MERRA report, p. 18.
91. PRO FO371/42781 W8384. Minute by A. Randall, 5 June 1944.

4 THE RELIEF EFFORTS ON BEHALF OF 'AMNESTIED' POLES

1. Sikorski to Kot, 28 August 1941. In *Documents on Polish–Soviet Relations*, Vol. 1. (henceforth *DPSR*). London, 1961, p. 161.
2. R. Buczek, 'Działalność opiekuńcza ambasady R.P. w ZSRR w latach 1941–43.' *Zeszyty Historyczne* (Paris), Vol. 29 (1973), p. 53. This is also quoted by Z. S. Siemaszko, in his *W sowieckim osaczeniu*. London, 1991, pp. 230–1.

   In the course of 1942 Freyd was replaced by Stefan Gacki.
3. *DPSR*, p. 141.
4. Ibid., p. 146.
5. Ibid.
6. Ibid., p. 160.
7. Cripps, in his conversation with Vyshinsky on 3 November, 1941,

   then cited the case of the 16 people who arrived here dead from the North the other night (of which Vyshinsky) had not before heard and suggested it must be due to illness. To which I replied that according to my information it was starvation and not illness.

   Ibid., pp. 191–2.
8. Sikorski's instructions to Kot, 25 August 1941. Ibid., p. 160.
9. E. Rozek, *Allied Wartime Diplomacy*. Boulder, Col., 1958, p. 38. Although the Soviet authorities assured Polish Ambassador Grzybowski that they had no knowledge of Matuszyński's whereabouts.
10. S. Kot, *Conversations with the Kremlin and Despatches from Russia*. London, 1963, p. 39. Letter to Raczyński, 22 September 1941.
11. J. Ciechanowski, *Defeat in Victory*. London, 1948, p. 57.
12. This was not a completely unknown situation to the Bolsheviks, however. In 1922 the (Hoover) American Relief Administration attempted to bring help to the Russian people wracked by war, revolution and famine. They created a huge relief network in Soviet Russia which saved countless lives, although it was not permitted to operate for long. The Soviet authorities suspected that espionage activities were being conducted under the guise of the relief network and the whole network was wound up,

stores seized and a considerable number of its personnel arrested. Buczek, op. cit., pp. 113, fn.
13. Kot, op. cit., p. 60. Letter of 10 October.
14. Ibid., p. 61. Letter of 11 October.
15. Ibid., p. 63. Letter of 12 October.
16. Ibid., p. 12. Indeed, Molotov, in his talks with Kot on 15 November, seemed unaware of the Commission's existence. *DPSR*, Vol. I, p. 216.
17. Ibid., pp. 153–4.
18. M. Dubanowicz, *Na Mongolskich Bezdrozach*. London, 1980.
19. Kot, op. cit., p. 70. Letter to Sikorski, 20 October 1941.
20. Z. S. Siemaszko, op. cit., p. 234.
21. Sikorski's conversation with Stalin at the Kremlin, 3 December 1941. *DPSR*, p. 234.
22. Ibid. But note that the Polish Embassy had already anticipated such an agreement. Ambassador Kot wrote to Sikorski exactly two months before this (3 October 1941):

> We are posting delegates in several districts in several provinces of European Russia.... We are sending Gruja as delegate to Archangel, and also to take over civilian transports, and with him a skilled office worker, to deal with the problems of our refugees in that part of the north. We are preparing to send a delegate to Vologda, Viatka (Kirov) and the Komi Republic.

Kot, op. cit., pp. 45–6.
23. The directors of the firm were S. Mikołajczyk, Kirkor, T Zamojski and L. Grosfeld. Archiwum Akt Nowych, Warsaw (hereafter AAN). File no. 1544.
24. AAN. File no. 1543.
25. *Jewish Chronicle*, 16 January 1942.
26. AAN. File no. 1549.
27. On 3 December 1941 the Polish Council of Ministers authorised Ambassador Ciechanowski to begin purchasing warm clothing, underclothes, boots and blankets ('on the same principles as Lend-Lease') to the value of $8 million. AAN. File no. 1550.
28. A breakdown of Lend-Lease relief supplies sent to the Poles reveals the following:

	% by value	*% by weight*
Food	35	67.6
New and used clothing	61	29.5
Medical aid	1.6	0.2

AAN. File no. 1550.

29. In December 1941 the American Red Cross offered the Poles its entire stock of blankets, condensed milk, canned foodstuffs and medicines from local stores in the Middle East. AAN. File no. 1551.
30. Kot to Sikorski, p. 45.
31. Between them, in the period from October 1941 to January 1943, these organisations shipped clothing, footwear, foodstufs, medical supplies and

field hospitals to the value of almost half a million dollars. PIGSM File A.11/49 (Sow) 32. 'Report on the Relief Accorded to Polish Citizens in the USSR', p. 18.

32. PIGSM A.18/6.
33. AAN. File no. 1556.
34. PIGSM. A.18/16.
35. AAN. File no. 1551.
36. PIGSM A.18/16.
37. PIGSM A.11/49 (Sow) 32. pp. 18–19.
38. It is important to remember that the Polish Army too played an important role in civilian welfare. Many civilian refugees, including the families and dependents of recruits, flocked to the vicinity of Polish camps in the hope of being cared for. Units set about organising help energetically and created welfare committees. They provided food and shelter and set up homes and orphanages where they could. They also made attempts to employ people capable of work.

    The Polish Forces created a Social Welfare Council on 17 March 1942 to coordinate relief for the civilian population.
    Polskie Siły Zbrojne w II Wojnie Swiatowej, Vol. 2, part 2. London, 1975, p. 269 (footnote). Also J. Romanowski, 'Moje Zawiłe Losy'. (In conversation with B. Herbich. Romanowski was Anders' adjutant during this period.) *Polityka* (Warsaw), no. 12, 25 March 1989.

39. AAN. 1551.
40. PIGSM A. 18/16.
41. Ibid.
42. AAN. 1551.
43. Goods obtained under Lend-Lease agreement accounted for 92.5 per cent of these goods by weight and 75 per cent by value. The remainder were gifts provided by voluntary and charitable agencies among which Jewish organisations were very prominent. These goods were conveyed in 380 transports of which 353 were seaborne and 27 airborne. By the northern route 1707 tons were sent on 40 ships; by the southern route, 5704 tons were sent on 74 ships. AAN. 1550.
44. *DPSR*, p. 414.
45. Buczeck, op. cit., p. 81.
46. *DPSR*, pp. 257–8.
47. Ibid., p. 104. Also, PISM Dziennik Cyznności N.W. 8/42, document entitled 'Likwidacja delegatur Ambasady R.P. przez władze sowieckie' (report written for the Polish Council of Ministers on 11 August 1942 by W. Arlet, a Polish diplomat expelled by the Soviets the previous month).

    However, a further document states that the number of 'men of confidence' ('a few months after the beginning of the distribution of relief goods') was 387 – of which, 297 were Poles, 82 Jews, and eight Ukrainians or Byelorussians. Quoted in *DPSR*, p. 608.

    Czesław Bloch, on the basis of documents found in the Hoover Institution, states that by January–February 1943 the number of 'men of confidence' had reached 421. C. Bloch, 'Losy Polaków poza granicami Kraju w latach II wojny światowej'. *Wojskowy Przegląd Historyczny*, Vol. 35 (1990), 1–2, p. 89.

48. Kot informed the Soviet Vice-Commissioner for Foreign Affairs, Salomon Lozovsky, on 17 September 1941, that he (i.e. the Polish Embassy) was receiving about one thousand letters every day from Poles scattered about the USSR. Kot maintained that he could not answer them all. Kot, op. cit., p. 23.
49. S. Skrzypek, *Rosja jaką widziałem*. Newtown, Wales, 1949, p. 48.
50. Buczek, op. cit., pp. 64–5.
51. PISM. A.7/307/43 Sprawozdanie Działu Opieki Społ. Amb. R.P., pp. 30–1. This Report was compiled by workers from the Embassy Relief Department: J. Aszkenazy, J. Ponikowski, L. Gronkowski, A. Treszka, T. Kozioł.
52. Ibid.
53. The question of discrimination in the distribution of Polish welfare supplies in the USSR, especially with regard to Polish Jews, is discussed in K. Sword, 'The Welfare of Polish-Jewish Refugees in the USSR, 1941–43; Relief supplies and their distribution', in N. Davies and A. Polonsky, *Jews in Eastern Poland and the USSR, 1939–46*. London, 1991, pp. 145–60.
54. A case in point is that of Edward Dubanowicz, 'man of confidence' in Ayaguz who, suffering from an advanced state of exhaustion, was evacuated in April 1942. He died in the following year. M. Dubanowicz, op. cit.
55. PIGSM A.7/307/43, p. 8.
    It is perhaps worth comment that a number of these relief workers were in fact '*women* of confidence': by December 1942, of the 387 'men of confidence' known to the Embassy, there were 324 men and 63 women. An Embassy report, in drawing attention to these statistics, points out that women were playing an increasing role in the welfare apparatus and this was a positive phenomenon since, as a rule, women enjoyed greater freedom of action and relatively greater personal safety. However, a woman – Urszula Muskus – was among the first relief workers arrested by the Soviet authorities in the spring of 1942.
56. PIGSM A.7/307/43, p. 9.
57. Weronika Hort's book, *Tułacze dzieci* (Beirut, 1948), contains much on the fate of Polish children in the USSR. Hort was the pen-name of Hanka Ordonówna, who was well-known in prewar Warsaw as a singer and actress. In 1940 she was deported together with her husband, Count Michał Tyszkiewicz. Following the 'amnesty' in 1940, the pair began work to rescue Polish children and were involved in the work of the Polish orphanage at Aschabad.
58. PIGSM A.7/307/34.
59. Republic and oblast authorities often revealed the view that they regarded the setting-up of Polish orphanages as pointless; they argued that the equivalent Soviet institutions could carry out the same task. The Poles naturally feared that this would result in the children being 'denationalised' and reared in the communist spirit. Letters from Polish children in Soviet *dietdomy* asking for help, resulted in fraught attempts to extract them. In some cases the children simply ran away. PIGSM A.7/307/34.
60. Ibid. Letter dated 24 September 1942.
61. Ibid. Letter dated 2 September 1942.
62. *PSZ*, Vol. II, part 2, p. 55.
63. See J. Erickson, *The Road to Stalingrad*. London, 1983, Ch. 7.

64. See *DPSR*, p. 227. Note from the Narkomindiel of 3 December and Embassy reply of 9 December.
65. Ibid., pp. 267–8, 23 January 1942.
66. Ibid., pp. 268–9, 272–4 and 284–5. Correspondence between Sikorski and Soviet Ambassador Bogomolov concerning an article written by Foreign Minister, Edward Raczyński, for *The Sunday Times* on the question of Poland's eastern border.
67. The question of evacuating 50 000 Polish children from the USSR was raised by General Sikorski in a letter to Roosevelt of 17 June 1942 (DPSR, p. 372). The Poles attempted to bring British and American pressure to bear on the Soviet leadership to permit this evacuation. The matter had some urgency as the mortality rate of children in areas of the southern republics during 1942 was as high as 40 per cent. Siedlecki, op. cit., p. 104. See also previous chapter.
68. For example, in the Semipalatynsk oblast, the Polish schools and other educational institutions which had been set up with the blessing of the Soviet authorities in February–March, were closed down in mid-June, as were reading rooms and loan libraries. Some classes continued in private, in spite of the ban. Account of Ms Lapicka, 'man of confidence' in Gieorgiewka (Zarminsk *oblast*). PIGSM A.7/307/34, p. 138.
69. *DPSR*, p. 374.
70. Kot, op. cit., pp. 230–1.
71. *DPSR*, p. 369.
72. Ibid., p. 377.
73. Ibid., pp. 378–80.
74. Ibid.
75. Ibid., p. 375.
76. Ibid., p. 378.
77. Further embassy delegates, including Słowikowski (Chelyabinsk), were deprived of diplomatic status by the Soviet authorities. See Ibid., (doc. 236) and Polish reply on p. 389 (doc. 242).
78. Ibid., p. 383.
79. Ibid., p. 417.
80. Ibid., p. 420.
81. Kot, op. cit., pp. 255–70. Also in shortened form in *DPSR*, pp. 381–6.
82. Sikorski's letter introducing the new ambassador, T. Romer, was sent to Stalin on 26 October. *DPSR*, p. 441.
83. Ibid., pp. 418–19.
84. Ibid., p. 445.
85. Kot raised the issue of evacuating some 50 000 Polish children from the USSR during talks with Vyshinsky on 2 June 1942 (see note 67 above). Despite couching the evacuation in positive terms from the Soviet point of view (it helped alleviate the economic situation), Vyshinsky was annoyed by the suggestion and would not agree to it. *DPSR*, pp. 361–3.
    Kot returned to the issue of Polish children in his farewell conversation with Vyshinsky on 8 July. Kot, op. cit., p. 266.
86. J. Siedlecki, *Losy Polaków w ZSRR w latach 1939–1986*. London, 1987, p. 102. Yet Aleksander Wat claims that Poles close to the Delegatures

made use of their proximity and privileged positions to take more than their share of welfare supplies:

> Wagons arriving with gifts from America and England rescued a million people from death – not only Poles but how many Russians too. There were innumerable trains with supplies. Of course, not all of them arrived complete. Already at the railway junctions, at the frontier, things disappeared. And there was such a number of thefts, such a number. When they arrived at Alma-Ata, a gang of porters was recruited from among the stronger Poles. A powerful gang of these strong Poles was formed. But they had certain rules. They only took a certain percentage of the goods.

A. Wat, *Mój Wiek.* London, 1981, p. 281.

87. See article by T. Romer, 'Moja misja jako ambasador R.P. w Związku Radzieckim'. *Zeszyty Historyczne*, no. 30 (1974), p. 145.

88. S. Świaniewicz, *W cieniu Katynia.* Warsaw, 1990. Świaniewicz writes that, upon his arrival at the Polish Embassy in Kiubyshev, he had a conversation with Stanisław Kot in the course of which the ambassador complained that the army, prompted by the British, was carrying out intelligence activity which might well endanger the emergency welfare programme (pp. 223–4). Unfortunately, the author does not indicate the precise date of this conversation.

See also the section on the role of Embassy delegate and army officer, Rola-Janicki, who was expelled by the Soviet authorities in June 1942 (pp. 238–44).

89. W. Pobóg-Malinowski, *Najnowsza Historia Polityczna Polski 1864–1945*, Vol. III. London, 1981, p. 239 fn.

90. A. Wat, op. cit., pp. 283–4.

91. *DPSR*, p. 456. 19 November 1942.

92. J. Siedlecki, op. cit., p. 103.

93. *DPSR*, p. 604.

94. PISM A.11.49 (Sow) 32. On 15 January, the day before passing the decree which ordained that henceforth all those present in Eastern Poland on 1 and 2 November 1939 would be considered Soviet citizens, the Council of People's Commisars of the USSR passed a decree that all of the relief institutions of the Polish Embassy were to be taken under Soviet management and administration.

95. *DPSR*, p. 473. Polish protest and Sikorski's intervention with Churchill on 9 February 1943.

The result of the 15 January nationality decree and the 'paszportizatsiya' process meant that only a fraction of the 265 000 Poles with whom the Embassy had been in contact were henceforth considered by the Soviet Government as Polish citizens. The Australian Legation estimated that it was between 10 000 and 30 000. Sir P. Heydon, 'Protecting Polish Interests in the USSR 1943–1944: An episode in Australian representation', *Australian Journal of Politics and History*, Vol. XVII, 2 (1972), p. 200.

96. The Australian Legation took over some small quantities of food and medicine, which it was able to issue at various times to needy Poles. It

also took charge of a Polish bank account holding 3 601 000 roubles. When it became more widely known that the Australians were representing Polish interests, appeals from Poles for help began to pour into the Legation. When the applicant's name appeared in lists supplied by the Polish Government, the Australian Legation sent out money remittances of 400 roubles by telegraph. Heydon, op. cit., pp. 198–201.

5 THE ROLE OF THE POLISH COMMUNISTS IN THE USSR, 1943–45

1. I have in mind here both the Congress of Polish communists and other left-wing elements, organised at Saratov in November–December 1941 (see note 12 below). Also the statement made by Stalin in late January 1943 to Aleksander Kornieczuk, husband of Wanda Wasilewska:

   > the situation looks as though it is heading towards a decisive conflict between the Polish émigré government and the Soviet Union, and in such an eventuality we consider that Wanda could accomplish a great deal.

   F. Tych (ed.), 'Wanda Wasilewska. Wspomnienia (1939–1944)', *Archiwum ruchu robotniczego*, VII (1982), p. 383. Hereafter referred to as Wasilewska, 'Wspomnienia'.

2. On the liquidation of the prewar Polish Communist Party (KPP) see M. K. Dziewanowski, *The Communist Party of Poland: an outline history*. Cambridge, Mass., 1976, pp. 149–54; R. Staar, 'The Polish Communist Party 1918–48', *Polish Review*, no. 1, 1956, pp. 41–59; A Korboński, 'The Polish Communist Party, 1938–42', *Slavic Review*, xxvi (1966). 430–44; also I. Deutscher, 'The Tragedy of Polish Communism Between Two World Wars', in *Marxism in Our Time*. London, 1972.

   It has never been clear precisely how many Polish communists died in labour camps and before firing squads after being summoned to Moscow. However, in the mid-1980s the Paris-based historical journal *Zeszyty Historyczne* began to publish lists of victims, some of whom had earlier been members of Róża Luksembourg's SDKPiL. See A. A. Myszkowski, 'Słownik Biograficzny Komunistów Polskich Represjonowanych w ZSSR'. *Zeszyty Historyczne*, no. 69 (1984), pp. 40–80. Myszkowski writes (on p. 73):

   > The repressions involved, above all, the leadership of the KPP. The majority of those condemned carried out important functions in the Party apparatus or in the Soviet administration. The higher a given person was placed in the hierarchy, the less chance he had of surviving the purge.

   By a sad irony some of the Polish communists liquidated in 1937 and 1938 had earlier been arrested by the Polish authorities and, under an agreement with the Soviet government, exchanged for Poles arrested in the Soviet Union. See W. Materski, 'Polska-radziecka wymiana więźniów politycznych, 1921–1937'. *Z pola walki*, no. 1 (1977), pp. 37–68.

3. In his biography of Władysław Gomułka, Andrzej Werblan writes:

the majority of former communist activists in the middle levels of the organisation, who possessed even minimal experience in propaganda and administration, found themselves in the ranks of the 1st Army and of the ZPP.

A. Werblan, *Władysław Gomułka. Sekretarz Generalny PPR.* Warsaw, 1988, p. 213. However, their numbers were not large.

4. Wasilewska recalled, from everyday experience in Lwów during the period September 1939 to June 1941, that former membership not only of the KPP and KPZU (Communist Party of Western Ukraine), but membership of any organisation whatsoever, had 'frightened our Soviet comrades' ('odstraszała radzieckich towarzyszy'). Wasilewska, 'Wspomnienia', p. 356.

5. K. Sobczak, 'Wanda Wasilewska – Bojowniczka o Postęp Społeczny, Niepodległość i Socjalizm', *Wojskowy Przegląd Historyczny*, no. 1 (79), 1977, p. 11.

Wasilewska was born in 1905, the daughter of Leon Wasilewski, PPS member and close colleague of Piłsudski. She had been a student in Kraków during the years 1923–27 and a schoolteacher in the same town during the years 1928–33. She was eventually dismissed because of her political views and activities ('a teacher such as this cannot be allowed to shape the views of the young') and thereafter could not find work in Kraków.

She moved to Warsaw in 1934 with her second husband, Marian Bogatko (her first husband, Roman Szymański, had died in 1931). For a time, Wasilewska worked for the publishing section of the Polish Teachers' Union. However, she devoted an increasing amount of her time and energy to political activity (it was at this time that she established contact with the communists) and to writing. She wrote a number of novels in the 1930s which, in literary terms, were thought of as no more than average works, but were printed in large numbers in the Soviet Union. (One Polish report states that immediately following the Soviet occupation of Lwów in 1939, she was paid royalties of 40 000 roubles.)

With the outbreak of war in September 1939 and the Soviet occupation of eastern Poland, she moved to Lwów, where she was active in cultural and literary circles. She became a Soviet citizen and was accepted into the Soviet communist party. Following the German attack on Soviet Russia, she joined the Red Army. In 1943 she was a leading force behind the creation of the Union of Polish Patriots (for which she edited its journal, *Wolna Polska*) and the 1st Polish ('Kościuszko') Division. In July 1944 she was deputy chairman of the Polish Committee of National Liberation (PKWN – the 'Lublin' Committee). After the war she chose to remain in the Soviet Union, living in Kiev. She died in 1964. Sources: K. Sobczak (op. cit.); *Słownik Wspołczesnych Pisarzy* (ed. K. Korzeniowska), 3rd volume, Warsaw 1963; Polish Institute and Sikorski Museum, London. (PIGSM) A.XII, 3/43. (Intelligence report supplied to the Polish C-in-C, by the Political Department of the Ministry of National Defence.)

6. The activities of this cultural group in Lwów are discussed and analysed in B. Czaykowski, 'Soviet Policies in the Literary Sphere: Their Effects

230 *Notes*

and Implications', in K. Sword (ed.), *The Soviet Takeover of the Polish Eastern Provinces, 1939–41*. London, 1991. For personal accounts of this period, see J. Stryjkowski, *Wielki Strach*. Warsaw, 1980; J. Kowalewski, *Droga Powrotna*. London, 1974.

7. The presence of Dzierżyńska and Usiejewicz is a reminder of a cosmopolitan tendency which Dziewanowski noted among Polish radical socialists in the late nineteenth and early twentieth centuries. Often, he suggests, they felt more at home among Russian socialists than among Poles. See the chapter 'Social democrats versus social patriots?' in M. K. Dziewanowski, op. cit.

8. M. Turlejska, *Prawdy i Fikcje*. Warsaw, 1968, p. 647.

9. Z. Kumos, *Związek Patriotów Polskich*. Warsaw, 1983, p. 45.

10. J. Broniewska from 'Z notatnika korespondenta wojennego' (Warsaw 1953), quoted in W. Pobóg – Malinowski, *Najnowsza Historia Polityczna Polski, 1864–1945*, Vol. III. London, 1981 (Second Edition), p. 211.

11. The article 'Słuchając braci Polaków' appeared in *Izvestia* on 2 December 1941.

12. See Pobóg-Malinowski, op. cit., p. 210; E. J. Rozek, *Allied Wartime Diplomacy. A Pattern in Poland*. Boulder, Col., 1958, p. 95; Dziewanowski, op. cit., p. 162 suggests that the conference was deliberately called for that date so as to put pressure on Sikorski. K. Sobczak makes the same point, albeit his reading of the situation reflects the communist view:

> It was . . . a warning to General Sikorski, who at that time had arrived on an official visit to the Soviet Union . . . that there existed a considerable number of the Polish community in the USSR who wished for a sincere and genuine rapprochement and cooperation with the Soviet Union.

Sobczak, op. cit., p. 15.

13. Pobóg-Malinowski, op. cit., p. 211. Ehrlich and Alter were executed by the Soviet authorities soon after being rearrested, although their fate did not come to light until February 1943. See also: D. Engel, 'The Polish Government-in-Exile and the Erlich–Alter affair', in N. Davies and A. Polonsky, *Jews in Eastern Poland and the USSR, 1939–1946*, London, 1991, pp. 172–82. (*NB* Both spellings – 'Ehrlich' and 'Erlich' – are found in the literature.)

14. Wasilewska, 'Wspomnienia', pp. 378–9.

15. Kumos, op. cit., p. 45. F. Zbiniewicz, *Armia Polska w ZSSR*. Warsaw, 1963, p. 26.

16. This conversation took place in Moscow, 25 October 1942. Kumos, op. cit., p. 50.

17. Ibid., pp. 50–1. See also Sobczak, op. cit., p. 19.

18. Ibid., p. 52.

19. 'Wspomnienia', p. 283. See also Kumos, op. cit., p. 53.

20. Wasilewska later commented that even members of the ONR (the prewar National Radical Camp, an extreme right-wing grouping) had asked to join! 'Wspomnienia', p. 395.

21. *Wolna Polska* quickly reached a print-run of 40 000. It continued publication until August 1946 when it ceased to appear, as a result of the

ending of the ZPP's activities. *Dokumenty i Materiały do Historii Stosunków Polsko-Radzieckich*, Vol. VII (1973), p. 406.
22. Quoted in Kumos, op. cit., p. 53.
23. Quoted in P. Zaron, *Ludność polska w Związku Radzieckim w czasie II wojnie ś wiatowej*. Warsaw 1990, p. 264.
24. *Wolna Polska*, no. 1, 1 March 1943. The reference to 'fratricidal murders was a reference to the clashes that were occurring in eastern Poland between Home Army units loyal to the London Polish Government and Soviet partisans.
25. *Wolna Polska*, no. 2, 8 March 1943.
26. Kumos, op. cit., p. 54.
27. There were several ironies, in fact. Her father, Leon Wasilewski, was one of the Polish negotiators who, at the Riga Conference in 1921, had helped establish the Polish–Soviet frontier – the same frontier that twenty years later his daughter proved so ready to alter in Stalin's favour.
     Furthermore Wasilewska herself had studied in Krakow under the historian, Professor Stanisław Kot. This was the same man who became Sikorski's ambassador to the Soviet Union during 1941–42.
28. Furthermore she was highly dismissive of Dimitrov and the Comintern:

    I did not sort out any matters with Dimitrov or through Dimitrov. Having access to people who had more power to take decisions than Dimitrov, I certainly had no need to go to him. ('Wspomnienia', p. 366.)

    Wasilewska also claimed to have 'managed' the question of the Polish Army by herself. The Union of Polish Patriots did, she admitted, have a Military Department, but 'that sorted out purely technical matters . . .'. Ibid., p. 396.
29. Sobczak, op. cit., p. 11.
30. Stalin revealed that he had requested Wasilewska to ask Polish officers about serving in Red formations ('exactly a year ago') during talks with Polish ambassador, Stanisław Kot, at the Kremlin, 14 November 1941. *Documents on Polish–Soviet Relations 1939–1945* (edited for the General Sikorski Historical Institute, London), Vol. I (1961), doc. 149, p. 212.
31. Turlejska writes that, in June 1941, immediately following the German attack, more than 100 Poles in the Soviet Union who had formerly served with the 'Dąbrowski Brigade' in Spain volunteered to fight against the Nazis. The men were based at three centres outside Moscow and included men who had arrived from camps in the south of France in the first quarter of 1941 (presumably via German-held territory). Some ninety were selected as being fit for service and were directed to training centres near Schodnaya on the Moscow–Leningrad line. After a two-week period of intensive training – which included parachute instruction – they were dropped during July–September in several small groups in the frontline area. The majority of them disappeared without trace. Only two of them were known to have survived the war. Turlejska, op. cit., p. 642.
32. Kumos, op. cit., pp. 56–7.
33. Upon his arrival in Britain, following the collapse of France, Sikorski sent a note to the British Government in which he raised the possibility of creating a 300 000-strong army from the Polish manpower under Soviet

occupation or deported to Soviet territory. The army would be used against the Germans, whose defeat, he agreed, should be the principal war-aim. The note proved an embarrassment to Sikorski, since he had embarked on this policy initiative without the agreement of the President or Cabinet. *DPSR*, Vol. 1, doc. 76, p. 95. See also Pobóg-Malinowski, op. cit., pp. 151ff.

Over a year later, and following the German attack on the Soviet Union, Sikorski informed Churchill that of the 1 500 000 Poles in the USSR, over 100 000 could be called up to the Polish Army – but equipping them would be a problem. Note of 17 September 1941 for Churchill. *DPSR*, Vol. 1, doc. 123, pp. 167–9.

34. The full text of this speech (in Polish) is in *Dokumenty i Materiały*, Vol. VII, doc. 247, pp. 404–6.

35. Ibid., doc. 250, pp. 408–9 (in Russian).

A Soviet–Czechoslovak Agreement was signed on 18 July 1941 allowing for the formation of Czechoslovak military units on Soviet territory. The 1st Independent Czechoslovak Battalion began to form on 5 February 1942 under the command of Ludvik Svoboda. On 8 March 1943 the battalion went into combat near the town of Sokolovo in the Charkov region.

36. No reference was made to those murdered by the NKVD at Katyn and other sites, although it seems more than likely that Wasilewska was aware of the crime.

37. Ibid. See also *Polski Czyn Zbrojny w II Wojnie Światowej. Ludowe Wojsko Polskie 1943–1945*. Warsaw, 1973, pp. 31–2. Berling's own account of these events can be read in his memoirs *Wspomnienia* (3 vols). Warsaw, 1990–91.

Zygmunt Berling, born in 1896, had his army career in Poland suspended in the spring of 1939 when he was withdrawn from active service. In 1939, he made his way to Vilnius, where he was apprehended by the Soviets when they seized the city in September 1939. He was interned with other Polish officers initially in the POW camp at Starobielsk but was one of a group of 64 from that camp who avoided the fate of their comrades at Katyn and were subsequently moved to Griazoviets camp (Vologda) in the summer of 1940.

In the autumn of 1940 a change of Soviet policy on the Polish question took place. This was probably connected to Hitler's unexpectedly speedy defeat of France and a sense in the Kremlin of exposure to the German leader's growing appetite for territory. The Soviets attempted to recruit Polish officers sympathetic to their cause from among the 'internees', but could find only 15, of whom Berling was the most senior. The group were separated from their compatriots and placed in a special NKVD centre at Małachówka near Moscow, for indoctrination and training. The centre became known as the *Villa Szczęścia* (villa of delight) because of the favourable conditions the group enjoyed there.

Following the signing of the Sikorski–Maisky Agreement and the Polish–Soviet military accord in the summer of 1941, Anders set about forming Polish units in the Soviet Union and the 'Małachowka group' were released to join them. Berling became Chief of Staff of the 5th Infantry Division (until suspended from duty following a difference of opinion with its commander, General Boruta-Spiechowicz), and acted as base superviser during the last of the evacuation operations. As the last transports left Krasnovodsk for Persia on 31 August 1942, he had remained behind, effectively deserting.

38. Berling's own letter to Soviet authorities. See Kumos, op. cit., p. 58; Kersten, op. cit., p. 10.
39. Kersten writes that Berling was summoned to the Kremlin in the middle of February when 'Stalin commissioned him to organize Polish units. The military question though, like the ZPP, remained in suspension until the end of April. . . .' K. Kersten, *The Establishment of Communist Rule in Poland, 1943–1948* (1991), p. 10.
40. *Dokumenty i Materiały*, Vol. VII, docs 255, 256. See also Z. Berling, *Przeciw 17 Republice. Wspomnienia* (part 2). Warsaw, 1991, p. 93.
41. Kumos, op. cit., p. 59.
42. Ibid.
43. This was a young priest named Kubsz. According to one version, he had been arrested at his parish near Pińsk and imprisoned by the Germans. Having managed to escape, he joined a partisan band operating in the Polesie region. However, it is not clear how he was spirited across the front line to Soviet-held territory.
    According to another version, Kubsz was kidnapped by Soviet partisans in Poland and taken to Soviet territory. J. Garliński, *Poland in the Second World War*. London, 1985, p. 196.
44. The Polish text reads, in part: 'Przysięgam dochować wierności sojuszniczej Związku Radzieckiemu, który mi dał do ręki broń do walki ze wspólnym wrogiem, przysięgam dochować braterstwa broni sojuszniczej Armii Czerwonej.' Sobczak, op. cit., p. 26. The oath is also reproduced in its entirety in Berling, op. cit., p. 177.
45. *Polski Czyn Zbrojny*, pp. 32–3.
46. *Soviet Monitor* (issued by Tass), no. 2948. 13 May 1943.
    In the English-language copy of this bulletin, the name of the Kościuszko Division's commander-designate – unfamiliar no doubt to the translators – is rendered as 'Sigmund Behrling'.
47. L. Woodward, *British Policy in the Second World War*, Vol. II. London, 1971, p. 633.
48. PRO FO371. C5431/258/55. Minute by F. K. Roberts, 14 May 1943. Roberts was commenting on an interview with Berling which appeared in the Soviet Army journal *Krasnaya Zviezda* (Red Star) and in *Wolna Polska* and which had been reproduced in *The Times*.
49. Ibid.
50. J. Erickson, *The Road to Berlin. Stalin's War with Germany*. London, 1983, p. 88.
51. This account by Berling was given on Polish television on the occasion of the 35th anniversary of the creation of the People's Polish Army. It is quoted in B. Dańko, *Nie zdążyli do Andersa. (Berlingowcy)*. London, 1992, pp. 9–10. Also Berling, op. cit., p. 113.
52. The only references to ill-health I have found concern precautionary vaccinations and medicines being dispensed to counter malaria. *Polski Czyn Zbrojny*, p. 49.

53. Dańko, op. cit., pp. 34, 55, 94.
54. Quoted in Ibid., op. cit., p. 19.
55. See, for example, the accounts in Dańko, op. cit., pp. 34 and 106, where it is not made at all clear why the individual concerned did not join up at the earlier stage.
56. Ibid., op. cit., p. 74.
57. As an example:

> Those who left with Anders were predominantly officers and their families, senior officials and the Sanacja administration, landowners, capitalists and the like. The evacuation itself therefore imposed a kind of selection upon the Soviet 'Polonia'. Those who remained in the USSR, however, were working people, mainly farming settlers ('osadnicy'), lower ranking officials, workers, artisans, members of the forestry service, etc.

Ignacy Blum, 'O składzie socjalno-demograficzynym Polskich Sił Zbrojnych w ZSSR'. *Wojskowy Przegląd Historyczny*, no. 2 (1963), p. 12.
58. The classification of members of the 1st Polish Division according to social class (on the basis of 'family background', which presumably meant father's occupation) was as follows:

workers	2106 (25%)
peasants	3615 (43%)
white-collar	1063 (13%)
artisans	1069 (13%)
trade	107 (1%)
others	423 (5%)
	8383

However, it should be pointed out that these figures are from April 1944 and therefore relate to the reconstituted division – not the original division which fought at Lenino in October 1943 and suffered such high losses. Blum, op. cit., p. 15.
59. Ibid., p. 30. According to the author, a total of 979 women served in uniform, of whom 132 were officers.
60. This document comes from the Mikołajczyk papers, Hoover Institution, Stanford.
61. Statistics of recruitment are as follows (Blum, op. cit., p. 14):

10.6.1943	6 092
1.7.1943	14 380
30.9.1943	24 925
25.11.1943	28 209
22.1.1944	32 643
15.3.1944	40 262
30.4.1944	55 552
1.6.1944	77 922
1.7.1944	90 977
10.8.1944	123 000

62. Blum states (op. cit., p. 23) that of 684 officers in the 1st Polish Division in July 1943, 448 (65 per cent) had served previously with the Red Army, while 195 (29 per cent) had served with the Polish Army until 1939.

W. Jurgielewicz maintains that for the period from 14 May 1943 to 20 July 1944 some 4686 Soviet officers were directed to the Polish Army in the east. This represented 52.5 per cent of the officer cadre of the Polish army, whose overall number was 8925. W. Jurgielewicz, 'Pomoc Związku Radzieckiego w Utworzeniu Ludowego Wojska Polskiego'. *Wojskowy Przegląd Historyczny*, no. 1 (60), 1972, pp. 106–28.

See also *Polski Czyn Zbrojny*, pp. 88, 92, 120.

63. On 30 July 1945, the High Command of the Polish Army issued a note of thanks to those Soviet officers who were leaving the Polish Army and returning home. *Dokumenty i Materiały*, Vol. VIII, doc. 308 (in Russian), p. 567. The Polish text can be found in Jurgielewicz, op. cit., p. 127.

64. Wasilewska, 'Wspomnienia', p. 389.

65. I. Blum asserts that there was no attempt to ensure Party domination of the political apparatus in the army! In fact, as he makes clear, the communists were simply not strong enough in numerical terms to be able to do this. There were only 200 members of the prewar Polish Communist Party (KPP) in the Polish Army in the USSR; however, 70 of these were among the first 181 political officers named by the command of the 1st Polish Corps in July 1943. By December 1944 the Polish Divisions had 2809 *politruks* and by October 1945, 5385. Blum, op. cit., pp. 26ff.

66. *Polski Czyn Zbrojny*, p. 49.

67. Ibid., p. 49; also J. Franczak, 'My spod Lenino' in *Karta* (Warsaw) no. 7 (1992), p. 87. C. Podgórski, meanwhile, claims that 1378 Germans were killed and 229 taken prisoner. 'Rola ZPP w utworzeniu Polskich Sił Zbrojnych w ZSRR', *Wojskowy Przegląd Historyczny*, no. 1 (60), 1972, p. 91.

68. PISM A.XII 3/46. This information, from the news service of the Gouvernement General (in Polish), was picked up by the Polish Ministry of Information in London and relayed to the Ministry of National Defence in a letter of 25 November 1943.

69. Wasilewska, 'Wspomnienia', p. 391.

70. Ibid., p. 388.

71. Sobczak, op. cit., p. 27.

72. Ibid.

73. T. Żenczykowski, 'Geneza i kulisy PKWN'. *Kultura* (Paris), 7/322–8/323 (1974), p. 138.

74. See, for example, Podgórski, op. cit., p. 91; *Polski Czyn Zbrojny*, p. 73.

75. Żenczykowski, op. cit., p. 138.

76. PISM A.XII 3/46. Intelligence report to the Polish Ministry of National Defence. The news came via the ZPP journal *Wolna Polska*.

According to W. Rostafiński, on 11 November 1943 the Polish and Soviet communists gave out eleven Virtuti Militari crosses (Vth class) to those who had distinguished themselves in the Lenino battle. At a later period, the communist regime in Warsaw decorated Soviet marshals Zhukov and Rokossowsky. They even decorated NKVD general Serov –

architect of the mass deportations of 1940–41 – and other members of the Soviet security apparatus.

Rostafiński points out that there was a precedent for this shameful bestowal of medals on people who had trampled on Polish freedom. After the November 1831 Rising, when the remnants of Poland's freedom disappeared and it became just another province of the Russian empire, Tsar Nicholas I decreed not that the Virtuti Militari order be suspended, but that it should be issued as a commemorative medal to those who had played a part in crushing the Rising! W. Rostafiński, 'Trzykrotne pohańbienie orderu', *Tydzień Polski* (London), 6 June 1992.

77. Wasilewska, 'Wspomnienia', p. 423.
78. Ibid.
79. From Wasilewska's speech to the ZPP Congress, quoted in Kumos, op. cit., p. 72.
80. The Polish text of the Ideological Declaration, which was drafted by Alfred Lampe, can be found in *Dokumenty i Materiały*, pp. 449–56.
81. Kumos, op. cit., p. 72.
82. In late October 1943 communist ideologues attached to Berling's division drafted a document entitled 'What are we fighting for?' This was intended as a blueprint for political education within the division and became known as the 1st Division's 'Thesis'. The document aroused much ire and criticism, however, for its suggestion that the army would be the leading force in liberated Poland and should introduce a 'controlled' or 'organised democracy' to Poland. It diverged in many respects from the 'Ideological Declaration' of the ZPP, and rather gave the game away about the communists' ultimate objectives. A particular point of criticism was that it did not do justice to the 'comrades' who were fighting in the homeland. It was revised and redrafted during November and became the basis for political work within the division. C. Podgorski, op. cit., pp. 94ff; A. M. Cienciała, 'The Activities of Polish Communists as a Source for Stalin's Policy Towards Poland in the Second World War', *International History Review*, Vol. VII, no. 1, February 1985, p. 137; Kumos, op. cit., p. 103ff.
83. Ibid., p. 74.
84. Evidently none of the Wasilewska group applied to the Polish Embassy during 1941–42 for papers of Polish citizenship (few also had applied to join Anders' units). Wasilewska, of course, had earlier become a Soviet citizen voluntarily and, one may assume, because of her marriage to Kornieczuk, wished to remain one. It may be also that she felt too compromised by her activities between 1939 and 1941 to make any approach to the Embassy. However, Polish Government sources suggest that Helena Usiejewicz 'sounded out' the Polish embassy in Kuibyshev on Wasilewska's behalf.

    See Polish Government memorandum on the Union of Polish Patriots prepared for the Foreign Office in mid-May 1943. PRO FO371/34575 C5480/258/55.
85. Jewish officers played an important part in the organisation of the First Polish Corps and thereafter of the First Army. They were particularly prominent in the political apparatus, where they made up more than one-

third of all the political officers. K. Nussbaum, 'Jews in the Kościuszko Division and the First Polish Army', in N. Davies and A. Polonsky, *Jews in Eastern Poland and the USSR, 1939–1946.* London, 1991, pp. 183–213.

86. PRO FO371/34579 C6673/258/55.
87. PRO FO371/34581 C7049/258/55. Understandably, Stalin's reply to the greetings telegram he received from the ZPP Congress was couched in friendly and encouraging tones. Wishing them success in their work he assured them that the Soviet Union would do all that was possible 'in order to speed the defeat of the common enemy, Hitlerite Germany, to strengthen Polish–Soviet friendship, and by every possible means to aid the creation of a strong and independent Poland'. *Dokumenty i Materiały*, Vol VII, pp. 433–4.
88. *Dziennik Polski* (London), 21 June 1943.
89. A. Głowacki, 'Opieka Związku Patriotów Polskich w ZSSR nad Rodzinami Wojskowych. (1943–46) *Wojskowy Przegląd Historyczny*, no. 4 (98), 1981a, p. 25. The latter quotation contains a significant admission that there was hostility and agitation in the Berling units against the Soviet regime and its Polish collaborators.
90. As a result of General Sikorski's visit to Moscow in December 1941 and his conversations with Stalin at the Kremlin, Stalin had agreed to grant the Poles a 100-million-rouble loan in order to help create a welfare network for the Poles deported to Soviet territory in 1939–41 and subsequently 'amnestied' as a result of the Polish–Soviet Agreement of July 1941. See *DPSR*, p. 235.
91. Głowacki (1981a), p. 26.
92. A. Głowacki, 'Powstanie, Organizacja i Działalność Wydziału Opieki Społecznej Zarządu Głownego Związku Patriotów Polskich w ZSRR (1943–1946)'. *Acta Universitatis Lodziensis*, Folio Historica 8 (1981b), p. 110).
93. A. Głowacki (1981a), p. 26; Kumos, op. cit., p. 71. The ZPP resolution on the distribution of welfare supplies, approved at their opening congress, stated that

> In spite of former practices aid should be distributed on a basis of equality to all refugees in the Soviet Union, irrespective of the social origins, or political beliefs of the recipients, or whether they possessed documents confirming Polish or Soviet citizenship.

Dokumenty i Materiały, Vol. VII, pp. 434–5.
94. Głowacki writes (1981b, p. 110):

> The Congress set out only general guidelines regarding the direction and form welfare activity should take. It seems that it tied them down rather too closely to the functioning of the Soviet institutions. This caused initially a single-track attitude on the part of Polish functionaries in carrying out their task – which showed itself mainly in the distribution of charitable gifts. Only with the passage of time was the scope of the welfare programme widened – among other means, by self-help.

Apart from wondering what was meant by 'self-help' – there was an official allocation of ground for cultivation – it is not difficult to conclude from this rather opaque passage that policies had to be changed when the supplies of Western aid in the warehouses were exhausted.

95. Quoted in A. Głowacki (1981a), p. 29.
96. The Polish communists and ZPP élite had their own privileged sources of supply, as the following account from U.S. diplomatic sources makes clear:

> Gastronom No. 1 was the largest and best supplied of the commercial stores in Moscow. The list of luxury foods one could buy included cheese, black caviar, red caviar, all kinds of canned vegetables, beef and veal, cooked ham, chicken, canned cocoa, cubed and granulated sugar, fresh strawberries, dried apricots and raisins. . . . One section of the store was reserved for the pro-Soviet Poles living in Moscow during the war. Prices for the Poles were significantly lower than the prices for the Russians and some U.S. products were sold.

   Report from the United States Embassy in Kuibyshev dated July 1944; quoted in W. Moskoff, *The Bread of Affliction. The Food Supply in the USSR during World War II*. Cambridge, 1990, p. 179.
97. 'Uprosobtorg' (Uprawlenije Osoboj Torgowoli – Department for Special Trade). According to Głowacki (1981b, p. 109) it was established by an order of 21 May 1943.
98. Witos states in his report that there were 11, rather than 14, and lists them as Archangel, Syktyvkar, Kirov, Barnaul, Krasnoyarsk, Chkalov, Petropavlovsk, Pavlodar, Semipalatynsk, Samarkand, and Aschabad. *Dokumenty i Materiały*, Vol. VIII, doc. 41, p. 89.

   All of these towns were the site of Polish embassy stores during 1942, and this provides additional evidence that the ZPP bases were simply the appropriated stores of foreign relief supplies sent in to the USSR over the previous two years, intended for distribution by the Polish Government's representatives.
99. P. Heydon, 'Protecting Polish Interests in the USSR, 1943–44. An episode in Australian representation'. *Australian Journal of Politics and History*, Vol. XVII, 2, 1972, p. 201; *Foreign Relations of the United States*, 1943, Vol. III, p. 467: U.S. Chargé in the Soviet Union (Hamilton) to the Secretary of State. 30 September 1943.
100. Wasilewska, 'Wspomnienia', p. 395.
101. Głowacki (1981a), p. 30.
102. Ibid.
103. Ibid.
104. Głowacki (1981b), p. 123 states that 27 000 Poles were allowed to transfer from harsher regions of the country by the Soviet authorities in March 1944, but gives no further details. As a result of decisions by the Soviet of People's Commissars, on 5 May and 11 July 1944 some 60 000 Poles were transferred from the northern regions to areas of a milder climate. Fifteen thousand were transferred from the Komi Republic. *Dokumenty i Materiały*, Vol. VIII, pp. 129–30.
105. Głowacki (1981a), p. 32.
106. Ibid., pp. 34–5.

107. Ibid.
108. E. Trela, *Edukacja dzieci polskich w Związku Radzieckim w latach 1941–1946*. Warsaw, 1983.
109. Zaron, op. cit., p. 274.
110. Ibid., p. 285. The organisational structure of the ZPP included on Organising Committee for Polish Jews in the USSR, Kumos, op. cit., p. 80.
111. Zaron, op. cit., p. 274.
112. Jaruzelski (born 6 July 1923 at Kurow, near Lublin) had been deported with his family during 1940 and worked as a labourer in the north-eastern regions of the USSR. In May 1943 he volunteered for the Polish Army and was sent to officers' school in Riazan. Subsequently he fought with the 2nd (Dąbrowski) Infantry Division as commander of a reconnaissance platoon.

6 RENEWED DEPORTATIONS FROM POLISH TERRITORY, 1944–45

1. A. Albert, *Najnowsza Historia Polski 1918–1980*. London, 1989 (Second Edition), p. 423.
2. J. Garliński, *Poland during the Second World War*. London, 1985, p. 250; F. Zbiniewicz, *Armia polska w ZSRR*. Warsaw, 1963, p. 331.
3. At the end of November 1943, when the heads of the three Great Powers assembled in Teheran for the first of their wartime conferences, Polish premier Stanisław Mikołajczyk was excluded from the discussions. Nevertheless he addressed a memorandum to Churchill, in which he asked the British prime minister to intervene with Stalin with a view to restoring Polish–Soviet relations. His main concern was to safeguard the interests of the Polish state and the life and property of its citizens after Soviet troops had entered Poland. He made it clear that it was impossible for the Polish Government to abandon her eastern frontiers. Yet it was here at Teheran that Churchill suggested to Stalin the idea of moving Poland bodily to the west – ceding territory to the USSR and being compensated at Germany's expense in the west. From the time of the Teheran Conference, the fate of the Polish eastern provinces was settled. Henceforth, whether they accepted it or not, the Poles' eastern frontier was to lie on the River Bug.
    The history of the diplomatic negotiations surrounding the Polish–Soviet frontier dispute has been discussed at length elsewhere. See, for example, E. Rozek, *Allied Wartime Diplomacy. A Pattern in Poland*. Boulder, San Francisco and London, 1989. Also S. M. Terry, *Poland's Place in Europe. General Sikorski and the Origin of the Oder–Neisse Line, 1939–1943*. Princeton, 1983.
    See also the many diplomatic exchanges in *Documents on Polish–Soviet Relations 1939–1945* (henceforth DPSR) 2 vols. London, 1961 and 1967.
4. DPSR, Vol. II, p. 68; also *Polskie Siły Zbrojne w II wojnie światowej* (henceforth PSZ), Vol. III (Armia Krajowa). London, 1950, pp. 552–6.
5. PSZ, Vol. III, pp. 556–9.
    General Sikorski, first prime minister of Poland's exiled government during the war years, had anticipated the problems attendant upon the

entry of Soviet troops to Poland almost a year earlier. On 28 November 1942 he had written to AK commander General Rowecki:

> To wage an armed struggle by the Underground Army against Soviet troops entering Poland would be sheer madness. To keep secret the military organization of whose existence the Soviet Government is well informed would lead to an open fight of the Soviet troops against the Underground Army, a fight on which Communist propaganda would spread distorted views in the camp of the Allied nations. In this eventuality, I order therefore, to prepare the Underground Army for coming out into the open, and to start its mobilization. Its strength should be as great as possible, and it should emphasize its sovereign status and its positive attitude towards the Soviet Union.

> *DPSR*, Vol. II, p. 458.

6. *PSZ*, Vol. III, p. 559.

   The Poles are famed for their political jokes and their grim homour in adversity. A contemporary tale (from 1944) had a Russian major cajoling Poles to join the Red Army, maintaining that the Poles should fight at their side against the common fascist enemy. One of the 'recruits' turned to the Russian officer and asked:

   Have you ever seen two dogs fighting over a bone?

   Yes, I have. – came the answer.

   And – continued the Pole – did the bone take an active part in the struggle? Quoted from article 'Gomułka! Ten to całował. . . .' *Dziennik Polski* (Kraków), 10 August 1990.

7. Ibid., pp. 590–9.
8. Ibid.
9. Ibid.
10. W. Pobóg-Malinowski, *Najnowsza Historia Polityczna Polski 1864–1945*, Vol. 3 (1939–1945). London, 1981, p. 397.
11. Ibid. Also *Armia Krajowa w Dokumentach*, Vol. VI. London, 1989, p. 364. Also J. Erdman, *Droga do Ostrej Bramy*. London, 1984, pp. 242–3. Erdman suggests that the Ponomarenko mentioned in the order was the same Pantelejmon Ponomarenko who was first secretary of the Central Committee of the Byelorussian Communist Party, 1938–47. Erdman also quotes from a resolution of the Central Committee of the Byelorussian Party from 22 June 1943, in support of his contention that the action against the Polish underground was planned at the highest level.
12. *DPSR*, Vol. II, p. 143 (doc. 81).

   The Polish report to London, having conveyed the wording of the Soviet order, continued:

> one of the detachments of the Polish Underground Army was surrounded by Soviet partisans in December 1, 1943; 9 officers and 135 men were taken. Their Polish distinctions were torn off. The men were forbidden to use their language, and the commander of the detachment and four officers shot. The fate of the remaining officers and men is unknown. During the disarming of this detachment, 7 men were killed and 12 wounded.

13. *PSZ*, Vol. III, pp. 597–9; Albert, op. cit., p. 429.
14. *PSZ*, Vol. III, pp. 609–16; Pobóg-Malinowski, op. cit., pp. 587–8; Z. Szczęsny-Brzozowski, *Litwa-Wilno 1910–1945*. Paris, 1987, pp. 113–18.
15. B. Kuśnierz, *Stalin and the Poles. An Indictment of the Soviet Leaders*. London, 1949, p. 218.
16. Even at this stage friendly Soviet officers warned Poles not to walk about the city alone, but in groups; otherwise they would be arrested by the NKVD. Szczęsny-Brzozowski, op. cit., p. 119.
17. *PSZ*, Vol. III, p. 615; Szczęsny-Brzozowski, op. cit. pp. 118–19.
18. Pobóg-Malinowski, op. cit., p. 589; *PSZ*, Vol. III, p. 615.
19. Erdman, op. cit., pp. 640ff.
20. M. M. Bilewicz, *Wyszedłem z mroku*. Warsaw, 1990. p. 114.
21. Pobóg-Malinowski, op. cit., p. 590; *PSZ*, Vol. III, pp. 616–21.
22. Michał 'Rola'–Żymierski was at this time a member of the presidium of the KRN and commander of the Armia Ludowa, the underground 'People's Army', which owed allegiance to the communists. Later he became Minister of Defence in the Polish Committee of National Liberation (PKWN). For something of his background we may read from a poster prepared by the Polish underground in May–June 1945:

    Michał Żymierski has come to public notice in Poland for a second time. We remember very well the court case in 1927 in which Żymierski, as Deputy Administrative Chief of the Army, was sentenced to five years' hard labour, stripped of his honours and expelled from the army for the scandalous profiteering involved in the purchase of gas masks which were not serviceable.

    Żymierski could not find a place in the secret work of the military underground during the German occupation, involving himself with difficulty on the margins of the independence movement . . . (he) chose to make his career in the service of the Soviet agency known as the PPR, when his attempts to collaborate with right-wing organisations were rejected.

    And it is not surprising that the Soviet agency did not find anyone more worthy of the post in the so-called 'Polish Army' created in Russia. No honest, self-respecting Polish officer would take on such a role. One thing is perfectly clear, that Żymierski does not bring honour either to his superiors, or to those he now commands.

    AKwDok, VI, p. 470.
23. Pobóg-Malinowski, op. cit., p. 590; *PSZ*, Vol. III, p. 616. See also the account of these events in J. Węgierski, *W lwowskiej Armii Krajowej*. Warsaw, 1989.

    The Soviet charges against Filipkowski were that he had (1) collaborated in the killing of two Soviet soldiers in Lwów; (2) concealed part of the Home Army's reserve of weapons; and (3) inflicted violence on the Ukrainian population.(!) *AKwDok*, VI, p. 412.
24. *PSZ*, p. 590.
25. *DPSR*, Vol. II, p. 306. The message was passed to Foreign Secretary Anthony Eden on the following day.
26. Albert, op. cit., p. 424.

27. M. K. Dziewanowski, *The Communist Party of Poland. An Outline of History*. Cambridge, Mass. and London, 1976, pp. 174–7; A. Polonsky and B. Drukier (ed.), *The Beginnings of Communist Rule in Poland. December 1943–June 1945*. London, 1980, pp. 23ff; W. T. Kowalski, *Walka diplomatyczna o miejsce Polski w Europie 1939–1945*. Warsaw, 1970, Ch. 9.

There was still uncertainty among Polish communists and pro-Moscow leftists as to what Stalin's intentions were with regard to Poland. One at least, Wanda Wasilewska – Chairman of the Union of Polish Patriots! – hoped that the new Poland would be incorporated into the Soviet Union as the 17th republic. A. Albert, op. cit., p. 447.

28. 'Agreement between the Polish Committee of National Unity and the Government of the USSR on the Polish–Soviet State frontier', 27 July 1944. *Dokumenty i Materiały do Historii Stosunków Polsko–Radzieckich*, Vol. VIII. Warsaw, 1974, pp. 158–9.

29. 'Agreement between the Polish Committee of National Unity and the Government of the USSR concerning relations between the Soviet Commander in Chief and the Polish administration following the entry of the Soviet forces on to Polish territory', 26 July 1944. Ibid., pp. 155–7.

30. M. Turlejska, *Te pokolenia żałobami czarne.... Skazani na śmierć i ich sędziowie, 1944–1954*. London, 1989, p. 34.

31. Turlejska (op. cit.), p. 33. PKWN representatives protested about the number of arrests since it destroyed any chance they might have had of forming a wider basis of support in Polish society. Ironically, Stalin is reported to have queried whether the Soviet military and security organs knew they were not empowered to carry out arrests. Polonsky and Drukier, op. cit., p. 31.

32. The KRN decree is reproduced in *Dokumenty i Materiały do Historii Stosunków Polsko-Radzieckich*, pp. 142–3.

33. Kowalski, op. cit., p. 498.

34. Nikolai Bulganin (1895–1975) was active in the Bolshevik Party from 1917 and a member of the Party's Central Committee from 1934. He was premier of the Russian Federative Republic in 1937–38 and vice-premier of the USSR, 1938–41. In 1944 he held honorary rank in the Red Army and was the representative of the Council of People's Commissars to the PKWN. Subsequently, on two occasions (1947–49 and 1953–55), he was to be Soviet Minister of Defence.

35. Who was General Iwanov-Serov? I got to know him in 1944 when he was chief NKVD plenipotentiary in Poland. Under his control there were numerous NKVD operational groups scattered throughout Poland and advancing gradually to the west behind the Red Army. Sierov was not involved with military operations. His task was the political organisation of the country immediately behind the front line and thus, in simple terms, preparing the terrain to impose a communist government on Poland.

J. Błażyński (ed.), *Mówi Józef Światło. Za kulisami bezpieki*. London, 1985, pp. 60–1.

36. Albert, op. cit., p. 447.

Stanisław Jerzmanowski relates the sad tale of Ina Karczewska, daughter of a landowner from the Białystok region who was deported to Siberia with her family in 1940. When the amnesty was declared for Poles in 1941, Ina and her father joined the Polish units, leaving the mother in Siberia. But just before the evacuation to Iran, Ina contracted typhus and had to remained in a Soviet hospital. From there she was taken to prison where, for unknown reasons, she began to collaborate with the NKVD. In 1944–45 she was working for the NKVD in the Skrobów camp, attempting to recruit informers and collaborators. S. Jerzmanowski, 'W potrzasku. (Przyczynek do dziejów likwidacji niepodległosci w Polsce w 1945 roku przez sowieckich okupantów)', *Zeszyty Historyczne*, no. 54 (1980), pp. 75–6.

37. Polonsky and Drukier, op. cit., pp. 54ff; Albert, op. cit., p. 447.

Śląski points out that more members of the AK than the AL (communist underground) fought and died in the Polish Army's Berlin and Prague operations, not only because the AK was at least ten times larger in numerical terms – and hence there were more potential recruits – but because the AL people were regarded as more reliable and were directed to the MO and other security organs in order to keep the new authorities in power. J. Śląski, *Skrobów. Dzieje obozu NKVD dla żołnierzy AK 1944–1945*. Warsaw, 1990, p. 7.

38. Tumidajski died on 4 July 1947 during an attempt to force-feed him at a camp in Riazan. He had been on hunger-strike. T. Żenczykowski, *Polska Lubelska 1944*. Paris, 1987, p. 233.

39. Kuśnierz, op. cit., pp. 211–12.

40. Ibid.

41. *PSZ*, Tom III, p. 837.

42. Albert, op. cit., p. 448.

43. *Armia Krajowa w Dokumentach*, VI, p. 412.

44. Ibid., p. 414.

45. Ibid., p. 415.

46. Ibid., p. 419.

47. Ibid., p. 420.

48. Ibid., p. 431.

49. Ibid., p. 434.

50. Ibid., p. 435.

51. Ibid., p. 441.

52. Ibid., p. 459.

53. Ibid., p. 461.

54. Kuśnierz, op. cit., p. 229.

The Rembertów internment camp, site of a military academy before the war, lay on the outskirts of Warsaw. During the war it had been used by the Germans for the execution of AK prisoners (there is a memorial at the nearby railway station). However, far more Polish prisoners were held there by the Soviets in the period 1944–45. They organised a transit camp there on the site of a former factory. Among those held were not only AK personnel, but also Polish 'civilians'. . . .

The camp was mixed in another way. There were large numbers of German prisoners there too. Perhaps because of this the rumour spread

outside the camp that the inmates were Germans and Volksdeutsche collaborators, and prisoners who were led outside the camp to work were
often stoned by the local people. The Soviets favoured the Germans, giving them more responsible functions (medical orderlies, kitchen staff, etc.)
and more authority within the camp. M. Pyzel, 'Obóz NKVD w
Rembertowie', *Dziennik Polski* (London), 30 October 1992.

Another writer confirms that ex-Vlasov soldiers were interned in
Rembertów as well as Germans and that the enemy POWs were given a
monopoly of responsible positions there. On the night of 20/21 May 1945
two AK partisan groups launched an attack on the camp and freed almost
all (over 1400) prisoners. J. Śląski, op. cit., pp. 80–1.

55. A Home Army organisational directive of 6 November had instructed
some members of the underground to penetrate the army and militia where
possible. An estimated 10 per cent of the officer corps of the People's
Army had formerly served in the AK. Although this was not a large
percentage and more than 50 per cent of the entire officer corps were on
loan from the Red Army, nevertheless the prestige and authority of the
AK men was high. See Polonsky and Drukier, op. cit., p. 56.
56. Polonsky and Drukier, op. cit., pp. 33–4. Also I. Blum, 'Sprawa 31 pp.,
tło, przebieg i charakter masowej dezercji żołnierzy 31 pp. w 1944r.'
Wojskowy Przegląd Historyczny, 1965, no. 3.
57. Polonsky and Drukier, op. cit., p. 359.
58. Śląski, op. cit., p. 22.
59. A delegation from the PKWN had visited Moscow between 28 September
and 3 October 1944. According to Bolesław Bierut, reporting on this
mission to the Politburo on 9 October, Stalin had told the PKWN group
that 'a revolution (in the countryside) must be carried out by revolutionary methods. Comrade Stalin did not see us using these revolutionary
methods and criticized us for it.' 'Jak Stalin rozpętał wojnę domową w
1944 r.' *Zeszyty Historyczne*, no: 91 (1990), pp. 190–8. (This article contains the text of the decree.) Also Żenczykowski, op. cit., pp. 84–5.
60. Ibid.
61. Polonsky and Drukier, op. cit., p. 66 state that the deaths of PKWN personnel until October 1944 had numbered barely 40 or 50, but by the end
of December the number had risen to 400; see also pp. 30 and 33.

See also M. Turlejska, op. cit., pp. 41–5. Since Turlejska's book is a
study of the death-sentences carried out in the years following the establishment of communist rule in Poland, the legal background to the estimated
2500 death-sentences carried out in Poland between 1944 and 1948
(p. 26) is of obvious significance. It is worth noting, however, that the
court cases she cites in some detail include those of members of the
Militia and UB charged with acts of violence against the civilian population.

Recent documents passed to the Polish Ministry of Justice suggest that
more than 20 000 people died in prisons and work camps on Polish territory in the period 1945–57. See *Dziennik Polski* (London), 7 April 1993.
62. Rozek op. cit., pp. 183ff.; Kowalski, op. cit., pp. 594ff.
63. *PSZ*, Vol. III, p. 926. General Komorowski was by this time a prisoner
of the Germans, having been taken into captivity following the capitulation of the Warsaw insurgents.

64. Rozek, op. cit., pp. 370–2 and 390. Pobóg-Malinowski, op. cit., pp. 865ff; Z. Stypułkowski, *Invitation to Moscow*. London, 1951.
65. Wincenty's brother, Andrzej Witos, who had been used by the communists in the Soviet Union (Union of Polish Patriots) as a figurehead and had later joined the PKWN ('Lublin Committee') was dismissed from his post as head of the Committee's Agriculture and Land Reform Department at the beginning of October 1944. Polonsky and Drukier (op. cit.), pp. 68–9.
66. A. Chmielarz, *Polska 1944–1945* (pamphlet). Warsaw, 1990, p. 4.
67. Ibid., p. 5.
68. Ibid. See also *Armia Krajowa w Dokumentach*, Vol. V. London, 1981, p. 419.
69. 'Anonymous', 'Polacy znad Wilii, Niemna, Narwi i Bugu w łagrach sowieckich w latach 1944–47.' *Zeszyty Historyczne*, no. 67, p. 159.
70. I. Caban, *Polacy internowani w ZSRR w latach 1944–1947*. Lublin, 1990, p. 8.
71. Indeed, under the repatriation agreements, those living on Soviet territory were compelled to 'opt' for Polish citizenship if they wanted to transfer to west of the Bug.
72. M. Kulczyńska, *Lwów–Donbas 1945*. Warsaw, 1988, p. 5.
73. See, for example, *PSZ*, Vol. III, p. 926. Pobóg-Malinowski, op. cit., pp. 924–6.
   Krzyżanowski refers to 50 000 people being deported, without specifying whether or not this number only referred to those who belonged to the 'London' underground forces. J. R. Krzyżanowski, 'Ostatni Etap: Stalinogorsk', *Zeszyty Historyczne*, no. 70 (1984), p. 139.
   In a document from 21 October 1945 recently released from the Moscow archives, Beria reported to Stalin that 27 000 citizens of Polish nationality had been arrested and interned (by the NKVD) on Polish territory in the course of mopping-up operations in the rear of the Red Army. The USSR NKVD had found it possible to release and return to Poland 12 289 persons arrested and convicted of minor criminal offences, army deserters and lower-ranking members of the Home Army. However, some 14 721 Polish citizens had been arrested for spying, as members of sabotage–terrorist groups, of fascist organisations, or as Home Army commanders and were to remain in NKVD camps. M. McCauley (ed.), *The Deportation of Soviet Nationalities, 1920–1957* (forthcoming).
   This is an improbably low figure, unless one recognises that it refers only to those arrested on 'Polish territory' – i.e. presumably west of the River Bug, where the Polish security forces under Radkiewicz would have been carrying out most such tasks. (Beria actually wrote that it had proved possible to 'release and return' 12 289 persons, which must indicate that they were taken east to Soviet territory before being allowed back.) Those taken in the eastern territories, beyond the Bug, probably numbered several times this figure.
74. Kulczyńska, op. cit., 1988, p. 6.
75. M. Turlejska, writing under the pen-name Ł. Socha. Quoted in J. Siedlecki, *Losy Polaków w ZSSR w latach 1939–1986*. London, 1987, p. 207.
76. Caban, op. cit., p. 7.
77. Surprisingly perhaps, the Soviets conveyed some of the internees to the

USSR not by the established means of transport – rail – but also by road and by air. For example, on 11 August, 3, 7 and 14 September, air transports took AK personnel to Kiev (in the first instance) and Charkov (the remaining three). Caban, op. cit., pp. 12ff.

78. Caban writes that ten senior AK officers from the Vilnius district, including the regional commander, General 'Wilk' Krzyżanowski, were moved from NKVD care to the camp at Ostashkov only in June 1945. Caban, op. cit., pp. 11 and 45.

79. Ibid., p. 46.

80. Polaczek, op. cit., pp. 173–4.

The Hungarian historian Tamas Stark has estimated that the Soviets took 600 000 prisoners-of-war from Hungary alone during 1944–45. A large number of these people were not in fact combatants, but – as in the Polish case – civilians who were picked off the street. He concludes that some 200 000 never returned. T. Stark, 'Two Hundred Thousand Missing. The untold story of Hungarian prisoners in the Soviet Union.' *New Hungarian Quarterly* (Budapest), Spring 1990, pp. 56–63.

81. Caban, op. cit., pp. 42–3.

82. Ibid., pp. 32–3. Also J. R. Krzyżanowski, 'Teatr AK w sowietach'. *Zeszyty Historyczne*, no. 54 (1986), pp. 59–70.

83. Caban, op. cit., p. 38. Polaczek mentions the episode briefly, before discussing the fate of one group of the prisoners in the camp who were taken to the Maryjsk Republic, op. cit., p. 154, Żenczykowski, op. cit., pp. 226–8, discusses the episode in a little more detail.

84. Polaczek, op. cit., p. 159.

85. Ibid., p. 166.

86. A. Popławski, *12 lat łagru*. Paris, 1987.

Adolf Popławski was one of six sons born in Vilnius to Polish parents. Their story is an example in microcosm of the tragedy that befell Poles in the region in the first half of the twentieth century. The eldest son volunteered for the Polish Army in 1919 and was killed during the Polish–Bolshevik War. The second son was arrested in 1944 for membership of the AK and sentenced to 10 years in Siberia; he died a year later. The third son (Adolf himself) was sentenced to 15 years in the labour camps, returning in 1956. The fourth son was mobilised in 1939 as a reserve lieutenant and was killed by German bullets during the siege of Lwów in September 1939. The fifth, also a reserve officer, died at Katyn. The sixth and youngest, sentenced together with his brother Adolf, to ten years' corrective labour, served eleven years before returning home.

Thus the parents raised six sons, only two of whom survived them. However, their last years were spent in loneliness, as neither of the surviving sons was at hand. By the time Adolf and his younger brother returned from Soviet labour camps their parents were no longer alive.

87. M. Wierzbicka, 'Więzienie, Łagry, Zesłanie. 1944–1955' (typescript).

Ostrowski had been a Professor of Law at Lwów University before the war. After his move to post-Yalta Poland he became at various times Deputy Minister of Internal Affairs, ambassador in Sweden, *wojewoda* for the Kraków region, and Director of the publishing concern PIW.

88. Wierzbicka's case was unusual, however, in that she was pregnant when

arrested and gave birth to a son while still in prison (24/25 March 1945).
She was allowed to hand over the child to her mother, who had remained
in Lwów despite the large-scale westward movement of the Polish population. Soviet law, despite its limitations, recognised that a child, although
born in such unpromising circumstances, could not be held guilty of the
crimes committed by its parents. Having parted with her son as a baby,
she was next to see him as an 11-year-old boy. Travelling to Poland at
the end of the 1955, following her release, she contacted friends who
were caring for the boy (her mother had died during her term of exile).
She was able to meet them at the railway station in Lwów and take the
boy with her to her new home. Her husband returned from the Gulag the
following year.
89. Buca is best known for his part in the famous Gulag strike which followed the death of Stalin and began in July 1953. The strike alarmed the
Gulag authorities, since coal supplies were severely disrupted, and a high-
level team was sent from Moscow to investigate the complaints. The strike
ended in bloodshed, with some sixty or seventy prisoners thought to have
lost their lives. Buca and the other perpetrators faced further charges.
However camp conditions later began to improve. E. Buca, *Vorkuta*. London,
1976. See also F. Król, 'Pierwszy strajk w Gułagu. Workuta 1953'. *Zeszyty
Historyczne*, no. 95 (1991), pp. 73–90.
90. Ibid., p. 344.
91. M. Urbanek, 'Łagier nr. 0310'. *ITD* (Warsaw), June 1989.
92. Kulczyńska (op. cit.), pp. 5–7.
 Much of this is confirmed in other accounts. Urbanek's article, for
example, mentions the presence in the Krasny Don camp of professors
from the Lwów schools of higher education. However, Kulczyńska states
with some precision that the number taken in the transport was 1760;
over a thousand men and more than seven hundred women. This is a
little over half the number mentioned by Krzaklewski.
93. Szczęsny-Brzozowski, op. cit., p. 120.

7 REPATRIATION FROM THE SOVIET UNION, 1944–48

1. K. Kersten, *Repatriacja ludności polskiej po II wojnie światowej*. Wrocław,
1974, p. 225.
2. J. Czerniakiewicz, *Repatriacja ludności polskiej z ZSSR 1944–1948*. Warsaw,
1987, p. 161 gives a figure of 50 000, but earlier writes (p. 53) that a
further 65 000 were recruited between 25 February and 26 July 1944 on
the former Polish territory incorporated into the western Soviet republics.
3. J. Schechtman, *Postwar Population Transfers in Europe, 1945–1955*.
Philadelphia, 1962, p. 168. However, Czerniakiewicz, quoting KRN archival
sources, estimates that 100 000 left the Western Ukraine before the formal repatriation schemes were set in motion, op. cit., p. 46.
4. Mentioned by Kersten, op. cit., p. 225.
5. The decree was signed by Kalinin, Chairman, and Gorkin, Secretary of
the Supreme Soviet. It is reproduced in Russian in *Dokumenty i Materiały*

do Historii Stosunków Polsko-Radzieckich, Vol. VIII. Warsaw, 1974, doc. 96, p. 191.

6. J. Drewnowski, *Cynga. Wspomnienia z Łagrów Północy 1940–1944*. Warsaw, 1989, p. 150. Indeed, Drewnowski's release from prison camp did not automatically mean that he had regained his liberty or was free to return to Poland. The 'amnesty' freed him from his sentence of hard labour and from the confines of the camp, but he soon learned that he did not have the right to leave the Komi republic. He was advised to apply for a Soviet passport in Uchta and register himself as a permanent resident there. Only by a complicated procedure of (a) taking Soviet citizenship; (b) attempting to enlist for the Red Army; and (c) once with the military authorities, stating his preference to join the Polish forces, did he eventually make his way back to Polish territory. There he was promptly arrested by the communist authorities and interned in the former German concentration camp at Majdanek.

7. Kersten, op. cit., pp. 11–12 and 99.
8. Schechtman, op. cit., p. 57; Czerniakiewicz, op. cit., pp. 31 and 237 fn.
9. *Documents on Polish–Soviet Relations 1939–1945*, Vol. II. 1943–1945 (henceforth *DPSR*). London, 1967, p. 401.
10. See below, note Schechtman, op. cit. pp. 162–3; Kersten, op. cit., p. 225; Czerniakiewicz, op. cit., p. 237.
11. Kersten, op. cit., p. 92.
12. Ibid., pp. 90–2.
13. Kersten, op. cit., p. 96. A copy of this decree in English can be found in *DPSR*, dok. 148, p. 270. An original Russian version is in *Dokumenty i Materiały*, op. cit., doc. 53, p. 118.
14. As with the later repatriation agreements, the Polish Government in London protested against this decree, whereby the Soviet Government arrogated to itself the right to confer Polish citizenship. While the Polish Government welcomed Moscow's retreat from the position of regarding as Soviet citizens all Poles who were within the reach of Soviet executive power, nevertheless it could not regard as lawful or legally binding the granting of Polish citizenship to Soviet citizens who had no previous connection with Poland. This measure, it concluded, was 'probably designed to justify the fact that the Polish Army in the USSR and the so-called Partisans in Poland are officered mainly by Soviet citizens'. 'Note verbale' to the British and American Governments, 17 July 1944. *DPSR*, dok. 160, p. 286.
15. Stefan Jędrychowski, PKWN ('Lublin Committee') representative in Moscow, quoted in Kersten, op. cit., p. 97.
16. Kersten, op. cit., p. 36.
17. According to Kersten's researches, the appeal document was dated 13 October, op. cit., p. 97 fn 134. However, it is not listed in the otherwise detailed *Dokumenty i Materiały* collection; neither is there any indication from Kersten that a reply came from the Soviet authorities. To a certain extent, events had been overtaken by the September decrees covering Poles and Jews in the annexed eastern territories.
18. Czerniakiewicz, op. cit., pp. 58–9, table 3.
19. Schechtman, op. cit., p. 158.

20. Czerniakiewicz, op. cit., p. 32. Interestingly, the Poles managed to persuade the Lithuanian authorities – although with great difficulty – to open repatriation offices *beyond* the 1939 Polish–Lithuanian frontier in Kaunas (Kowno) and other towns to repatriate Poles who had been Lithuanian citizens before the war. (Ibid., p. 39.)
21. Schechtman, op. cit., p. 157.
22. Quoted in ibid., op. cit., p. 168.
    However, there must be some doubt as to the veracity of this information. Having quoted this TASS report, Schechtman states on the following page that the only 'repatriates' who entered Poland before the end of 1944 were from the Western Ukraine. This is confirmed in a detailed breakdown of statistics by Czerniakiewicz, who makes no reference to a movement of repatriates from Byelorussia before the end of 1944. See table in Czerniakiewicz, op. cit., p. 54.
23. Czerniakiewicz, op. cit., p. 36 emphasises the fact that the speedy settlement of Poles was felt to have a real influence on the permanence of the new western borders; their colonisation of the region created a *fait accompli*, which nobody could later change. Molotov himself made use of this argument in 1946 when the United States and Britain questioned the positioning of Poland's western border. People, he insisted, were not pawns in a game of chess to be moved here and there according to the demands of the players. (Molotov's statement was made to a representative of the Polish Press Agency on 16 September 1946.) This was a fairly breathtaking comment from the representative of a regime which over the previous decade had forcibly transported hundreds of thousands – and probably millions – of people with impunity.
24. 'The tendency to escape from the Russians to the West, especially mass desertion by the Polish people from territories where there are compact settlements, should be avoided, as it would mean a liquidation of the Polish position in those territories.' 'Order of the Home Army Commander to Home Army units on operating in the open in front of the advancing Soviet troops.' *DPSR*, dok. 54, pp. 88–9.
25. Czerniakiewicz, op. cit., p. 37.
26. Ibid.
27. Ibid., p. 45.
28. Ibid., p. 38.
29. Schechtman, op. cit. p. 169.
30. In a memorandum to the premier and chairman of the KRN. Quoted in Czerniakiewicz, op. cit., p. 35.
31. Ibid., p. 54 (table).
32. Ibid., pp. 195ff. (tables).
33. According to Schechtman, op. cit., p. 165, Modzelewski broadcast the terms of the Agreement over Moscow radio on 7 July.
34. *Dokumenty i Materiały*, Vol. VIII, pp. 501–4 contains the Polish text of the Agreement and the attached Protocol. The first two paragraphs of the Agreement are reproduced in English in *DPSR*, p. 661.
35. Ibid. Agreement, article 4.
36. Ibid. Agreement, article 5, Also see P. Zaron, *Ludność polska w Związku Radzieckim w czasie II wojny światowej*. Warsaw, 1990, p. 349; Kersten,

op. cit., p. 227 states that mixed marriage pairs attempted to return together, although these cases often ran into difficulties.

37. *Dokumenty i Materiały*, pp. 501–4. Paragraphs 6 and 7 of the supplementary protocol.

38. Ibid. Agreement, article 8 and Protocol, para. 3.
   In December 1945 it had three million roubles at its disposal for the task, although the Soviet government contributed additional funds. Zaron, op. cit., p. 349; Schechtman, op. cit., p. 165.

39. It is true, however, that some Poles had already been moved from the remoter and harsher regions of the USSR to more central areas. On 18 March 1944 the Executive Committee of the ZPP sent a message to Stalin, with an appeal to improve the material position of the Polish population in the USSR, especially in the remoter districts. The result was an order from the Board of People's Commissars of 5 April, allocating additional material help. A further order was issued on 11 July 1944 by the Committee of People's Commissars for the partial evacuation of the Polish population. It seems that this order must have been the result of the same initiative from the ZPP, or else from renewed representations from the PKWN, or perhaps both, as a result of the second order; some 60 000 Poles were transferred from the northern regions of the USSR, including some 15 000 from the Komi Republic, to areas with a milder climate. (See *Dokumenty i Materiały*, pp. 74–9 and 129–30.) See also Kersten, op. cit., p. 38.

40. Czerniakiewicz, op. cit., pp. 60–1.

41. Maria Łęczycka, who acted as ZPP representative in the Semipalatynsk region of Kazakhstan and was herself involved in listing the names of Poles due for repatriation, wrote that pregnant women were also given preference, although they were not a category marked out for special attention in the original Protocol to the 6 July 1945 Agreement. M. Łęczycka, *Zsyłka*. Wrocław, 1989, p. 267.

42. *Dokumenty i Materiały*, p. 503.

43. Archiwum Akt Nowych, Warsaw. Files of the Union of Polish Patriots (ZPP), no. 399. Quoted in Kersten, p. 228.

44. Kersten, op. cit., p. 99.

45. Zaron, op. cit., p. 353.

46. Łęczycka, op. cit., p. 255.

47. Schechtman, op. cit., p. 162.

48. Zaron, op. cit., p. 350.

49. Kersten, op. cit., p. 227.

50. Łęczycka, op. cit., p. 269.

51. Ibid., pp. 292–4.

52. Ibid.

53. Zaron, op. cit., p. 357.

54. Ibid., p. 359. Wasilewska mentions this event in her memoirs. F. Tych (ed.), 'Wanda Wasilewska. Wspomnienia (1939–1944)' *Archiwum ruchu robotniczego*, VII (1982), p. 420.

55. Zaron, op. cit., p. 360.

56. See Czerniakiewicz, op. cit., table on p. 79.

57. Quoted in Zaron, op. cit., p. 367.

58. Łęczycka, op. cit., pp. 265–6.
59. Ibid., p. 254.
60. AAN ZPP file 1009, p. 16. Quoted in Zaron, op. cit., p. 352.
61. Łęczycka, op. cit., p. 268.
62. AAN ZPP file 399. Quoted in Kersten, op. cit., p. 228.
63. Zaron, op. cit., pp. 353–4.
64. Łęczycka, op. cit., pp. 261ff.
65. Zaron, op. cit., p. 354.
66. Kersten, op. cit., pp. 100–1.
67. Czerniakiewicz, op. cit., p. 54 (table).
68. A. Albert, *Najnowsza Historia Polski 1918–1980*. London, 1989, p. 518.
69. Zaron, op. cit., p. 356.
70. Z. Warhaftig, *Uprooted: Jewish Refugees and Displaced Persons after Liberation*. New York, 1946, p. 59. Quoted in Schechtman, op. cit., pp. 173–4.
71. Czerniakiewicz makes the strange remark, op. cit., p. 55, that in 1946 all who wanted to return to Poland, did so. It is not clear precisely what he means by this, since from his own table (p. 54) it is clear that more than 18 000 returned during 1947 and 1948 (although they comprised less than one-and-a-half per cent of the total returning under these agreements).
72. Kersten, op. cit., p. 227.
73. Schechtman, op. cit., p. 175. See also A. Skrzypek, 'O drugiej repatriacji Polaków z ZSRR (1954–1959)', *Kwartalnik Historyczny*, no. 4 (1991), pp. 63–74.
74. J. Siedlecki, *Losy Polaków w ZSRR w latach 1939–1986*. London, 1987, pp. 235–6. During the winter of 1962–63 eight hundred Poles – mostly Home Army soldiers seized and deported during the years 1944–47 – returned to Poland from a camp near Omsk. The returnees stated that there were still some 27 000 Poles being held in camps in the locality. Op. cit., p. 246.
75. Ibid., p. 238.
76. There is a suggestion in a letter quoted in ibid., p. 242, that the release of camp prisoners was linked in some way to Adenauer's first visit to the USSR and his efforts to have imprisoned German nationals freed.
77. Ibid., p. 240.

Select Bibliography

ARCHIVAL MATERIALS CITED

(i) **Archiwum Akt Nowych (Archive of Modern Records, Warsaw)**
Files of the Polish Embassy in London
Files of the Union of Polish Patriots (ZPP)

(ii) **Hoover Institution, Stanford, California**
Anders Collection

(iii) **Polish Institute and General Sikorski Museum, London**
A.7 Files of the Polish Embassy in the USSR
A.9 Files of the Ministry of Internal Affairs
A.11 Files of the Ministry of Foreign Affairs
A.18 Files of the Ministry of Labour and Social Welfare
A.XII Papers of the Ministry of National Defence
Dziennik Czynności Naczelnego Wodza (Diary of Activities of the Polish
    Commander-in-Chief, General Sikorski)
Kol. 5 Papers of Tadeusz Romer
Kol. 138 Papers of Col. W. Bąkiewicz
Kol. 210 Papers of Lt-Col. J. Lis

(iv) **Public Record Office, London**
FO371 Foreign Office General Correspondence Files
PREM 3 Prime Minister's Files
WO204 War Office (Joint Planning Staff – Liaison Section)
WO208 Directorate of Military Intelligence

(v) **Studium Polski Podziemnej (Polish Underground Study Trust, London)**
3.19.1 Okupant Sowiecki, 1939–1941

PERIODICALS CITED

(i) **Polish**
Akta Universitatis Lodziensis
Aneks (London)
Antemurale (Rome)
Czerwony Sztandar (Lwów)
Dziennik Polski (Kraków)
Dziennik Polski (London)
Dzieje Najnowsze
Gazeta Wyborcza
ITD
Karta
Kwartalnik Historyczny

Kultura (Paris)
Kultura (Warsaw)
Niepodległość (London–New York)
Polityka (Warsaw)
Tydzień Polski (London)
Wiadomości (London)
Wojskowy Przegląd Historyczny
Wolna Polska
Zeszyty Historyczne (Paris)
Z pola walki

(ii) **English**
Australian Journal of Politics and History
East European Politics and Society
International History Review
Jewish Chronicle
Journal of Contemporary History
New Hungarian Quarterly (Budapest)
Polish Review
Slavic Review
Soviet Monitor
The Sunday Times
The Times

(iii) **Other**
Izvestia
Krasnaya Zviezda

UNPUBLISHED SECONDARY SOURCES

Dubanowicz, E., 'Pod Sowiecką Inwazją' (325-page typescript produced in 1942 for the Polish Ministry of Information in London. Copy in Polish Library, London.)
Litvak, Y., 'Polish-Jewish Refugees in the USSR, 1939–46'. PhD Thesis, Hebrew University of Jerusalem, 1983.
Wierzbicka, M., 'Więzienie, Łagry, Zesłanie. 1944–1955'. (290-page typescript. Copy in the possession of the author.)

PUBLISHED SOURCES

Albert, A., *Najnowsza Historia Polski, 1918–1980.* London, 1989.
Armia Krajowa w Dokumentach 1939–1945. (Vols I–VI). London, 1970–89.
Anders, W., *Bez Ostatniego Rozdziału. Wspomnienia z lat 1939–46.* (Tenth Edition) London, 1989.
Anonymous, *The Dark Side of the Moon.* London, 1946.
Begin, M., *White Nights.* London, 1977.
Berling, Z., *Wspomnienia.*
  I. (Z łagrow do Andersa.) Warsaw, 1990.

II. (Przeciw 17 republice.) Warsaw, 1991.
Bilewicz, M. M., *Wyszedłem z mroku.* Warsaw, 1990.
Błazyński, Z., *Mówi Józef Światło. Za kulisami bezpieki i partii.* London, 1985.
Bloch, C., 'Losy Polaków poza granicami Kraju w latach II wojny światowej'. *Wojskowy Przegląd Historyczny,* Vol. 35 (1990), no. 1–2, pp. 79–109.
Blum, I., 'O składzie socjalno-demograficznym Polskich Sił Zbrojnych w ZSSR'. *Wojskowy Przegląd Historyczny,* no. 2 (1963), pp. 3–34.
Bohusz-Szyszko, Z., *Czerwony Sfinks.* Rome, 1946.
Buca, E., *Vorkuta.* London, 1976.
Buczek, R., 'Działalność opiekuńcza ambasady R.P. w ZSRR w latach 1941–43'. *Zeszyty Historyczne,* Vol. 29 (1973), pp. 42–115.
Caban, I., *Polacy internowani w ZSRR w latach 1944–1947.* Lublin, 1990.
Ciechanowski, J., 'Armia polska w Rosji w świetle dziennika Szefa Sztabu z 1942 roku'. *Zeszyty Historyczne,* no. 57 (1981), pp. 92–127.
Cienciała, A. M., 'The Activities of Polish Communists as a Source for Stalin's Policy Towards Poland in the Second World War'. *International History Review,* Vol. VII, no. 1, February 1985, pp. 129–45.
Conquest, R., *The Nation-Killers. The Soviet Deportation of Nationalities.* London, 1970.
Czapska, M., *Polacy w ZSRR, 1939–42.* Paris, 1963.
Czerniakiewicz, J., *Repatriacja ludności polskiej z ZSRR, 1944–1948.* Warsaw, 1987.
Dallin, D. J. and Nicolaevsky, B. I., *Forced Labour in Soviet Russia.* London, 1947.
Dallin, A. and Breslauer, G. W., *Political Terror in Communist Systems.* Stanford, 1970.
Dańko, B., *Nie Zdążyli do Andersa (Berlingowcy).* London, 1992.
Davies, N., *God's Playground. A History of Poland.* Vol. II. Oxford, 1982.
Documents on Polish-Soviet Relations, 1939–45. (2 vols.) London, 1961 and 1967. (Edited by the General Sikorski Historical Institute.)
Dokumenty I Materiały Do Historii Stosunków Polsko-Radzieckich. Warsaw, 1973–74 (Vol. VII: Jan. 1939–Dec. 1943); 1974 (Vol. VIII: Jan. 1944–Dec. 1945).
Drewnowski, J., *Cynga. Wspomnienia z łagrów północy, 1940–1944.* Warsaw, 1989.
Dubanowicz, M., *Na mongolskich bezdrożach.* London, 1980.
Dziewanowski, M. K., *The Communist Party of Poland.* London, 1976.
Erdman, J., *Droga do Ostrej Bramy.* London, 1984.
Erickson, J., *The Road to Stalingrad.* London, 1983.
Fainsod, M., *How Russia is Ruled.* Cambridge, Mass., 1964 (Revised Edition).
Fałkowski, R. S., 'Polacy w czerwonej armii (1940–1945)'. *Zeszyty Historyczne,* no. 101 (1992), pp. 115–142.
Garliński, J., *Poland in the Second World War.* London, 1985.
Głowacki, A., 'Opieka Związku Patriotów Polskich w ZSSR and Rodzinami Wojskowymi (1943–46)'. *Wojskowy Przegląd Historyczny,* no. 4 (98), 1981a, pp. 25–42.
Głowacki, A., 'Powstanie, Organizacja i Działalność Wydziału Opieki Społecznej Zarządu Głównego Związku Patriotów Polskich w ZSSR (1943–1946)'. *Acta*

Universitatis Lodziensis, Folio Historica 8 (1981b).

Głowala, J., *Purga. Wśród więzniów i zeszłanców w ZSRR, 1941–1955.* Warsaw, 1990.

Goetel, F., *Czasy Wojny.* London, 1955.

Goetel, F., 'Główne kierunki rozwoju Polonii w ZSRR w okresie mię dzywojennym.' *Przegląd Polonijny* (Kraków), Vol. XIV (1988), no. 3, pp. 61–72.

Gross, J. T., 'Okupacja Sowiecka i Deportacje do Rosji w Oczach Dzieci'. *Zeszyty Historyczne*, XLVIII, 1979, 55–83.

Gross, J. T., 'Wywózki'. *Aneks* (London), no. 51–52 (1988).

Gross, J. T. and Grudzińska, I., *'W czterdziestym nas matko na Sybir zesłali...'* *Polska a Rosja 1939–42.* London, 1983.

Grubiński, W., *Między Młotem a Sierpem.* London, 1948.

Halpern, A., *Liberation – Russian Style.* London, 1945.

Herling-Grudziński, G., *Inny Świat. Zapiski sowieckie.* London, 1953.

Heydon, P., 'Protecting Polish Interests in the USSR 1943–1944: An episode in Australian representation.' *Australian Journal of Politics and History*, Vol. XVII (1972), no. 2, pp. 189–213.

Hort, W., *Tułacze Dzieci.* Beirut, 1948.

Iwanow, M., *Polacy w Związku Radzieckim w latach 1921–1939.* Wrocław, 1990.

Iwanow, M., 'Polonia w Związku Radzieckim okresu międzywojennego. Kontrowersje wokół liczebności.' *Dzieje Najnowsze* (Warsaw), Vol. XIX (1987), no. 4, pp. 29–51.

Januszkiewicz, M., *Kazachstan.* Paris, 1981.

Jurgielewicz, W., 'Pomoc Związku Radzieckiego w utworzeniu Ludowego Wojska Polskiego'. *Wojskowy Przegląd Historyczny*, no. 1 (60), 1972, pp. 106–128.

Kamińska, R. T., *Mink Coats and Barbed Wire.* London, 1979.

Karol, K. S., *Solik. Life in the Soviet Union, 1939–1946.* London, 1986.

Kersten, K., *Repatriacja ludności polskiej po II wojnie światowej.* Wrocław, 1974.

Kersten, K., *The Establishment of Communist Rule in Poland, 1943–1948.* Berkeley/Los Angeles, 1991.

Kochanowicz, T., *Wspomnienia z pobytu w ZSRR (1939–1942).* Warsaw, 1989.

Kot, S., *Conversations with the Kremlin and Despatches from Russia.* London, 1963.

Kowalewski, J., *Droga Powrotna.* London, 1974.

Kowalska, J., *Moje Uniwersytety.* London, 1971.

Kowalski, W. T., *Walka dyplomatyczna o miejsce Polski w Europie, 1939–1945.* Warsaw, 1970.

Król, F., 'Pierwszy strajk w Gułagu. Workuta 1953.' *Zeszyty Historyczne*, no. 95 (1991), pp. 73–90.

'Krystyna' (Kawecka, Z.), *Journey Without a Ticket.* Nottingham, 1989.

Krzyżanowski, B., *Wileński Matecznik 1939–44.* Paris, 1979.

Kulczyńska, M., *Lwów–Donbas 1945.* Warsaw, 1988.

Kumos, Z., *Związek Patriotów Polskich.* Warsaw, 1983.

Kuśnierz, B., *Stalin and the Poles.* London, 1949.

Kwapiński, J., *1939–1945 – Kartki z Pamiętnika.* London, 1947.

Łęczycka, M., *Zsyłka.* Wrocław, 1989.

Lipińska, G., *Jeśli zapomnę o nich. . . .* Paris, 1988.

Liszewski, K., *Wojna polsko-sowiecka.* London, 1987.

Liszewski, K., *Wojna polsko-sowiecka 1939r.* London, 1939.

Lizak, W., 'Szkic o dziejach Polaków w ZSRR, 1917–1939/47'. In J. Leszkiewiczowa (ed.), *Polacy w ZSRR 1917–1947.* Warsaw, 1990.

Mitkiewicz, L., *Z generałem Sikorskim na obczyźnie.* Paris, 1968.

Młynarski, B., *W niewoli sowieckiej.* London, 1974.

Myszkowski, A. A., 'Słownik biograficzny komunistów polskich represjonowanych w ZSSR'. *Zeszyty Historyczne* (Paris), no. 69 (1980), pp. 40–80.

Mora, S. and Zwierniak, P., *Sprawiedliwość Sowiecka.* Rome, 1945.

Moskoff, W., *The Bread of Affliction. The Food Supply in the USSR during World War II.* Cambridge, 1990.

Możejko, E., 'Wierność i cierpienia: o Polakach w Związku Sowieckim przed 1939r.' *Zeszyty Historyczne*, no. 100 (1992), pp. 3–22.

Naglerowa, H., *Sprawa Józefa Mosta.* London, 1953.

Obertyńska, B., *W Domu Niewoli.* Chicago, 1968.

Pawłowski, E., 'Polacy w Armii Radzieckiej'. *Wojskowy Przegląd Historyczny* (Warsaw), no. 2, 1984, 309–11. (Reprinted in *Zeszyty Historyczne*, no. 70.)

Piekut, S., *Pod krwawym niebem. Z Polski do Rosji Stalina.* London, 1986.

Pobóg-Malinowski, W., *Najnowsza Historia Polityczna Polski*, Vol. 3, (1939–45). London, 1981.

Podgórski, C., 'Rola ZPP w utworzeniu Polskich Sil Zbrojnych w ZSSR'. *Wojskowy Przegląd Historyczny*, no. 1 (60), 1972. pp. 81–105.

Polaczek, J., 'Zołnierze AK w obozach Maryjskiej ASSR'. *Zeszyty Historyczne* (Paris), no. 97 (1990), pp. 154–75.

Polonsky, A. and Drukier, B., *The Beginnings of Communist Rule in Poland. December 1943–June 1945.* London, 1980.

Polska Wschodnia 1939–1941. Rome, 1945. (Published and printed by the Press and Cultural Unit of the Polish Second Corps.)

Polski Czyn Zbrojny w II Wojnie Światowej
    Vol. III Ludowe Wojsko Polskie, 1943–1945. (ed. W. Jurgielewicz). Warsaw, 1973.
    Vol. IV Walki Formacji Polskich na Zachodzie, 1939–1945. (ed. W. Biegański). Warsaw 1981.

Polskie Siły Zbrojne w Drugiej Wojnie Światowej. (Edited by the General Sikorski Historical Institute), Vol. III (London, 1950) and Vol. II, part 2 (London, 1975).

Popławski, A., *12 lat Łagru.* Paris, 1987.

Putrament, J., *Pół Wieku.* (Vol. II. Wojna). Warsaw, 1969.

Rozek, E. J., *Allied Wartime Diplomacy. A Pattern in Poland.* London, 1958.

Rudnicki, K., *The Last of the War Horses.* London, 1974.

Schechtman, J., *Postwar Population Transfers in Europe, 1945–1955.* Philadelphia, 1962.

Siedlecki, J., *Polacy w ZSRR w latach 1939–1986.* London, 1988.

Siemaszko, Z. S., 'O Polakach w ZSSR'. *Zeszyty Historyczne*, no. 31 (1975), pp. 175–200.

Siemaszko, Z. S., '17 Września i jego skutki' (na tle wspomnień prof. Swianiewicza). *Zeszyty Historyczne*, no. 44 (1978).

Siemaszko, Z. S., 'Problemy Polaków w Sowietach.' (Series of articles in the *Dziennik Polski* (London), appearing between 22 April 1985 and 17 June 1986.)

Siemaszko, Z. S., 'Jeńcy wojenni. (ZSSR 1939–1941)'. *Zeszyty Historyczne*, no. 82 (1987), pp. 86–105.

Siemaszko, Z. S., 'Sprawy religijne wśród Polaków w Sowietach, 1939–42'. *Duszpasterz Polski Zagranicą*, rok XXXIX (1988), no. 1/166 (Rome) pp. 97–121.

Siemaszko, Z. S., *W sowieckim osaczeniu.* London, 1991.

Skrzypek, S., *Rosja Jaką Widziałem.* Newtown, Wales, 1949.

Slaski, J., *Skrobów. Dzieje obozu NKWD dla żołnierzy AK, 1944–1945.* Warsaw, 1990.

Sobczak, K., 'Wanda Wasilewska – Bojowniczka o Postęp Społeczny, Niepodległość i Socjalizm.' *Wojskowy Przegląd Historyczny*, 1 (79), 1977, pp. 3–36.

Sobolewski, H., *Z ziemi wileńskiej przez świat Gułagu.* Warsaw, 1990.

Sosnkowski, K., 'Układ polsko-rosyjski z 30 lipca 1941.' *Kultura* (Paris), no. 42 (1951), pp. 122–3.

Stypułkowski, J., *Droga do wojska.* London, 1967.

Sukiennicki, W., 'Z ziemi nieludzkiej – relacje obcych i swoich'. *Kultura* (Paris), no. 36 (1950), pp. 121–57. (Review article of five works on deportation to the Soviet Union.)

Sulek, L. A., 'Wojenne losy Polaków żolnierzy Armii Czerwonej (1940–1945)'. *Zeszyty Historyczne*, no. 99 (1992), pp. 30–9.

Świaniewicz, S., *Forced Labour and Economic Development. An enquiry into the experience of Soviet industrialization.* London, 1965.

Sword, K. (ed.), *The Soviet Takeover of the Polish Eastern Provinces, 1939–1941.* London, 1991.

Szczęsny-Brzozowski, Z., *Litwa–Wilno 1910–1945.* Paris, 1987.

Tęczarowska, D., *Deportacje w nieznane. Wspomnienia, 1939–1942.* London, 1981.

Torańska, T., *Oni.* London, 1985.

Trela, E., *Edukacja dzieci polskich w Związku Radzieckim w latach 1941–1946.* Warsaw, 1983.

Turlejska, M., *Prawdy i Fikcje.* Warsaw, 1968.

Turlejska, M., *Te pokolenia żałobami czarne..... Skazani na śmierć i ich sędziowie, 1944–1954.* London, 1989.

Ulam, A., *Expansion and Coexistence. Soviet Foreign Policy, 1917–1973.* London, 1968.

Umiastowski, R., *Russia and the Polish Republic, 1918–41.* London, 1945.

Vincenz, S., *Dialogi z Sowietami.* London, 1966.

Wasilewska, E., *The Silver Madonna.* London, 1970.

Wasilewska, W., 'Wspomnienia (1939–1944)'. *Archiwum Ruchu Robotniczego*, VII, Warsaw, 1975.

Wat, A., *Mój wiek.* London, 1981.

Węgierski, J., *W lwowskiej Armii Krajowej.* Warsaw, 1989.

Wielhorski, W., *Los Polaków w Niewoli Sowieckiej.* London, 1956.

Wirski, S., *Polityka ZSSR wobec ziem polskich, 1939–41.* Warsaw, 1985.

Zarod, K., *Inside Stalin's Gułag.* Lewes, Sussex, 1990.

Zaron, P., *Armia polska w ZSRR, na Bliskim i Srodkowym Wschodzie*. Warsaw, 1971.

Zaron, P., *Ludność polska w Związku Radzieckim w czasie II wojnie światowej*. Warsaw, 1990.

Zbiniewicz, F., *Armia polska w ZSSR*. Warsaw, 1963.

Żenczykowski, T., *Polska lubelska 1944*. Paris, 1987.

Index

259